# THE
# CONCISE
# CATHOLIC
# DICTIONARY

**THE ANGELUS PRESS**
**2918 Tracy Avenue**
**Kansas City, MO 64109**

**April, 1992**

# THE CONCISE CATHOLIC DICTIONARY

Kansas City, Missouri

Nihil obstat:   H. B. RIES
              *Censor librorum*

Imprimatur:   ✠ MOSES E. KILEY
              *Archbishop of Milwaukee*
       October 16, 1943

# COOPERATING EXAMINERS

In the interest of accuracy and completeness, important portions of the manuscript of the Dictionary have been examined and approved by a group of specialists. The compiler is grateful to the following reverend gentlemen for their service:

*Religious Ceremonies and Ritual:* REVEREND MATTHEW BRITT, O.S.B., Lacey, Washington.

*General Entries:* REV. FRANCIS M. SCHNEIDER, S.T.D., St. Francis, Wis.; and VERY REV. DONALD F. MILLER, C.SS.R., Oconomowoc, Wis.

*Theological Terms:* REV. L. J. FALLON, C.M., S.T.D., St. Louis, Mo.

*Canon Law:* REV. ADAM C. ELLIS, S.J., St. Marys, Kansas.

*Liturgy:* REV. GERALD ELLARD, S.J., PH.D., St. Marys, Kansas.

*Moral Theology:* REV. FRANCIS J. CONNELL, C.SS.R., S.T.D., Washington, D. C.

*Sacred Scripture:* REV. GEORGE J. ZISKOVSKY, L.S.SC., PH.D., S.T.D., St. Paul, Minnesota.

*Religious Orders:* REV. JOSEPH B. CODE, D.SC. HIST., Kansas City, Mo.

*Philosophy:* A DOMINICAN.

## PREFACE

WHILE ALL MODERN languages undergo constant change, the language of the Traditional Catholic is, for the most part, static except in various additions which may be made from time to time.

This dictionary was compiled to present a concise statement of definitions of words which are used in Church language. It was based on the solid conviction that people, whether members of the Faith or not, would better understand the Roman Catholic religion if they had a clearer and more concise knowledge of words which are peculiar to the expression of that religious belief.

It was also a conviction that Catholics would have a better understanding of their faith and its Liturgy if they learned the words in which their faith is enunciated.

As with all dictionaries the actual test is in the service it renders. It was toward this end our compilation was made.

This dictionary is not, by any means, the first of its type. A number of Catholic Encyclopedia Dictionaries have been produced over the years. Most were found wanting in many respects. In some instances they were confusing to many of the faithful. Added to that shortcoming was the fact their expense made them prohibitive to many, especially students.

This is not an encyclopedia dictionary. By that is meant that words are not presented in comprehensive detail, along with information containing their origin. Biographical and historical entries which usually make up encyclopedia dictionaries have been purposely omitted.

We have, however, endeavored to bring to readers the following:

- A concise and simplified statement of definition of 1900 words, clearly and briefly stated for ready reference and as precise as technical limitations permit. These words are of the Roman Rite, except where frequent use of other words demanded their inclusion. Many of the entries are illustrated.
- The basic derivation and pronunciation of words, which larger sources lack.
- An appendix of 350 foreign words and phrases which frequently appear in the vernacular, together with literal translations.
- An appendix of abbreviations generally used in the Church.
- An appendix containing a list of the Popes, together with the dates of their reigns and a list of the Ecumenical Councils and the doctrines they defined.
- An appendix of titles and terms of address given to Ecclesiastical authorities has been added.

For students the dictionary will serve:

- as a valuable adjuct to the courses in traditional religious instruction;
- as a functional aid as indispensable as the English school dictionary;
- as a basic tool in the library, and as a handy and quick reference.

# NOTES ON PRONUNCIATION

WORDS in ecclesiastical language have the same accepted standard pronunciation as English words of the same spelling even though the meaning attached may be entirely different. The only exception to this general rule is where we have the adoption of a foreign word, not Anglicized, and used it as it was in the original language. To make clear this exception there is given below a guide to pronunciation of Latin words. Because the English words have the same pronunciation regardless of their usage we recommend that the reader for a complete statement consult the sections on pronunciation found in the standard unabridged English dictionaries. However, for immediate convenience we briefly include the following:

ā as in day, hate, labor
ā as in vacation, cordate
â as in dare, air
ă as in has, apt, accept
ă as in infant, vacant
ä as in dark, far
à as in castle, ant, cast
a as in sofa, abound

ē as in evil, eve
ê as in create, detect
ĕ as in devil, relic
ĕ as in silent, angel
ē as in average, fern

ī as in idea, time
ĭ as in pity, bill
i as in charity, direct

ō as in old, go
ŏ as in obey, potato
ô as in order, cord
ŏ as in God, not
ŏ as in combine, occur
o͞o as in moon, food
o͝o as in foot, wood

ū as in cube, use
û as in unite, nature
û as in burn, furl
ŭ as in under, up
ŭ as in pious, circus

# PRONUNCIATION OF LATIN WORDS

THE CATHOLIC CHURCH has drawn largely directly from the Latin language and many words are used in their Latin form. For the most part these words have been Anglicized in their pronunciation, and where such Latin words do not appear with Anglicized pronunciation, no pronunciation has been given. There is no prescribed manner of pronouncing Latin words, but that preferred in Church language is the Italian or "soft" pronunciation, and for the convenience of those who wish to apply this to Latin words or phrases, we supply the following chart.

## Vowels

ā as *a* in father
ē as *a* in late
e as *e* in met
ī as *i* in machine
i as *i* in pin
ō as *o* in rope
o as *o* in obey
ū as *oo* in food

## Diphthongs

ae as *a* in fate
oe as *a* in hate
au as *ow* in now

## Consonants

c before *e* and *i* as *ch* in chess
c as *k* before a, o, u, au and h
g before *e* and *i* as *g* in gentle
v as in English
gn as *ni* in onion
sc before *e* and *i* as *sh* in ship
ti as *tsi* in tertiary

# ACCENT AND RULES OF PRONUNCIATION

In Latin the last syllable is never accented. In words of two syllables the first receives the accent. In words of more than two syllables the accent is on the second last syllable if (1) the vowel is long; (2) it has a diphthong; (3) it is a vowel followed by *j*, *x*, or *z* or by two consonants. If *l* or *r* appear in the second syllable it is not long. The accent is on the third last syllable when the second last syllable is not long.

Every consonant except *h* is sounded.

Vowels not followed by a consonant in the same syllable are pronounced long while vowels followed by a consonant within the same syllable are pronounced short.

## ABBREVIATIONS USED IN THIS COMPILATION

*Etymological*

- *Aram.* —Aramaic
- *A.S.* —Anglo Saxon
- *Celt.* —Celtic
- *D.* —Dutch
- *Fr.* —French
- *Ger.* —German
- *Gr.* —Greek
- *Heb.* —Hebrew
- *It.* —Italian
- *Jav.* —Javanese
- *L.* —Latin
- *M.E.* —Middle English
- *O.E.* —Old English
- *O. Fr.* —Old French
- *Scand.* —Scandinavian
- *Sp.* —Spanish

*Others*

- *Abbre.* —Abbreviation
- *Adj.* —Adjective
- *Colloq.* —Colloquial
- *n.* —Noun
- *obs.* —Obsolete
- *pl.* —Plural
- *v.t.* —Verb, transitive
- *v. intr.* —Verb, intransitive
- *Bib.* —Bible or biblical

# THE CONCISE CATHOLIC DICTIONARY

# ✢ A ✢

**Abbess** (ăb'ĕs), n.; L., Fr. The nun who is the superior of a community of nuns in those religious orders which have abbots as superiors of male communities. An abbess has domestic or temporal authority but no spiritual jurisdiction.

**Abbé** (Fr. abbot) (à'bā'), n.; L., Fr. Title given to an abbot, but generally to a secular ecclesiastic in France; often used colloquially to refer to any cleric.

**Abbey** (ăb'ĭ), n.; L., Fr. Properly a monastery or convent governed by an abbot or abbess; also the community of monks or nuns numbering at least twelve in a canonically erected monastery or convent. Generally refers to the entire group of buildings, but sometimes only to the church building.

**Abbot** (ăb'ŭt), n.; Gr., L. The superior of a community of men in an abbey. The one directing a group of men in an abbey who live under religious vows according to a rule or laws for the community. The abbot is elected for life. His authority is the administration of the property of the abbey, the enforcing of the rule, the exercise of quasi-episcopal powers, as he has the privilege of conferring Tonsure, and Minor Orders, and a limited use of the Pontificals, and he may at times pontificate.

**Abbreviator** (ă·brē′vĭ·ātēr), n.; L. A notary or secretary employed in the Papal Chancery and entrusted with the work of abbreviating and copying papal documents.

**Abdias** (ăb·dī′ăs), n.; Gr.; Bib. The Greek name of Abadiah, author of the shortest prophetical book of the Old Testament.

**Abduction** (ăb·dŭk′shŭn), n.; L. The forceful carrying off or detention of a woman by a man which forms a diriment impediment to marriage between such a man and woman so long as she is in his power against her will for the purpose of marriage.

**Abjuration** (ăb′jōō·rā′shŭn), n.; L. (1) The renunciation or denial under oath of an apostasy, heresy or schism before apostates, heretics or schismatics are validly absolved from excommunication. (2) Required as a preliminary of a convert's confession of faith previous to the reception of Baptism.

**Ablegate** (ăb′lĕ·gāt), n.; L. An envoy of the Papal service who bears the red biretta to a new cardinal who is not residing in Rome; a legate from the Holy Father with this mission.

**Ablution** (ăb·lū′shŭn), n.; L., Fr. The wine and water with which the celebrating priest washes remaining particles of the communion host from his thumb and index finger after the Communion in the Mass. In the Mass, the washing and consuming by the priest of this wine and water. Also the process of purifying the chalice during Mass.

**Abrogation** (ăb′rô·gā′shŭn), n.; L. In canon law, the repeal or cancellation of a law; the total revoking of a law.

**Absolution** (ăb′sô·lū′shŭn), n.; L. (1) The remission of sin by an authorized priest in the Sacrament of Penance; the judicial act of forgiving; sacramental forgiveness. Conditional absolution is that given when the Sacrament is in danger of nullity or when, if it is not given or is denied, the penitent might suffer spiritual loss. General absolution is that given to a group simultaneously when private confession is impossible. Those so absolved are obliged to mention their sins when they next have an opportunity to go to confession. (2) Absolution from censures is the removal of penalties imposed by the Church; it grants reconciliation with the Church. (3) Absolution for the dead is that ceremony performed over the body of the dead after a requiem Mass, and in which the priest implores the remission, indirectly, of the penalties of sin. If the body is not present, the service is held over the catafalque. (4) Absolutions in the breviary are those short petition prayers said before the lessons in matins.

**Abstinence** (ăb′stĭ·něns), n.; L., Fr. (1) The act whereby one forgoes or deprives oneself of something pleasing to the senses, such as alcoholic beverages. (2) The obligation attached to certain days on which the Church forbids Catholics the eating of meat and soups of meat stock, gravy or sauces made from meat. On days of complete abstinence, these foods may not be eaten at all; on days of partial abstinence, they may be eaten once, at the principal meal. The law of abstinence binds all over 7 years of age. Days of complete abstinence are: Fridays, Ash Wednesday, the vigils of Immaculate Conception and Christmas; partial days are: Ember Wednesdays and Saturdays, and vigils of Pentecost.

**Accident** (ăk′sĭ·děnt), n.; L., Fr. That which is apt to exist only in another being; it has no independent existence, its existence is not self-sufficient. As spoken of regarding the Blessed Sacrament, the accidents are what the senses perceive. Philosophical term in distinction to substance.

**Accidie** (ăk′sĭ·dĭ), n.; L. The sin of spiritual laziness. Indifference toward a spiritual good because one is obliged to live up to its troublesome requirements. In itself it is a venial sin, but is mortal when it leads to the neglect of a grave obligation.

**Acclamation** (ăk′lă·mā′shŭn), n.; L. (1) Naming one to an ecclesiastical dignity unanimously by the electors without balloting, or by vocal acclaim. One of three ways of electing a Pope. (2) A brief liturgical formula such as, *"Laus tibi Christe."*

**Accommodation** (ă·kŏm′ŏ·dā′shŭn), n.; L.; Bib. An adaptation of the words of Scripture to express ideas different from those intended by the author. The adapting of the words of Scripture to a speech or subject to illustrate it; an adapted application of Scripture.

**Accomplice** (*ă*·kŏm′plĭs), n.; L. One who cooperates in the sin of another; one who gives physical or moral aid to another in the commission of a sin or the planning of a sinful act.

**Acoemetae** (*ă*·sĕm′ē·tē), n. pl.; Gr. Also acoemeti. Certain Eastern nuns or monks who kept perpetual prayer; "sleepless monks," so called because they chanted the divine office in relays day and night without intermission.

**Acolyte** (ăk′ŏ·līt), n.; Gr., L. An escort; an attendant. His office is that of assisting the priest at Mass, of performing the duties of Mass-server. (1) The name given to the highest of the four minor orders; a sacramental. (2) A Mass-server or assistant of a priest at any ritualistic ceremony.

**Act (of worship)** (ăkt), n.; L., Fr. The Mass and the divine office which are the principal services of the Catholic Church and the chief acts of worship. Generally, the adoration of God.

**Action** (ăk′sh*ŭ*n), n.; L., Fr. (1) The Canon of the Mass. (2) The discussion of a single subject in a session of a council. (3) Used in the phrase "Catholic Action" to denote the acts commissioned by the hierarchy for the participation of the laity in the liturgy, prayer, conversion duties, and work of the Catholic hierarchy. Work to advance the cause of Christ in temporal and spiritual matters: first, personally; second, in the family; and third, in the associations of social life.

**Acts** (ăkts), n. pl.; L., Fr. (1) The proceedings and their recording in a court of justice. (2) "Acts" of the Martyrs, accounts of their confessions of faith and death. (3) The "Acts of the Apostles" which is the section of Sacred Scripture wherein their activities are recorded. (4) Prayers by which one declares his faith in God, hope in Him, charity or love of Him, and sorrow for sin because of offending Him.

**Actual Grace** (ăk′tū-ăl grās), adj. & n.; L. The internal gift of God to the soul which after the manner of a motion influences the will and understanding, lasting as long as the action for which it is given lasts. Actual grace may be that which excites the mind to act, or it may be that which assists the mind to complete an action already begun. (Cf. Grace.)

**A.D.** abbre.; L. Abbreviation for the Latin words *Anno Domini* meaning literally "in the year of the Lord," and denoting the years after the Incarnation of the Son of God from which time we now reckon our calendar.

**Adam** (ăd′ăm), n.; Heb.; Bib. Proper name used for the first man created by God. He from whom all mankind is descended.

**Adamites** (ăd′ămī-ts), n. pl.; Heb., L. (1) An obscure Gnostic sect of the second century. (2) A fanatical sect of the Middle Ages given to nudism.

**Adjuration** (ăj′ōō-rā′shŭn), n.; L. The act of begging

earnestly or of commanding in God's name, or in the name of some holy person or thing, in order to urge the person addressed to act or to desist from acting.

**Administrator** (ăd·mĭn′ĭs·trā′tẽr), n.; L. He who is in charge of a diocese when the bishop is lawfully absent or when the diocese is vacant by resignation or removal of the bishop, or during the interim between the death of the bishop and the arrival of his successor. Also applied to a priest who directs and governs a parish temporarily but is himself not the permanent rector or pastor.

**Admonition** (ăd′mô·nĭsh′ŭn), n.; L. The penal remedy required by canon law before a censure can be imposed; a warning to cease doing an evil act or simply some misconduct before a censure is imposed; usually there are three given.

**Adoration** (ăd′ô·rā′shŭn), n.; L. (1) Acts of divine worship directed to God; (2) Perpetual — Continuous exposition of the Blessed Sacrament, day and night, during which time adorers take turns in offering prayers and devotion. (3) Adoration of the Cross: the ceremony of Good Friday, so called by long use, which is an act of venerating the crucifix. (Cf. Latria.)

**Adultery** (a·dŭl′tẽr·ĭ), n.; L. Act of infidelity, by carnal intercourse, to the bond of marriage by either husband or wife. Sin against chastity and also against justice. If a married man and a married woman, each unfaithful to his or her spouse, commit this sin with each other and make an agreement of marrying in the future, they incur a diriment impediment which prevents them from marrying each other even though their respective partners die.

**Advent** (ăd'vĕnt), n.; L. The time of preparation for the Feast of the Incarnation, which in the Church calendar consists of three or four weeks between Advent Sunday, the Sunday nearest the Feast of St. Andrew, and Christmas eve. The first liturgical season of the Church calendar. The period of spiritual preparation for Christmas.

**Advocate** (ăd'vŏ·kāt), n.; L., Fr. A lawyer in an ecclesiastical court, either cleric or lay, who pleads a case.

**Advowson** (ăd·vou'zŭn), n.; L. The right by which one founding a benefice could present some cleric to the bishop when the benefice was vacant. (obs.)

**Aequiprobabilism** (ē'kwĭ·prŏb'a·bĭ·lĭz'm), n.; L., Fr. Also equiprobabilism. The system of moral theology which teaches that (*a*) in a strict doubt as to the existence of a law, the law need not be obeyed. There is a strict doubt when the opinions are equally probable for the law and for liberty; (*b*) in a strict doubt as to whether a certain law has ceased to bind, the law must be obeyed; (*c*) liberty may never be favored when the opinion for the law is certainly more probable. The basis of this system is the obligation of the human mind to seek truth, and if it cannot find what is certainly true, to accept what seems nearer to truth. (Cf. Probabilism.)

**Affinity** (ă·fĭn′ĭ·tĭ), n.; L. Relationship of persons arising from a valid Christian marriage, whether consummated or not. It exists between either party to the marriage and the blood relations of the other party. In canon law an impediment to marriage; it annuls possibility of marriage in all degrees in the direct line of blood relationship and to the second degree inclusive of the collateral line.

**Agape** (ăg′à·pĕ), n.; Gr., L. An obsolete feast or meal, sometimes called brotherly or love feast, taken in common following an early practice of the Greeks. It was in commemoration of the Last Supper and was probably taken before the celebration of Mass.

**Age** (āj), n.; L. The canonical age is that time fixed when one incurs certain obligations or can receive certain dignities or privileges. The canonical age is reckoned from the day of birth and not from the day of baptism. The canonical age affects the life of a Christian in the following: (*a*) at the age of seven a child becomes subject to the laws of the Church, e.g. Sunday Mass, abstinence, etc.; it is presumed that at that age one has the use of reason; there are exceptions, however: a child is obliged by the law of annual confession and Paschal Communion as soon as he attains to the use of reason, even though he has not completed his seventh year. (*b*) Marriage contracted by males under sixteen or by females under fourteen is null and void. Males attain the age of puberty at the end of the fourteenth year, and females at the end of the twelfth year of age; those who have not reached the age of puberty are not subject to penalties *latae sententiae;* Godparents at Baptism must normally be at least fourteen years of age. (*c*) At the age of twenty-one the obligation to fast begins, and this obligation ceases for both men and women at the beginning of the sixtieth year.

**Aggeus** (ă·gē′ŭs), n.; L. The Latin for the Hebrew name Haggai. He is the tenth among the minor prophets; the recording of his prophecies in the Old Testament is called the Book of Aggeus.

**Agnus Dei** (ăg′nŭs dē′ī), n.; L. (1) The prayer in the Mass, shortly before the Communion, beginning with these words, in English, "Lamb of God." (2) Name given to disks of wax on which are impressed the figure of a lamb and which are blessed at regular seasons by the Pope; they may be oblong, round or oval in shape and vary in size; the figure of the lamb usually has a banner or cross accompanying it.

Agnus Dei
(Cf. 2 of definition)

**Agrapha** (ăg′rȧ·fȧ), n. pl.; Gr. Sayings of our Lord not recorded in the canonical Gospels but handed down; one instance is found in inspired Scripture in Acts 20, 35.

**Alb** (ălb), n.; L. The white, full length, linen vestment with sleeves worn over the amice by the priest in celebrating Mass. It is bound close to the body by the cincture.

Alb

**Albigenses** (ăl′bĭ·jĕn′sēz), n. pl.; L. Heretics of the

twelfth and thirteenth centuries who held the Manichaean belief of two creative principles, one good and one bad.

**Alienation** (āl'yĕn·a'shŭn), n.; L. The transference of title on property rights to Church property to another; e.g. by sale, mortgage, exchange, lease, gift, etc.

**Aliturgical** (ăl'ĭ·tûr'jĭ·kăl), adj.; Gr. Term applied to those days of the year on which the celebration of Mass is forbidden; now only Good Friday.

**Allegorical** (ăl'ē·gŏr'ĭ·kăl), adj.; Gr., L. Said of a thing spoken in allegory.

**Allegory** (ăl'ē·gō'rĭ), n.; Gr., L. A story or metaphor used in Sacred Scripture; a parable; the description of one thing under the image of another thing.

**Alleluia** (ăl'ē·lū'yà), n., interj.; Gr., L. Word used in the liturgy of the Church as a joyful prayer of praise, meaning "praise the Lord."

**Allocution** (ăl'ō·kū'shŭn), n.; L. A pronouncement on an important matter of the moment, made by the Pope to the cardinals gathered in secret consistory; a papal announcement of policy either of ecclesiastical or civil affairs.

**All Saints** A.S., L. The feast celebrated on the first of November commemorating all the Saints of the Church, whether canonized or not.

**All Souls** A.S. The feast celebrated on the second of November in solemn commemoration of and as prayer for the souls in Purgatory. The priest is permitted to celebrate three Masses on this day.

**All-wise** (ôl·wīz), adj.; A.S. Descriptive of the attribute of God's knowledge, which means that His infinite wisdom prompts the planning, the foresight, and the ordering of all created things; thus, it contains within it God's providence. (Cf. Omniscience.)

**Almoner** (ăl′mŭn·ēr), n.; A.S. Formerly an ecclesiastic at a king's court in charge of the distribution of alms. Now sometimes applied to a chaplain of a charitable institution.

**Alms** (ämz), n.; A.S., Gr., L. Originally any temporal or spiritual work of mercy; now any material gift or aid given in Christian charity to one in need.

**Almuce** (ăl′mūs), n.; L., A.S. The garment for covering the head and shoulders worn by Canons while chanting the office in choir.

**Altar** (ôl′tēr), n.; L., A.S. A place of offering sacrifice. The table used for the celebration of the Sacrifice of the Mass. The altar stone is essential to the Mass, must be consecrated by a bishop, and if small and set into a wooden top must still be large enough to support the host and the greater part of the chalice. Within this stone relics are placed (*a*) The "fixed" or "im-

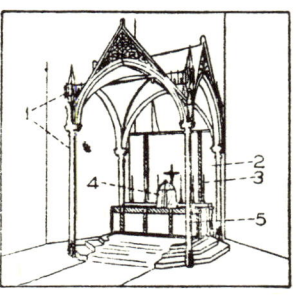

Altar with (1) *Ciborium Magnum* or canopy; (2) dossal; (3) one of the six candlesticks; (4) conopaeum; (5) antependium. The stipites are behind the antependium, and the crucifix is behind the covered tabernacle

movable" altar is a large stone table top together with stone supports (stipites) consecrated as a whole. (b) The "portable" or "movable" altar consists of a small altar stone alone which is consecrated by itself.

**Altar (high),** n.; L., A.S. The principal or main altar in a church. (a) An altar is designated as a *side* altar when it is an altar other than the high altar. (b) *Doubled* altar is an altar built so that Mass can be offered on either side of it. (c) A *fixed* altar is one solidly built of stone and immovable. (Cf. Altar.)

**Altarage** (ôl′tẽr·ĭj), n.; L., A.S. The offerings received by a priest from the laity for performing ceremonies such as baptisms, marriages, or funerals. (Obs.) (Cf. Honorarium, Stipend.)

**Altar breads** (ôl′tẽr brĕdz), n. pl.; L., A.S. Round wafers baked of fine, wheaten, unleavened flour and used in the Consecration at Mass. There are two sizes, the smaller for the Communion of the faithful, the larger for the priest's Communion of the Mass and for exposition. Also called hosts.

**Altar cards** (ôl′tẽr kărdz), n. pl.; L., Fr. The three cards placed at the center and two sides of the altar table and on which are printed some parts of the Mass which are constant, or contained in the ordinary of the Mass.

**Altar cloths** (ôl′tẽr klŏths), n. pl.; L., A.S. Three cloths, always of linen, required by the rubrics of Mass, which are spread over the top of the altar and are specially blessed for use on the altar.

**Altar piece** (ôl′tẽr pēs′), n.; L., A.S. A painting at the back of a main altar; decorative statuary on the altar.

**Altar stone** (ôl′tẽr stōn), n.; L., A.S. (1) The small square, consecrated stone which is the portable altar. (2) The entire top of the fixed or immovable altar. (Cf. Altar.)

**Ambo** (ăm′bō), n.; pl. ambos. Gr. A raised platform or pulpit approached by steps. It was placed in the nave of early churches from which pronouncements were made or where certain parts of the sacred liturgy, as the Epistle and Gospel of High Mass, were, and sometimes still are, sung. There may be two, one on each side.

**Ambry** (ăm′brĭ), n.; L. A closet or chest wherein the holy oils are kept on church property, usually attached to the wall of the sanctuary.

**Ambulatory** (ăm′bû·l*a*·tō′rĭ), n.; L. The two aisles of a church running up to and behind the high altar, forming a circular walk; a gallery or walking space in a cloister.

**Amen** (ā′měn′), interj.; Heb. A word meaning "truly," "certainly," "so be it." When said at the end of a Creed, it means assent; at the end of a prayer, it signifies desire to obtain the petition. Otherwise, the word is merely to mark the ending of a statement.

**Amice** (ăm′ĭs), n.; O.E. An oblong white linen cloth worn on the shoulders of the priest and fastened around the waist by ribbons attached to two corners. The first garment in the vesting of a priest for celebrating Mass, worn beneath the alb.

**Amos** (ā'mŏs), n.; Heb. A prophetical book of the Old Testament; the author of this book who lived in the eighth century B.C.

**Amulet** (ăm'ū·lĕt), n.; L. In pagan times a charm or good luck piece. Christians of the early Church replaced these objects with medals or emblems bearing an image or relic and worn for veneration.

**Anamnesis** (ăn'ăm·nē'sĭs), n.; L. Literally "a calling to mind." The words in the prayer of the Mass which declare that the Consecration is fulfilled in memory of Christ; in the Roman rite the first of three prayers after the Consecration of the Mass beginning with the words *Unde et memores*. (Cf. Anemnesis.)

**Anaphora** (à·năf'ô·rà), n.; Gr. The Canon of the Mass, including the Preface in Eastern rites.

**Anathema** (à·năth'ē·mà), n.; Gr., L. A thing given over to evil; that pronouncement by which the Church declares a person to be out of her communion, particularly because of the denial of a truth of faith; an excommunication.

**Anchor** (ăng'kēr), n.; Gr., L. The symbol of hope. In the days of early persecutions it was used to represent the cross.

**Anchorite** (ăng'kēr·ĭt), n.; Gr., L. A man who has given up the world and lives alone, dedicating his life to God. A hermit, especially one of the Eastern Church.

Anchor symbol

**Anemnesis** (à·něm·nā'sĭs), n.; Gr., L. A commemorative prayer. The term is usually applied to the commemoration of Christ's Passion, Resurrection, and Ascension in the prayer beginning *Unde et memores* which is said after the Consecration of the Mass. Also, anamnesis.

**Angel** (ăn'jĕl), n.; Gr., L. A spiritual being created by God superior in nature to man. Literally means "messenger," one sent. A pure spirit, a being that cannot be perceived by the senses because it has no body but which is a person since it possesses intellect and free will. Angels are innumerable in number. There are nine orders, or classifications, three in each hierarchy: (1) Seraphim, Cherubim, Thrones; (2) Dominations, Principalities, Powers; (3) Virtues, Archangels, Angels. This enumeration is not an article of faith.

**Angel (Guardian)**, n. pl.; Gr., L. The angel, one appointed to every human being, whose duty it is to aid men to avoid evil, to pray, and to help him guard his thoughts at all times, and who presents man's soul to God if he is saved.

**Angelical salutation**, n.; Gr., L. "The Hail Mary." The prayer so named because it begins with the Archangel Gabriel's words of greeting to the Blessed Virgin when he announced to her that she was to become the Mother of God. (Cf. Hail Mary, *Ave Maria*.)

**Angelicals** (ăn·jĕl'ĭ·kălz), n. pl.; Gr., L. An order of nuns, following the Augustinian Rule, founded about 1530 by Louigia de Lorelli, at Milan, Italy.

**Angelus** (ăn'jĕ·lŭs), n.; L. The devotion honoring the

Incarnation and venerating the Blessed Virgin at morning (6 o'clock), noon, and evening (6 o'clock) by the recitation of three Hail Marys, with words spoken by the Blessed Virgin at the Annunciation, and a final prayer. Also refers to the angelus bell which is rung at the three times of the day.

**Anger** (ăng'gēr), n.; O.E. The excessive desire or inclination to take revenge. It is excessive when the passion is unreasonably strong in the mind or in outward expression. It is grievous when it offends charity or justice in its expression. It is one of the capital or deadly sins because it easily leads to other sins. Its contrary virtue is meekness. (Cf. Capital Sins.)

**Anglican Orders** (ăng'glĭ·kăn), n. pl.; L. Holy Orders of controverted validity of the clergy of the heretical Church of England. Declared by the Church to be "absolutely null and void" in the Bull *Apostolicae Curae* (1896).

**Annates** (ăn'āts), n. pl.; L. Revenues for the first year of an ecclesiastical benefice. Benefits given to the Pope to aid in defraying the expense of his office and international work.

**Anniversary** (ăn'ĭ·vûr'sa·rĭ), n.; L. In ecclesiastical language, a Requiem Mass read on the third, seventh, and thirtieth day after the death of a person, or a year after the death.

**Annona** (ă·nō'na), n.; It. The store from which foodstuffs may be purchased by the residents of the Vatican State. The store is operated for Vatican City, and the price of goods is very low because there is no state tax on articles sold within the Papal domains.

**Annulment** (ă·nŭl′měnt), n.; L. (1) Declaration of the invalidity of a marriage by civil or ecclesiastical courts. (2) —of a vow, the withdrawal or suspension of the obligation by a lawful superior.

**Annunciation** (ă·nŭn′sĭ·ā′shŭn), n.; L. The statement made to Mary by the Archangel Gabriel that she was to be the Mother of the Son of God. (Luke 1:26–38.) This event is commemorated on March 25.

**Anointing** (à·noint′ĭng), n.; L. (1) Term applied to the act of tracing a mark in the form of a cross, with a holy oil, on a person or thing. (2) Referring to the sick, it usually means the administration of the Sacrament of Extreme Unction.

**Antependium** (ăn′tĕ·pĕn′dĭ·ŭm), n.; L. The cloth hanging down in front of the altar from the front edge of the table to the floor, varying in color with the liturgical season or the particular Mass being celebrated. Required by rubrics when the altar is not of stone. A frontal. (Cf. Frontal.)

**Anticamera** (ăn′tĭ·kăm′ĕr·à), n.; L., It. A room adjoining the study of the Pope; a waiting room to the Pope's office.

**Antichrist** (ăn′tĭ·krīst′), n.; Gr., L. The person or power to come before the second coming of Christ who will persecute the Church and cause many to apostasize.

**Anticipation** (ăn·tĭs′ĭ·pā′shŭn), n.; L. The practice of reciting, on the previous evening or after 2 p.m., matins and lauds of the divine office; permitted only in the recitation of the divine office in private.

**Anticlericalism** (ăn'tĭ·klĕr'ĭ·kăl·ĭsm), n.; L. Opposition to religion by attacking the clergy or attempting to stop their activities. This may be an attack against the clergy themselves or attempts to stop their work, or it may be simply an habitual spirit of antagonism.

**Antilogy** (ăn·tĭl'ô·jĭ), n.; Gr., L. An apparent contradiction between statements in Sacred Scripture.

**Antimension** (ăn'tĭ·mĕn'sĭ·ŏn), n.; Gr., L. A combination corporal and altar stone used in the Byzantine Rite. It is an 18-in. square piece of linen doubled, in which are sewn up relics anointed with chrism. It is generally ornamented with a design, representing the entombment of our Lord, with the four Evangelists and the instruments of the passion, printed in black ink. It corresponds somewhat to a portable altar. Also called the "Greek corporal."

**Antiphon** (ăn'tĭ·fŏn), n.; Gr.; L. (1) Words or verses prefixed to and following a psalm or psalms containing thoughts on the mystery considered by the Church in the divine office. (2) In the Mass, the prayers of the Introit, Offertory, and Communion are called antiphons.

**Antiphonary** (ăn·tĭf'ô·nĕr'ĭ), n.; Gr., L. Latin: *Antiphonale Romanum*. The book containing the antiphons of the breviary together with their musical notes, or those parts of the breviary which are sung in choir.

**Antiphoner** (ăn·tĭf'ŏ·nēr), n.; Gr.; L. One who intones the antiphons when the breviary is sung in choir.

**Antipope** (ăn'tĭ·pōp'), n.; Gr., L. A false, rival claimant to the Papacy. A pretender to the See of the Bishop of Rome.

**Antistes** (ăn·tĭs'tēz), n.; L. The title applied to a prelate or bishop in Church history and sometimes in prayers.

**Apocalypse** (*a*·pŏk'*a*·lĭps), n.; Gr., L. The name applied to the last book of the New Testament written by St. John the Evangelist and containing his revelation concerning the future of the Church.

**Apocrisiarius** (ăp'ŏ·krĭ'sĭ·ā'rĭ·*ŭ*s), n.; Gr., L. The Papal emissary to the court of the emperor in Constantinople from the fourth to the ninth centuries. (Obs.)

**Apocrypha** (*a*·pŏk'rĭ·f*a*), n. pl.; Gr., L. (1) Spurious scriptural books denoted by the Fathers of the Church as forgeries of heretics. (2) Books declared by St. Jerome to be writings not in the recognized canon of Scripture. (3) Writings held by some to be inspired, but rejected by the Church. The Protestant Apocrypha differs from that of the Church. (Cf. Canon of Scripture.)

**Apodictic** (ăp'ŏ·dĭk'tĭk), adj.; Gr., L. A form of argumentation or reasoning which deduces a conclusion from certain and evident premises; capable of being demonstrated. n. The study of the nature and basis of knowledge.

**Apollinarianism** (*a*·pŏl'l*ĭ*·när'ĭ·*ă*n·ĭz'm), n.; Gr., L.

The heretical doctrine taught by Apollinaris, bishop of Alexandria in the fourth century, denying the human intelligence of our Lord. It denied that Christ had a human rational soul but affirmed that He had a human sensitive soul, and that the Divine Word took the place of the rational soul. Therefore it denied the true humanity of Christ.

**Apologetics** (*å·pŏl'ō·jĕt'ĭks*), n. pl.; Gr. The science of defending and explaining the Christian religion and in particular Catholic doctrine.

**Apologist** (*å·pŏl'ō·jĭst*), n.; Gr. (1) A writer or speaker who defends Christianity and the Church from attacks by infidels and others. (2) An early Christian writer of the first four centuries who vindicated the faith against paganism.

**Apology** (*å·pŏl'ō·jĭ*), n.; Gr. A written or oral defense of the Church against attacks.

**Apostasy** (*å·pŏs'tå·sĭ*), n.; Gr., L. Defection from God through entire rejection of either one or more of the following after it had been previously accepted: (1) the Christian faith; (2) ecclesiastical obedience; (3) the religious or clerical state.

**Apostate** (*å·pŏs'tāt*), n.; Gr., L. One who possessed the Catholic faith and has rejected it entirely; also, one who apostasizes from Church obedience, or from the religious or clerical state.

**Apostle** (*å·pŏs''l*), n.; Gr., L. (1) One "sent" or "commissioned." Primarily one of the twelve Apostles of Christ, namely, Saints Peter, John, James the son of Zebedee, Matthew, Jude, Thomas, Philip, Bartholomew, James the son of Alpheus, Andrew,

Simon the Cananean, Mathias, later chosen to replace Judas, and later St. Paul. (2) The name often given to the first missionary to a country.

**Apostles' Creed** (krēd), n.; Gr., L. A prayer embodying the fundamental Christian teachings and a profession of belief in them; a liturgical prayer of the Catholic beliefs of faith. It is called Apostles' because it embodies a summary of Apostolic teachings. (Cf. *Credo*, Nicene Creed.)

**Apostolic Canons** (ăp'ŏs·tŏl'ĭk), n. pl.; G., L. Writings on ecclesiastical discipline supposed to have been dictated by the Apostles to St. Clement of Rome. Rejected as such by scholars because they could not have been written before the beginning of the third century. They are found appended to the Apostolic Constitutions.

**Apostolic Constitutions,** n. pl.; Gr., L. Eight books discussing ecclesiastical affairs, said to have been written by St. Clement of Rome. Recognized as spurious by scholars.

**Apostolic Delegate,** n.; Gr., L. Papal representative sent to a country having no regular diplomatic relations with the Holy See. One having special delegated powers.

**Apostolic Fathers,** n. pl.; Gr.; L. Early Christian writers who wrote on doctrinal subjects and whose writings were not done later than the opening of the third century.

**Apostolicity** (*à*·pŏs'tō·lĭs'ĭ·tĭ), n.; Gr., L. That one of the four marks of the Catholic Church by which it stems from the Apostles in its doctrine, authority, and organization.

**Apparel** (ă·păr′ĕl), n.; L., O.Fr. A panel of embroidery stitched on the upper center part of the amice and on the cuffs and hem of the alb.

**Apparition** (ăp′a·rĭsh′ŭn), n.; L. The visible presence of a supernatural being; a vision in human form.

**Approbation** (ăp′rō·bā′shŭn), n.; L. Judgment by a prelate of a priest, declaring him qualified by authorizing him to exercise some sacred ministry. The grant of faculties by a bishop to an ordained cleric.

**Apse** (ăps), n.; Gr., L. The sanctuary end of a church building, especially those of Romanesque or Gothic architecture; originally, the semicircular termination of the church, but later the shape became varied according to the general design of the building. In a basilica, that rounded or vaulted section in which are placed the bishop's throne and seats for the clergy, and in front of which the altar stands.

**Archangel** (ärk′ān′jĕl), n.; Gr., L. One of the nine choirs of angels.

**Archbishop** (ärch′bĭsh′ŭp), n.; Gr., L. The bishop of an archdiocese who has limited authority over the other bishops of his province. As head of an ecclesiastical province the archbishop is called the metropolitan, the other bishops are called suffragans. The title archbishop is sometimes given *honoris causa* to the bishop of an archdiocese which has no suffragan sees.

**Archconfraternity** (ärch′kŏn′fra·tûr′nĭ·tĭ), n.; Gr., L.

An association of confraternities. A confraternity which has received from the Holy See the power to aggregate to itself other confraternities similar tc it, and to share its privileges and indulgences with them. Also called Primary Union. (Cf. Confraternity.)

**Archdeacon** (ärch′dē′kŭn), n.; Gr., L. In early days of the Church the deacon selected by the bishop to assist him in his work, now obsolete. The vicar-general today corresponds to this early office.

**Archdiocese** (ärch′dī′ȯ·sēs), n.; Gr., L. A diocese or jurisdiction of an archbishop; usually it is the metropolitan see of an ecclesiastical province. (Cf. Archbishop.)

**Archiepiscopal (Cross)** (är′kĭ·ē·pĭs′kȯ·păl), adj.; Gr., L. A cross with two cross bars, the upper one shorter than the other. It is carried before the archbishop in processions in his own province. Also called Patriarchal Cross.

**Archives** (är′kīvz), n. pl.; Gr., L. The repository of the official records of a diocese or other moral person in the Church; it contains all necessary accounts of ecclesiastical affairs pertaining to the diocese or other moral personality.

**Archivist** (är′kĭ·vĭst), n.; Gr., L. One in charge of the archives.

**Archpriest** (ärch′prēst′), n.; Gr., (1) A dean; a head of a diocesan deanery. (2) In early times a special representative of a bishop.

**Arcosolium** (är′kȯ·sō′lĭ·ŭm), n.; L. A decorated arch-shaped recess in the wall of the catacombs used as a burying place.

**Arianism** (âr′ĭ-ăn-ĭz'm), n. The heresy originated by Arius (d. 336) denying the consubstantiality of God the Son with God the Father, consequently a denial of the true and eternal Godhead of Christ.

**Aridity** (ă-rĭd′ĭ-tĭ), n.; L. The lack of felt devotion and of consolation in prayer.

**Ark** (ärk), n.; L. (1) The boat built and used by Noe at the time of the deluge. (2) Ark of the covenant was the chest, carried by the Israelites in their wanderings, containing the Tablets of the Law. (3) Title of the Blessed Virgin because she is the instrument of the new covenant between God and man through Christ.

**Ascension (Feast of)** (ă-sĕn′shŭn), n.; L. The commemoration of our Lord's rising into heaven forty days after His Resurrection on Easter. It falls upon a Thursday.

**Ascension (of Christ)**, n. The rising into heaven of Christ from Mount Olivet forty days after His Resurrection; the Ascension was in virtue of His being God and characteristic of a blessed spirit.

**Ascetical (theology)** (ă-sĕt′ĭ-kăl), n.; Gr. The branch of the science of theology which treats of the rules of perfection; the systematized practice and theory of acquiring perfection.

**Ascetics** (ă-sĕt′ĭks), n. pl.; Gr. (1) The study embracing all of the theology of virtue and perfection and the means of gaining that perfection. (2) Those persons who apply the principles and teachings of ascetical theology; those using the practical means to acquire virtue and become perfect in order to achieve sanctity.

**Aseity** (á·sē′ĭ·tĭ), n.; L. A philosophical term applied to one existing independent of all else; a mode of existing of oneself. The prime distinguishing attribute of the divine substance.

**Ash Wednesday** (ăsh), n.; L., Ger., A.S. The first day of the Lenten fast. It derives its name from the custom of placing blessed ashes of burnt palms on the foreheads of the faithful in the form of a cross to remind them of death and the necessity of penance.

**Ashes (blessed)** (ăsh′ĕz), n. pl.; A.S. The burnt remains of palms which are blessed before the principal Mass of Ash Wednesday and placed on the forehead of each person to remind them of their last end and the necessity for penance; blessed ashes are a sacramental of the Church.

**Asperges** (ăs·pûr′jēz), n.; Gr., L. (1) The ceremony of sprinkling the altar, clergy, and people with holy water, performed by the celebrant before the principal Mass. This is only permitted on Sundays. (2) The first word of the psalm verse sung by the celebrant at this ceremony.

**Aspergill** (ăs′pĕr·jĭl), n.; L. Latin: *aspergillum*. An instrument for sprinkling holy water; usually a rod with a perforated metal bulb at the end from which holy water is shaken.

(1) Aspergill, (2) Aspersory.

**Aspersory** (ăs′pēr·sô′rĭ), n.; L. Latin: *aspersorium*. A portable vessel to hold holy water and into which the aspergill is dipped.

**Aspiration** (ăs′pĭ·rā′shŭn), n.; L. A short prayer; an ejaculation.

**Assessor** (ă·sĕs′ẽr), n.; L. A consultant of a judge in an ecclesiastical court.

**Assistant** (ă·sĭs′tănt), n.; L. (1) The priest aiding a parish priest; a curate. (2) One assisting the bishop in a pontifical function. (3) A newly ordained priest may have an assistant priest at his first Solemn Mass. (4) Assistant deacons, sometimes called chaplains, are those who assist the bishop at low Mass, walk at his side in procession, or sit beside him when, vested in *cappa magna*, he sits at the throne.

**Assumption** (ă·sŭmp′shŭn), n.; L. The taking up of the body of the Blessed Virgin into heaven and she was thereby preserved from bodily corruption after her death. The feast is celebrated on August 15 and is a holyday of obligation. (Dogma: Nov. 1, 1950)

**Atonement** (ă·tōn′mĕnt), n.; M.E. The reconciliation of man with God by Jesus Christ, the Son, through His sacrificial death on the Cross. The Redemption.

**Attention** (ă·tĕn′shŭn), n.; L. Advertence of the mind to what one is doing; required for prayer and for the lawful administering or receiving of the sacraments.

**Attributes (divine)** (ăt′rĭ·būts), n. pl.; L. Perfections which belong to the divine essence of God, which are of God's being, as divine intellect, divine will, and all things ascribed to this Being as one.

**Attrition** (ă·trĭsh'ŭn), n.; L. An imperfect sorrow for sin, distinguished from contrition by the motive, which is the fear of God's punishments or the heinousness of sin. Its motive is supernatural because it arises from faith but is not based on unselfish love of God. Sufficient for the reception of the sacraments of Baptism (by an adult) and Penance.

**Aumbry,** L., Fr. Variation of *ambry*.

**Audience (Papal)** (ô'dĭ·ĕns), n.; L., Fr. A formal hearing or interview with the Pope. It may be (*a*) public, when those having a special card of admission from the *Major Domo* are admitted to the Hall of the Consistory where the Holy Father speaks to them and hears their petitions; or (*b*) private, when the Holy Father grants a visit to an individual.

**Augustinians** (ô'gŭs·tĭn'ĭ·ănz), n. pl.; L. (1) Also called Assumptionists. The congregation of the Augustinians of the Assumption, formally approved in 1864. They were suppressed in France in 1900 but are active in England, United States and in the Orient. (2) The members of the religious order of the Hermits of St. Augustine founded by St. Augustine in 391.

**Aureole** (ô'rē·ōl), n.; L. (1) In art, the light or gold shading surrounding the figure depicted in a sacred picture. (2) In theology, a certain accidental reward over and above the essential bliss of heaven given to persons who

Aureole
(Cf. 1 of definition)

achieve heaven with extraordinary degrees of merit.

**Austere** (s·tēr′), adj.; Gr., L. Rigorous; practicing mortification; strict in observance.

**Austerity** (ôs·tĕr′ĭ·tĭ), n.; Gr., L. Bodily mortification for spiritual advancement, such as a fast or other penance painful to the body.

**Avarice** (ăv′a·rĭs), n.; L. See Covetousness.

**Azyme** (ăz′ĭm), n.; Gr. The unleavened bread used by the Jews in their sacrifices; sometimes applied to the Eucharistic bread.

**Azymites** (ăz′ĭ·mīts), n. pl.; Gr. Term used by Greek Schismatics for Christians of the Latin Church.

# ✧ B ✧

**Baianism** (bā'yăn·ĭz'm), n.; L., Fr. Erroneous teaching begun by Michael du Bay, known as Baius (1513–1589), who was a professor at Louvain University during the middle of the sixteenth century. By his interpretations Baius rejected the doctrine of original sin, grace, and declared man free of responsibility for personal sin since, he said, man acts, by concupiscence, independently of his will. Baius recanted his errors but he had contributed to the Protestant revolt.

**Baldacchinum** (băl'dà·kē'nŭm), n.; It. Also Baldacchino. (1) A canopy suspended over the main altar and its footpace from the roof or extending from the wall. It is called a ciborium when it is a domelike canopy resting on pillars. (Cf. Canopy, *ciborium magnum*.) (2) The canopy of cloth carried above the priest by means of four poles when the Blessed Sacrament is borne in procession. (3) The small canopy over an episcopal throne.

**Baldaquin** (băl′da·kĭn), n.; It., Fr. A canopy; a baldacchinum.

**Balm** (bäm), n.; Gr., L. The fragrant secretion of certain trees or plants which when mixed with olive oil forms chrism.

**Bandeau** (băn·dō′; băn′dō), n.; pl. **-deaux** (-dōz′), Fr. A circlet of cloth worn about the forehead to which a veil is attached, which forms the headdress of some nuns.

**Banner** (băn′ẽr), n.; L. A cloth upon which religious objects or mottoes are pictured. They are not attached to a single staff as a flag, rather the cloth hangs from a cross-bar which, together with the staff, forms a cross. Banners are borne in processions or displayed before religious groups or in a church.

**Banns** (bănz), n. pl.; L. (1) The public proclamation of an intended marriage by which all are informed that they must make known to the competent authorities any impediments which would prevent the ecclesiastical officials from permitting the marriage to take place. The banns must be announced in the parish churches of the contracting parties at the principal Mass on three successive Sundays or Holydays of obligation. If the marriage does not take place within six months of the final announcement, the banns must be again announced. (2) A pronouncement to determine if impediments exist made in the home parish of a man before being granted the privilege of receiving subdeaconship.

**Baptism** (băp′tĭz′m), n.; Gr., L. (1) A sacrament instituted by Christ by which through the infusion of grace original sin is taken away, and administered by the pouring of water on the head and saying, "I baptize you in the name of the Father, and of the Son, and of the Holy Ghost," and by which act one enters into the Church of Christ. There are three means of Baptism for gaining salvation: (*a*) Baptism of water which is performed by the act of pouring water. (*b*) Baptism of desire is the act of perfect love of God which suffices for adults in good faith if the formal baptism with water is impossible. (*c*) Baptism of blood, i.e., martyrdom which also forgives the effects of sin and remits the temporal penalties of sin. (*b*) and (*c*) are not sacraments.

Baptism is a necessary sacrament. It remits all sins—original and actual, may be given to all human beings, is ordinarily performed by a priest but in a case of necessity may be given by any person who has attained the use of reason. The matter of the sacrament is the washing with water; the form is the words "I baptize you, etc."

(2) Ceremonies of blessing church bells or ships were formerly called "baptisms."

**Baptismal Name** (băp·tĭz′măl), adj.; Gr., L. A name given to the person baptized, signifying he has become a new creature in Christ. It is prescribed that this be the name of a saint.

**Baptismal Robe** (rōb), n.; Gr., L. In the early Church the white garment worn by those to be baptized; it is now commemorated in the white linen cloth laid on the head of the infant being baptized.

**Baptismal Water,** n.; Gr., L. Water blessed on Holy Saturday and the vigil of Pentecost in the baptismal font by the priest and into which oil of catechumens and chrism is poured. This water must be used in administering solemn Baptism.

**Baptistery** (băp′tĭst·ēr·ĭ), n.; Gr., L. A small separate building or part of the church containing the font and set apart as the place for the administration of Baptism.

**Barbette** (bär·bĕt′), n.; Fr. The cloth head covering extending to the neck, the sides of the head and under the chin, worn by sisters or nuns of certain religious orders.

**Baruch** (bâr′ŭk), n.; Heb.; Bib. A prophetical book of the Old Testament named after its author.

**Basilica** (bȧ·sĭl′ĭ·kȧ), n.; Gr. A consecrated church usually built with the front facing east, generally constructed in one of the historic styles of architecture. The form is oblong in shape with the length forming the nave, at one end of which is the apse. It is now required that basilicas in order to be so titled contain some work of art. The major basilicas have an altar for the Pope, which no one else may use without his permission. There are thirteen basilicas in Rome, five major and eight minor.

**B.C.,** abbre. Abbreviation for the words "before Christ" meaning the years before the Incarnation of the Son of God from which event the present calendar is now reckoned.

**Beads** (bēdz), n. pl.; A.S. Colloq.: The Rosary. Any

form of beads on a chain or string to aid one in counting a repeated number of prayers.

**Beatific (vision)** (bē′a·tĭf′ĭk), adj.; L. The act of seeing God face to face which forms the essential happiness of angels and men in heaven. This "seeing of God" is through direct knowledge whereas the knowledge of God on earth is merely by reflection through created things and revealed images.

**Beatification** (bē·ăt′ĭ·fĭ·kā′shŭn), n.; L. The declaration made by the Church after due process of determining the sanctity of a deceased person; the process necessary to the declaration by the Church that one may be publicly venerated; a preliminary action to actual canonization. It bestows the title of "blessed" on the one beatified.

**Beatitude** (bē·ăt′ĭ·tūd), n.; L. That happiness or bliss which creatures find in the vision and love of God alone.

**Beatitudes (the eight)** (-tūdz), n. pl.; L. The eight blessings spoken by our Lord in the Sermon on the Mount. (Matt. 5:3-10.) They are: Blessed are the poor in spirit, for theirs is the kingdom of heaven; blessed are the meek, for they shall possess the earth; blessed are they who mourn, for they shall be comforted; blessed are they who hunger and thirst for justice, for they shall be satisfied; blessed are the merciful, for they shall obtain mercy; blessed are the pure of heart, for they shall see God; blessed are the peacemakers, for they shall be called the children of God; blessed are they who suffer persecution for justice' sake, for theirs is the kingdom of heaven.

**Beatus** (bē·ā′tŭs), n.; L. The title applied to one who

has been beatified; also applied to canonized saints; a soul who has reached heaven. Literally, "blessed one."

**Bedesman** (bĕdz'măn), n.; A.S. Also beadsman. One who prays for the soul of another or one charged with this duty. Also the one for whom one should pray. (Obs.)

**Beelzebub** (bē·ĕl'zē·bŭb), n.; Heb., Gr. Satan. The name applied to the "prince of devils" in the New Testament.

**Belief** (bē·lēf'), n.; L., A.S. The acceptance by the mind of Catholic teaching, because it comes from divine revelation; a single truth of Christian doctrine.

**Bell** (bĕl), n.; A.S. A hollow metallic vessel which emits a ringing sound upon being struck. The large church bell is usually kept in the church tower and is used to sound the Angelus or to call the faithful to divine service. A smaller bell also has place in the sanctuary where it is sounded during the Mass at the *Sanctus*, elevation, and when the priest spreads his hands over the host and chalice before the Consecration and at the *Domine, non sum dignus* before the priest's communion.

A type of hand bell used in the sanctuary

**Benedicite** (bĕn'ē·dĭs'ĭ·tē), L. imperative pl. The Latin word meaning "bless ye," used as a greeting in monasteries.

**Benedictines** (bĕn'ē·dĭk'tĭnz), n. pl.; L., Fr. The order of religious which follows the rule of St. Benedict.

**Benediction (of the Blessed Sacrament)** (běn'ē·dĭk'-shŭn), n.; L. The service during which the Sacred Host is adored while it is exposed in the monstrance or enclosed in the ciborium. During the service the hymn *O Salutaris Hostia* or some other hymn is sung and the consecrated Host is incensed; a litany and other prayers may follow; finally the *Tantum ergo* with its prayer is sung and the blessing given with the Blessed Sacrament. The act of Benediction is the blessing of the people with the Sacred Host in the form of a cross by the priest. The Host is then removed from the monstrance and replaced in the tabernacle.

**Benedictional** (běn'ē·dĭk'shŭn·ăl), n.; L. Latin: *Benedictionale*. A book containing the forms of blessing found in the Roman ritual, pontifical, and missal.

**Benedictus** (běn'ē·dĭk'tŭs), n.; L. The canticle of Zachary recited daily in the divine office. It is found in Luke 1:68–79.

**Benefice** (běn'ē·fĭs), n.; L. A perpetual right granted by competent Church authority to an ecclesiastic consisting of a sacred office and the right to receive the revenue which accrues from that office's endowment.

**Beneficiary** (běn'ē·fĭsh'ĭ·ĕr'ĭ), n.; L. (1) One who holds a benefice. (2) A cleric who aids the members of a chapter in their choral duties in a cathedral or collegiate church.

**Benemerente (medal)** (běn'ē·mĕr·ĕn'tā), n.; It. An honorary decoration given in recognition of outstanding military or civil services. It was instituted by Pope Gregory XVI and may be merited by either men or women. Pl.: *benemerenti*.

**Benignity** (bē·nĭg′nĭ·tĭ), n.; L. Kindness; one of the twelve fruits of the Holy Ghost.

**Berrettino** (bĕr′rĕt·tē′nô), n.; It. Literally a "little biretta." Name applied to the zuchetto. (Cf. Zuchetto, Solideo.)

**Betrothal** (bē·trŏth′ăl), n.; L., O.E. Formal engagement to marry; the espousal or promise to marry which is valid between Catholics and is canonically binding when made in writing signed by the parties, the parish priest or local ordinary, or by at least two witnesses.

**Bible** (bī′b'l), n.; Gr. Sacred Scriptures which have been pronounced authentic by the infallible authority of the Church. The writings are both of Jewish and Christian origin. The Bible records the revelation of God to man. There are 72 books contained in the Bible; 45 in the Old Testament; 27 in the New Testament. The name is taken from the Greek and literally means "the Books."

**Bigamy** (bĭg′à·mĭ), n.; Gr., L. In canon law that irregularity of marriage in which one of the contracting parties goes through the ceremonies of marriage while being validly married to a third party still living. In regard to holy orders bigamy is that irregularity which arises from the fact that a man has contracted two or more valid marriages successively.

**Bilocation** (bī′lô·kā′shŭn), n.; L. The act of being in two places at one time; used in reference to the presence of Christ in heaven and in the Blessed

Sacrament. Also refers to saints who have appeared in two places simultaneously.

**Bination** (bĭ·nā′shŭn), n.; L. Sometimes called duplication. The celebration of a second Mass on the same day by the same priest by permission of ecclesiastical authority.

**Biretta** (bĭ·rĕt′à), n.; L., It. Also berretta. A square cap of cloth with three or four leaves or projecting corners rising from the top. In the center of the crown there is a pom-pom or tassel. It is worn by priests or other clerics, and is found in the following colors: navy blue, black, red, or purple.

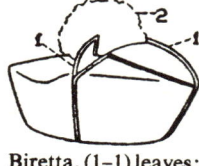

Biretta. (1-1) leaves; (2) pom-pom

**Biritualism** (bĭ·rĭt′ū·ăl·ĭz′m), n.; L. The use, in certain cases, by a priest belonging to the Latin rite of a rite other than his own. This is the practice of missionaries of the Latin rite who work among the Eastern Churches and use an Eastern rite or that of the people among whom they work.

**Bishop** (bĭsh′ŭp), n.; Gr., L. A member of the hierarchy of the Church. An ecclesiastic who has received the highest of the sacred orders and who has jurisdiction over a diocese; the ordinary. (1) Auxiliary—one raised to the dignity of the hierarchy and named a titular bishop and placed as an assistant to another ruling bishop. He does not enjoy jurisdiction by reason of his consecration, but receives it from the bishop whom he assists in the duties of the episcopal office. (2) Coadjutor—

one raised to the dignity of a bishop and given jurisdiction in part to govern the diocese of a bishop who is partly incapacitated. He usually has the right of succession. (3) An Administrator—a bishop given complete jurisdiction to govern the diocese of a bishop who is wholly incapacitated. (4) Suffragan—a diocesan bishop in an ecclesiastical province of a metropolitan who is subject to an archbishop. (5) Titular—one consecrated to a diocese or see which existed at one time but which now, because the faith has died out in that place, no longer exists.

**Blasphemy** (blăs′fĕ·mĭ), n.; Gr., L. Any word or act insulting to God or to holy things. It is a sin against religion and may be aimed directly at God, or indirectly by contempt for His Church, His saints, or sacred persons or things.

**Blessed** (blĕs′ĕd), n.; A.S. One who has been beatified; a soul enjoying the happiness of heaven. (Cf. Beatus.)

**Blessing** (blĕs′ĭng), n.; A.S. A prayer asking God's favor upon a person or thing. The person giving the blessing acts in God's name. Besides the blessing of persons, any place or thing used for the good of man may be blessed. Blessing does not permanently set aside the object blessed for religious purposes as does a consecration.

**Boat** (bōt), n.; A.S. The boat-shaped dish or vessel which holds the raw incense to be burned in the censer.

Boat

**Books of Wisdom,** n. pl.; Bib. Five books of the

Old Testament, namely *Job*, *Proverbs*, *Ecclesiastes*, *Wisdom*, and *Ecclesiasticus*. The sapiential books.

**Bow** (bou), n.; A.S. An inclination of the head or a bending of the body in respect or reverence. There are four kinds of bows used in the ceremonies of the Church: (*a*) a deep bow of the body; (*b*) a moderate bow of the body; (*c*) a deep bow of the head only; (*d*) a slight bow of the head.

**Brandea** (brăn′dē·à), n. pl.; L. Objects which have been touched to genuine relics or the remains of a saint; originally pieces of cloth lowered into the shrine or crypt of a saint.

**Brasses** (brăs′ĕz), n. pl.; L., A.S. Brass mountings used in decoration or for inscriptions on tombs or sepulchers where burial took place in church. (Obs.)

**Bread** (brĕd), n.; L., A.S. Unleavened bread of wheat used as one of the elements of the Sacrifice of the Mass.

**Breviary** (brē′vĭ·ĕr′ĭ), n.; L. The collection of prescribed prayers and readings contained in the divine office recited by those in major orders. It is a solemn formula of public prayer composed of psalms, lessons from the Old and New Testaments, passages from doctrinal writings and the lives of the saints, hymns, and special prayers. It is divided into four parts corresponding to the seasons of the year. Each day has as its office eight parts called "hours," namely, matins, lauds, prime, terce, sext, none, vespers, and compline.

**Brief** (brēf), n.; L. Also breve. A papal letter of the court of Rome signed by the Pope's secretary of briefs and sealed with the Pope's signet ring, called the fisherman's ring. (Cf. Bull.)

**Brothers** (brŭth′ẽrz), n. pl.; A.S. Members of a male religious community who have not taken Holy Orders or who do not aspire to Holy Orders but live a religious community life and devote themselves to various works of a religious nature.

**Bugia** (bū′jĭ·à), n.; L., It. A candlestick with a short handle; it is held by the chief assistant at the Mass of a bishop when the bishop is before the Missal for the reading of the Epistle or Gospel. The use of the bugia is conceded to abbots and to certain other prelates. More recently referred to simply as the "hand candle." Also called palmatoria or scotula.

Bugia

**Bull** (bool), n.; L. An official papal document or writing receiving its name from the lead or gold seal, called the *bulla*, bearing a representation of SS. Peter and Paul and the name of the reigning pontiff. Bulls are of strong parchment and are signed by the Pope and the chief members of the papal chancery. The bull is more formal than the brief and is used for more weighty pronouncements of the papal chancery. Today they are used only for very important and solemn occasions. Sometimes called a *bulla*.

**Bullarium** (boo·lȧ′ri·ŭm), n.; L. The name applied to a collection of papal bulls.

**Bursar** (bûr′sẽr), n.; L., Fr. The person who serves as treasurer of a religious community.

**Burse** (bûrs), n.; L., Fr. Also bursa or pera. (1) The square case in which the corporal used in Mass is carried. It is of the same color as the vestments. (2) The leather packet in which the pyx is carried. (3) An endowment given to an ecclesiastical institution for the support and education of one studying for the priesthood.

Burse (Cf. 1 of definition)

**Buskins** (bŭs′kĭnz), n. pl.; L., O.Fr. The ceremonial silk stockings worn over his purple stockings by a bishop at pontifical Mass.

**Bussolanti** (boōs′sō·län′tĭ), n. pl.; It. The lay chamberlains on guard in the anterooms which lead to the Pope's apartments in the Lateran Palace. They dress in red breeches, short cape, and silk stockings. They have the honor of carrying the Pope on the *sedia gestatoria*, and these are called *sediari* when performing this duty, and wear red capes over their uniforms. (Cf. Sediari.)

**B.V.M.**, abbre. The Blessed Virgin Mary.

**Byzantine Rite** (bĭ·zăn′tĭn), (n.), adj.; L. The celebrating of Mass, the administering of the Sacraments, and the performing of other liturgical functions after the manner now used by the Orthodox Eastern Church. Its ordinary language is Greek, but it is used in several other languages.

# ☩ C ☩

**Caeremoniale,** n.; L. See ceremonial.

**Caeremoniarius,** n.; L. See Master of Ceremonies.

**Calced** (kălst), adj.; L. Wearing shoes; certain members of religious orders who wear shoes distinguishing them from others belonging to another branch of their order who go barefoot or wear sandals.

**Calefactory** (kăl′ĕ·făk′tŏ·rĭ), n.; L. The common room or community room of a monastery; a room of the monastery in which there is a fireplace.

**Calendar (ecclesiastical)** (kăl′ĕn·dēr), n.; L. The days of the civil year set apart for religious celebrations; an arrangement marking the feasts of the Church assigned to each day of the year. A liturgical calendar gives the day by day course of feasts as followed by the Church in her liturgy; this begins with the first Sunday of Advent and continues in the cycle till the following first Sunday of Advent in the next year, and this calendar changes each year because many of the feasts of the Church are determined by the date of Easter.

**Caligae** (kăl'ĭ·jē), n. pl.; L. Buskins; leggings; liturgical stockings worn by a bishop for Pontifical Mass.

**Calotte** (ka·lŏt'), n.; It. A small skullcap worn by the Pope, bishops, and other prelates. A zuchetto, a berrettino.

**Calumny** (kăl'ŭm·nĭ), n.; L., Fr. A falsehood directed against the reputation of a person. Restitution must be made in as far as possible. (Cf. Slander, Detraction.)

**Calvary** (kăl'va·rĭ), n.; L. (1) The small hill to the west of Jerusalem where Christ was crucified. (2) A cross mounted on three steps.

**Camauro** (kä·mou'rō), n. It. A cap or headpiece made of red velvet trimmed with white fur worn by the Pope on occasions other than liturgical. One of white damask is worn during the Easter octave. This cap takes the place of the biretta.

**Camera** (kam'ĕr·a), n.; L., It. *Camera Apostolica*. An office of the Roman Curia, presided over by the Cardinal Camerarius, and entrusted with the administration of the Holy See, especially when the Holy See is vacant. The financial executor of the Holy See.

**Camerlengo** (kăm'ĕr·lĕng'gō), n.; It. Also Camerarius. The name attached to the cardinal holding the office of chamberlain of the Roman Church. The one holding this office certifies the death of the Pope and calls the conclave for electing a successor; he is in charge of the revenues of the sacred college of cardinals.

**Camillians** (kà·mĭl′ĭ·ănz), n. pl.; L., Fr. Members of the Clerks Regular for the Care of the Sick, a society founded in Rome by St. Camillus de Lellis in 1582 and dedicated to hospital work.

**Campanile** (kăm′pá·nē′lē), n.; It. (1) A bell tower. Originally, a form of bell tower which was developed by Lombardian architects and which is still used in Italy. The campanile is usually a slender tower, detached from the church building and crowned with a turret containing the bells; now it more frequently is attached to the church, or is found only in its similar construction, the steeple. (2) The name is also applied to an open construction on top of a roof in which a bell is placed.

Campanile

**Candelabrum** (kăn′dĕ·lā′brŭm), n.; L. Pl. candelabra. A multibranched candlestick or candle support, usually with five or seven branches.

**Candlemas** (kăn′d'l·más), n.; L., A.S. Common name attached to the Feast of the Purification of the Blessed Virgin, Feb. 2, and derived from the blessing of candles which takes place upon this feastday.

Candelabrum

**Candle** (kăn′d'l), n.; L., A.S. A cylindrical wax stick

or taper with a wick in the center used for illumination. Candles used in the church for liturgical purposes are of pure wax for the greater part and white in color except in Masses for the dead when they may be of yellow wax. The rubrics prescribe the usage of a specified number to be lighted during various ceremonies.

**Canon** (kăn′ŭn), n.; Gr., L. (1) Originally this meant a rule or measure. In the Church it has come to mean a rule of belief or conduct. A formal law of the Church. (2)—of a chapter, a member of the clergy forming a cathedral or collegiate chapter which lives in a semicommunity life. (Cf. Chapter.)

**Canon Law** (lô), n.; Gr., L., A.S. The name attached to that body of rules or laws for the direction of all faithful in matters of faith and conduct. It is that group of laws prescribed to Christians, i.e., baptized persons, by the authority of the Church regarding faith, morals, and discipline. Today we follow the New Code (*Codex Juris Canonici*) promulgated by Pope Benedict XV on May 27, 1917; its binding force began in full on May 19, 1918. The New Code is divided into five books: the first is introductory; the second treats of *persons* as affected by the law; the third treats of *things*, such as sacraments and sacramentals and the temporal affairs of the Church; the fourth gives the laws governing ecclesiastical procedure; the fifth deals with crimes and their penalties.

**Canon (of the Mass)**, n.; Gr., L. The portion of the Mass proper beginning after the *Sanctus* and ending just before the *Pater Noster*. The sacrificial action of the Mass.

**Canon (Pontificalis),** n.; Gr., L. A liturgical book containing the ordinary and Canon of the Mass and some liturgical forms proper to prelates. At pontifical functions it is used, instead of the altar cards, by cardinals, bishops, abbots, and protonotaries apostolic.

**Canon (of the Scripture),** n.; Gr., L. The books of Scripture recognized as authentic and prescribed as parts of the Bible by the infallible authority of the Church. The Canon recognizes the books of the Catholic Bible as true and inspired Scripture.

**Canonical Hours** (kȧ·nŏn′ĭ·kăl), (adj.), n. pl.; Gr., L. The eight hours or offices of the daily recitation of the breviary or divine office. They are: matins, lauds, prime, terce, sext, none, vespers, and compline.

**Canonicity** (kăn′ŭn·ĭs′ĭ·tĭ), n.; Gr., L. The recognition by the Church of a book of Sacred Scripture as inspired.

**Canonist** (kăn′ŭn·ĭst), n.; Gr., L. One who is skilled or learned in Canon Law; usually refers to one who has received the degree of Doctor of Canon Law. It also is used loosely to refer to a judge or official of an ecclesiastical court who is generally well trained in Canon Law.

**Canonization** (kăn′ŭn·ĭ·zā′shŭn), n.; Gr., L. The decree of judgment and the declaration of that judgment by the Church, given in a Papal bull, that a particular person lived a life of virtue in the heroic degree, that the prescribed number of miracles have been attested and proven, and that the person may be universally venerated and honored by the faithful as a saint.

**Canopy** (kăn′ô·pĭ), n.; Gr., L., It. (1) A cloth suspended on four poles and carried above the minister who bears the Blessed Sacrament in procession. (Cf. Baldacchinum. Also the similar word, baldaquin.) (2) Canopy of an altar is that rooflike covering of an altar and footpace usually so called when it is rigid, that is, made of masonry or wood, supported by columns; a civory; a *ciborium magnum*. (3) The tentlike veil or cloth covering the tabernacle. (Cf. Conopaeum.)

**Cantate Sunday** (kăn·tā′tā), n.; L., It. The fourth Sunday after Easter, so named from the first words of the introit of the Mass of that day.

**Canticle** (kăn′tĭ·k'l), n.; L. A sacred song or poem found in the Bible; e.g., one from the Old Testament as recorded in Daniel 3:52–57; or one from the New Testament as found in Luke 1:46–55.

**Cantor** (kăn′tôr), n.; L. The song leader of a choir; the precentor; a chanter.

**Capital (sins)** (kăp′ĭ·tăl), n.; L. The so-called "deadly sins," seven in number, called "capital" because they are the source of most other sins; called "deadly" because they easily lead to mortal sins. They need not be separate acts but can exist as habits or vices. The seven capital sins are: pride, covetousness, lust, anger, gluttony, envy, and sloth.

**Capitulary** (ka·pĭt′ū·lĕr′ĭ), n.; L. A set of "chapters"

each of which was a law. The name given to the canons or laws passed by provincial councils. Historically it refers to the laws, each called a "chapter," promulgated by the Frankish kings of the first and second dynasties.

**Cappa** (kăp′á), n.; L. A cape; a long cloaklike garment worn over the shoulders.

**Cappa Magna** (kăp′á măg′ná), n.; L. A long vestment with a hood lined with silk or fur, according to the season, worn by cardinals and bishops as a cape. The cappa magna is of scarlet silk when worn by cardinals and of purple wool when worn by a bishop. In procession the train of the cappa magna is usually carried by pages.

**Capsula** (kăp′sū·lá), n.; L. A metal vessel supported on a stand in which the Host for Benediction of the Blessed Sacrament is reserved. (Cf. Luna.)

**Capuchin** (kăp′ū·chĭn), n.; Fr., It. A religious order following the Franciscan rule whose name is derived from the cowl worn on the habit, or religious garb. The order was instituted in 1525 by Matteo da Bassi as a reform or return to the original observance of the rule of St. Francis. Its abbreviation is: O.F.M. Cap.

**Cardinal** (kär′dĭ·năl), n.; L., It. The name given to the members of the Sacred College appointed by the Pope; the number of these members should not exceed seventy. They govern in the Church and advise the Holy Father in council; upon the death of the Pope they gather to elect a successor. In the College of Cardinals there are three ranks of dignity ranging in order: Cardinal bishops, Cardinal priests, Cardinal deacons. (1) Cardinal Protector is one of the Cardinals of the Sacred College appointed to watch over the interests of a particular religious order, congregation, or nation but who has no jurisdiction over it. (2) Cardinal Vicar is the vicar general of the Pope as the Bishop of Rome who administers the spiritual affairs of the diocese; he is always a cardinal.

**Cardinal (virtues)**, n. (pl.); L., It. The four great moral virtues of prudence, justice, fortitude, and temperance, so named because of their importance since all other moral virtues are connected with one or other of these.

**Carmel** (kär′měl), n.; Heb., L. The original Hebrew word means a garden; it is a ridge of mountains in northwestern Palestine on the Mediterranean coast; sometimes the name given a Carmelite monastery.

**Carmelite** (kär′měl·ĭt), n.; L. An order of monks founded in the twelfth century and deriving their name from Mount Carmel, the place of their first monastery. Carmelite nuns were instituted in the fifteenth century.

**Carnival** (kär′nĭ·văl), n.; It., Fr. The three days preceding Lent which are a time of celebration before taking on the penances of the Lenten season. (Cf. Shrovetide.)

**Carthusian** (kär·thū′zhăn), n.; L. An order of monks founded by St. Bruno in the eleventh century.

**Cask** (kăsk), n.; L., It. One of two small containers of

wine given by the new bishop to his consecrator after the Offertory of the Mass of consecration.

**Cassock** (kăs′ŭk), n.; It., Fr. A tunic-shaped garment reaching from the neck to the heels worn as an outside garment by priests or clerics. In French, a soutane.

Cassock with sash

**Castel Gandolfo,** n.; It. The summer residence of the Pope near Rome.

**Casuistry** (kăzh′ū·ĭs·trĭ), n.; L., Fr. The science which treats of matters of conscience. Strictly, the study of moral principles through concrete cases; applied moral theology. (Cf. Moral theology.)

**Casus** (kā′sŭs), n.; L. A real or imaginary example used in teaching canon law or moral theology to illustrate a point and to give practice in applying general principles to particular circumstances.

**Catacomb** (kăt′à·kōm), n.; L., It. An underground place of burial of the early Christians which became a place of refuge during the persecutions, and where public services might be held. They were dug in the *tufa granolare*, a soft strata of earth adaptable to excavation. When used in the plural, they usually refer to those outside of Rome, but there are also catacombs at Syracuse and Palermo, and in Tuscany and Etruria.

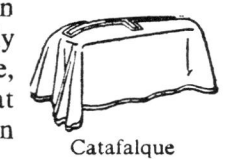
Catafalque

**Catafalque** (kăt′à·fălk), n.; It., Fr. (1) A frame shaped like a bier covered with a black cloth or pall and used during Masses of the dead when the coffin and corpse are not present and over which the absolution for the dead is given. (2) A stand or support on which the coffin (or sometimes a casket, when the body is absent) is placed during the funeral service. (3) A structure built in some places over the coffin and covered with a pall. Sometimes incorrectly called a hearse.

**Catechetics** (kăt'ē·kĕt'ĭks), n. pl.; Gr., L. The science and art of instructing the young in Christian doctrine; the teaching of catechism; instructions given to converts.

**Catechetical** (kăt'ē·kĕt'ĭ·kăl), adj.; Gr., L. Pertaining to catechetics; or the instruction in Christian doctrine; pertaining to the catechism or the work of the catechist.

**Catechism** (kăt'ē·kĭz'm), n. Gr., L. Instructions in Christian doctrine, usually of the question and answer form, by which the elements of faith or belief are taught to children or those preparing to enter the Church as converts. Also a collection of questions and answers, usually a book or booklet, used for instruction in Christian doctrine.

**Catechist** (kăt'ē·kĭst), n. Gr., L. One who teaches those preparing to receive Baptism; one giving instructions in catechism.

**Catechize** (kăt'ē·kīz), v.t. and intr.; Gr., L. To instruct in the teachings and doctrines of the Catholic religion; to teach the catechism; to convert; to evangelize; to ask questions pertaining to Christian doctrine.

**Catechumen** (kăt'ē·kū'mĕn), n.; Gr., L. One who is preparing to receive Baptism. In the early ages of the Church a period of two years or more was usually required before the instruction was considered complete and the sincerity of the person was proven.

**Catechumenate** (kăt′ê·kū′měn·āt), n.; Gr., L. A period of preparation preceding the reception of Baptism; a period of preliminary instruction. In the early Church this period lasted for two years or more. Sometimes referred to the place where the instructions were given.

**Cathedra** (ka·thē′dra; kăth′ê·dra), n.; Gr., L. (1) The chair in which the bishop sits; now termed a throne. (2) A symbol of the authority of the bishop; also a symbol of authoritative teaching. (3) *ex cathedra*, a term used to denote the Pope's supreme and infallible authority when he teaches the faithful regarding matters pertaining to faith and morals.

**Cathedral** (ka·thē′dral), n.; Gr., L. The home church of the bishop in his diocese; the church in which the chair of the bishop is located and from which it derives its name.

**Cathedraticum** (kăth′ê·drăt′ĭ·kŭm), n.; L. A small, determined tax, payable to the bishop by all churches and benefices of a diocese in token of subjection. In the United States, the tax due from each parish church for the maintenance of the bishop is popularly but mistakenly called cathedraticum. (Cf. Synodaticum.)

**Catholic** (kăth′ō·lĭk), adj. and n.; Gr., L. (1) Universal; the word was applied from very early ages to the true Church and today is recognized as the name of the Church. (2) A member of the Roman Catholic Church.

**Catholic Action,** n.; Gr., L. The acts of the laity in the liturgy, prayer, conversion, and work of the Catholic hierarchy upon approval and under the direction of the bishop. Work to advance the cause of Christ in temporal and spiritual matters: first, in ourselves; second, in our families; and third, in the associations of our social life.

**Catholicism** (ka·thŏl′i·sĭz′m), n.; Gr., L. The religion teaching the faith and morals revealed to man by God.

**Catholicity** (kăth′ô·lĭs′ĭ·tĭ), n.; Gr., L. (1) Universality. (2) That one of the four marks of the Catholic Church according to which the Church extends to all times and peoples, and teaches all the truths necessary for salvation.

**Cause** (kôz), n.; L., Fr. (1) That which produces an effect or result. (2) A course of action; a suit in court. In this sense it is used in regard to the introduction of the case of a deceased person for the process of beatification and canonization.

**Celebrant** (sĕl′ē·brănt), n.; L. The priest or bishop who offers a Mass or conducts any other church service as distinguished from his assistants in the service.

**Celebret** (sĕl′ē·brĕt), n.; L. A testimonial letter by a bishop or major superior of an exempt clerical institute to one of his clergy stating that the priest bearing the letter has been duly ordained and is free of canonical censure, and asking that he be allowed to celebrate Mass in other dioceses.

**Celestinians** (sĕl'ĕs·tĭn'ĭ·ăns), n. pl.; L., Fr. A branch of the Benedictine order founded by Peter of Morone, Pope Celestine V, in the thirteenth century.

**Celibacy** (sĕl'ĭ·bá·sĭ), n.; L. The state of being unmarried. A law in the western Church forbidding under pain of nullity the marriage of men in Holy Orders, beginning with the subdiaconate, and prohibiting a married man who has received Holy Orders from cohabiting with his wife.

**Cell** (sĕl), n.; L., O.Fr. (1) A small unit of a monastery. (2) The room or separate dwelling of a monk; his living quarters.

**Cellarer** (sĕl'ēr·ēr), n.; L. The procurator of a monastery; the one in charge of buying, storing, and dispensing food at a monastery.

**Cemetery** (sĕm'ē·tĕr'ĭ), n.; Gr., L. A burial ground; a place set aside for burying; a graveyard. Land consecrated and set apart for the burying of Christians; each lot may be consecrated individually. Burial in consecrated ground is a mark that the departed died in communion with the Church.

**Cenacle** (sĕn'á·k'l), n.; L., Fr. The upper room where Christ and His Apostles ate the Last Supper. Also a religious order of sisters devoted to the giving of retreats to lay women; Sisters of the Cenacle, or Cenacle Nuns, or the Institute of Our Lady of the Retreat in the Cenacle.

**Censer** (sĕn'sēr), n.; L., O.Fr. The vessel in which

incense is burned at certain liturgical functions. Also called thurible. (Cf. Thurible.)

**Censor** (sĕn'sẽr), n.; L. A person appointed by the bishop to pass judgment regarding correct doctrine of faith or morals contained in a book or other writing previous to publication. Usually a priest known for his learning.

**Censure** (sĕn'shẽr), n.; L., Fr. A spiritual and reforming penalty imposed by the Church on a baptized person for the correction of an offense. The censure deprives that one of spiritual advantages or benefits connected with spiritual matters. Absolution from censures is governed in accordance with the offense and the penalty attached; thus it may be reserved to one in authority, to the bishop, or to the Pope. In danger of death, any priest can absolve from all censures. (Cf. Reserved cases.)

**Cerecloth** (sēr'klŏth), n.; L. A linen cloth waxed on one side; it is cut to the dimension of the altar and is placed under the three linen altar cloths, with the waxed side to the table. It is most frequently used where the altar is of stone, and though not necessary, it serves as a protection for the other cloths against moisture or the oils of consecration on a newly consecrated altar. The chrismale.

**Ceremonial of Bishops** (sĕr'ē·mō'nĭ·ăl), n.; L. Latin: *Caeremoniale Episcoporum*. A liturgical book containing a detailed account of the order to be observed in religious ceremonies and divine worship. It is the Church's official manual of ceremonies. It contains no texts but is entirely composed of rubrics. It deals with the more solemn functions of the sacred liturgy as they are celebrated in cathedral or collegiate churches, especially when they are Pontifical, i.e., celebrated by, or in the presence of, the bishop. It is divided into three books, the first giving general rules for the bishop and his ministers; the second treating of the solemn celebration of Mass and the Divine Office, and of the chief functions of the liturgical year; the third is concerned with the rules for particular prelates who hold certain high offices.

**Ceremony** (sĕr'ē·mō'nĭ), n.; L., O.Fr. (1) An external act performed in the worship of God. (2) The action (attitude, gesture, etc.) of external worship. (3) The actual performance of a rite.

**Chair** (châr), n.; L., O.Fr. The cathedral seat or throne of a bishop.

**Chalice** (chăl'ĭs), n.; L., O.Fr. The cup-shaped vessel used in the Mass in which the wine is consecrated. It should be of gold or silver, or the cup should be of silver and gold lined; it is consecrated by the bishop with chrism and may not be touched except by those in Holy Orders or those to whom permission has been given.

Chalice. (1) cup; (2) node; (3) base

**Chalice veil** (-vāl), n.; L., O.Fr. A square silk veil used to cover the paten and chalice. Also called *peplum*.

**Chamberlain** (chām'bẽr·lĭn), n.; Fr. (1) An official of the papal court; one acting as a member of the Roman curia; a camerlengo. The camerlengo of the

Holy Roman Church is a cardinal and has charge of the properties and finances of the Holy See. The camerlengo of the Sacred College is the secretary-treasurer of the College of Cardinals. (2) Chamberlain is the title given to those who have duties about the papal apartments. They may be either clerics or laymen. The title is usually given as an honorary award.

**Chancel** (chăn′sĕl), n.; L., O.Fr. (1) That part of the church between the altar and the nave, deriving its name from the rails which form the separation. (2) A college (i.e., a corporation or organized body of persons with common duties and privileges) of clerics organized by ecclesiastical authority to carry out the sacred liturgy in a more solemn manner and to perform certain other ecclesiastical functions.

**Chancellor** (chăn′sĕ·lēr), n.; L., O.Fr. The one in charge of a diocesan chancery; the priest appointed by the bishop as a church notary whose duty it is to care for the diocesan archives, keep the records, and write up official documents.

**Chancery** (chăn′sēr·ĭ), n.; O.Fr. (1) Episcopal—the business office from which all documents pertaining to the exercise of the bishop's jurisdiction proceed; a place of retaining all legal papers in all matters pertaining to the fivefold jurisdiction of the bishop. (2) Apostolic—an office of the Roman Curia which expedites letters providing for the erection of new provinces and dioceses, and for other matters of greater importance.

**Chant (Gregorian)** (chănt), n.; L. The official music of the liturgy, called Gregorian because of its final development by St. Gregory, and prescribed for those parts of the liturgy which are to be sung.

**Chantry** (chăn′trĭ), n.; L., O.Fr. A place set aside from the body of the church where Mass was said for the benefit of the soul of some particular person. (Obs.)

**Chapel** (chăp′ĕl), n.; L. A building, smaller than a church, for divine worship; private or semipublic oratory; also a portion of a church set aside for celebrating Mass or for a particular devotion.

**Chaplain** (chăp′lĭn), n.; L., O.Fr. Literally, a priest given charge of a chapel; a priest appointed to exercise the sacred ministry in an institution such as a convent or hospital; one appointed to serve in a particular way, as, e.g., an army chaplain.

**Chaplet** (chăp′lĕt), n.; L., O.Fr. Originally a wreath worn about the head. A name sometimes applied to the rosary.

**Chapter** (chăp′tĕr), n.; L., O.Fr. (1) Cathedral—a group living a semi-community life, made up of dignitaries and canons attached to the cathedral of a diocese to carry on the sacred liturgy in a more solemn manner, to aid the bishop as his council and, when the see is vacant, to take his place in the administration of the diocese. It is chiefly a European term and institution. (2) Collegiate—a group of secular priests attached, not to the cathedral, but to another important church which they serve especially in the celebration of the sacred liturgy.

(3) Conventual—the assembly of delegated monks for the discussion, improvement, or change of the rules of their order. (4) Sometimes a short passage of Sacred Scripture in the Divine Office is called a "little chapter."

**Chapter house** (chăp'tēr hous), n.; L., O.Fr. A meeting place of the canons of the cathedral; also the meeting place of monks or religious within their monastery.

**Character** (kăr'ăk·tēr), n.; Gr., L. In theological usage, a spiritual mark imprinted upon the soul by the reception of the sacraments of Baptism, Confirmation, and Holy Orders.

**Charismata** (kȧr'ĭz·mȧ'tȧ), n. pl.; sing. charisma; Gr. Charisms. The extraordinary graces given to certain Christians for the benefit of others rather than for the spiritual welfare of the recipient; marks of favor. (Cf. *Gratiae gratis datae* in Appendix of foreign words.)

**Charisms** (kăr'ĭz'mz), n. pl.; Gr. A name applied to particular and wonderful gifts of grace, especially the gifts of the Holy Ghost; special gifts or favors of grace given for the benefit of others rather than for the spiritual welfare of the recipient. (Cf. Charismata.)

**Charity** (chăr'ĭ·tĭ), n.; L., Fr. A divinely infused virtue by which we prefer God as the sovereign good before all else and by which we do His will and are united with Him. The virtue that disposes us to love God, ourselves, and our neighbors for the sake of God.

**Charity (works of)**, n.; L., Fr. Spiritual and corporal works of mercy.

**Chastity** (chăs'tĭ·tĭ), n.; L., O.Fr. (1) The virtue excluding all voluntary pleasure or indulgence in acts arising from the sexual impulse in unmarried persons, and moderating within the bounds of right reason any deliberate pleasure arising from acts pertaining to sexual relations in the married. (2) The evangelical counsel which prompts one to vow permanently not to indulge in the natural sexual appetite. Such a vow is voluntarily made by those ordained subdeacons in the western Church and by monks and nuns and other religious at their professions. A vow of voluntary chastity may be made by a person privately.

**Chasuble** (chăz'ū·b'l), n.; L., Fr. The external garment or vestment worn by the priest in celebrating Mass, worn as a mantle over his shoulders and covering the body, front and rear, and descending to the knees. The Roman style of chasuble is more squarely shaped, while the Greek style is more circular in shape and hangs down on the upper parts of the arms.

Chasuble

**Cherubim** (chĕr'ū·bĭm), n. pl.; Heb. The second of the choirs of angels, near to the throne of God because of their more "full knowledge." Singular: cherub.

**Chevet** (chē·vĕ'), n.; Fr. A series of chapels placed around the east or apsidal end of a Gothic church; one or more small chapels arranged in order.

**Chirothecae** (kĭ′rō·thē′sē), n. pl.; L. See Gloves.

**Choir** (kwīr), n.; L., Fr. (1) The persons who sing certain parts of the liturgy; sometimes the place or gallery from which they sing. (2) An innumerable host of angels or one of the nine divisions of angels. (3) In cathedral, collegiate, and conventual churches, that part of the building raised up and closed off from the nave where the canons or monks (or nuns) have their stalls. (4) The clergy who are taking part in a liturgical function, seated in stalls arranged along the walls of the church between the sanctuary or apse and the nave or body of the church.

**Chorister** (kŏr′ĭs·tẽr), n.; L., Fr. A singer in a church choir; the name is generally applied to male singers.

**Chrism** (krĭz′m), n.; Gr., L., A.S. A mixture of olive oil and balsam blessed by the bishop and used in the administration of the sacraments of Baptism and Confirmation, but not in ordination of priests. Chrism is used in the consecration of bishops, the consecration of churches, altar stones, chalices, patens, and in the solemn blessing of bells and baptismal water. Chrism is blessed on Maundy Thursday. (Cf. Oils, holy.)

**Chrismal** (krĭz′măl), n.; Gr., L. *Chrismarium*, chrismatory. A vessel for containing holy chrism. Also the corporal or pall used in covering the chalice. Sometimes applied to a vessel holding a relic.

**Chrismale** (krĭz·mā′lē), n.; L. The cerecloth. (Cf. Cerecloth.)

**Christ** (krīst), n.; Heb., Gr., L. In its original meaning, the "anointed." In the Hebrew the word points to the Messiah. It is the official title of our Lord.

**Christening** (krĭs″n·ĭng), n.; L., A.S. Formerly a term applied to the sacrament of Baptism. The act of naming in the ceremony of administering Baptism.

**Christian (name)** (krĭs′chăn), adj.; L., A.S. The name given to the one receiving Baptism, hence a baptismal name.

**Christian** (krĭs′chăn), n.; Gr., L. In earliest times the name applied to a follower of Christ. Later used as (1) a term designating one who possessed a belief in Christ; (2) a Catholic; (3) a baptized person.

**Christ-life** (krīst′-līf′), n.; Gr., L., A.S. By Baptism one receives a vital influence of grace from Christ whereby one is united to Him and lives in Him; hence, the life of one in the Mystical Body; the Pauline doctrine of living intimately the life of Christ by manifesting Christ in all our actions. (Gal. 2:19, 20.) The basic motivation for Catholic Action.

**Christmas** (krĭs′măs), n.; Gr., L. The twenty-fifth day of December; the day celebrating the birth of Christ; the Feast of the Nativity.

**Christogram** (krĭs′tō·grăm), n.; Gr., L. A symbol of Christ; chiefly that made up of the first two Greek letters in the name of Christ, namely, *Chi* and *Rho*, which is formed thus. ☧.

**Christology** (krĭs·tŏl'ō·jĭ), n.; Gr. The formal study of Jesus Christ; scientific study of the doctrine and theory of Christ's natures and person.

**Christus** (krĭst'ŭs), n.; Gr., L. (1) The Latin name of Christ; (2) name applied to the chanter or singer who sings the words spoken by our Lord during the recital of the Gospel story of the passion. (Cf. Passion music.)

**Chronista** (krŏn·ĭs'tȧ), n.; Gr.; L. A narrator; the cleric who sings the narrative parts of the Gospel of the passion when it is sung solemnly by chanters. (Cf. Passion music.)

**Church** (chûrch), n.; Gr., A.S. (1) A group of Christians. (2) A place where Christians assemble. A building devoted to divine worship for use of the faithful in a group.

**Church History,** n. The account of the rise and continuance of the Catholic Church from its founding to the present time. The written account which gives the history of the Catholic religion. Eusebius, Bishop of Caesarea in the fourth century, is said to be the father of Church history.

**Church of Christ,** n. The Catholic Church. The body of Christians who profess the faith of Christ and believe in all the teachings of Jesus Christ, use the same means of grace, the sacraments, and obey the same authorities, their pastors, united under one visible head, the Pope, who is the representative of Christ on earth; that Church instituted by Christ with infallible authority under the visible head, the Pope; the Church which has as its mark oneness, apostolicity, holiness, and universality.

**Church Militant** (mĭl'ĭ·tănt), n.; L., Fr. Those members of the Catholic Church on earth; so named because these members are "fighting" to attain salvation, they are the "soldiers of Christ"; the Mystical Body of Christ, the Roman Catholic Church.

**Church property,** n. That which is possessed by the Church as a corporation or as a moral person. Any property, movable or immovable, owned by a moral personality created by the Church, such as a parish, religious house, and the like.

**Church Suffering,** n. A term used to describe those souls of the faithful who are suffering in purgatory; the poor souls.

**Church Triumphant,** n. The souls in heaven; all those who have triumphed over sin and won the victory of heaven by faithfully serving Christ; all the saints.

**Churching (of women)** (-ĭng), n.; Gr., L., A.S. A blessing given to women after childbirth; the custom of receiving such a blessing according to the ritual. This is also a public act of thanksgiving by the mother.

**Churchyard** (chûrch'yärd), n.; Gr., L., A.S. The land or property belonging to the church and immediately surrounding the church, often devoted to the burial of members of the congregation; sometimes called a cemetery.

**Ciborium** (sĭ·bō'rĭ·ŭm), n.; Gr., L. The vessel, chalice-like in shape and having a cover, in which communion hosts are kept in the tabernacle. The early meaning was that of a canopy over the altar. (Cf. Luna, Capsula.)

**Cilicium** (sĭ·lĭsh′ĭ·ŭm), n.; L. A garment worn for penance; a hairshirt.

**Cincture** (sĭngk′tūr), n.; L. A woven cord used as a belt about the waist to hold the alb; a girdle binding the alb. A cingulum.

Ciborium with cover

A cloth veil placed over the ciborium

**Cingulum** (sĭng′gŭ·lŭm), n.; L. A cincture; a girdle or cord symbolizing purity.

**Circumcision (Feast of)** (sûr′kŭm·sĭzh′ŭn), n.; L. The feast celebrated on January 1, commemorating the submission of Jesus to the Jewish law of circumcision.

**Circumincession** (sûr′kŭm·ĭn·sĕsh′ŭn), n.; L. The existence in each other of the three persons of the Holy Trinity. "I am in the Father, and the Father in Me." (John 14:10.)

**Circumninsession**, n.; L. See Circumincession.

**Cistercians** (sĭs·tûr′shănz), n. pl.; L. Monks of the Order of Citeaux begun by St. Robert in the eleventh century for a more strict observance of the rule of St. Benedict. There are two Observances, the Common and the Strict, or the Trappists. There are also Cistercian nuns who are always cloistered and live contemplative lives.

**Citation** (sī·tā′shŭn), n.; L., O.Fr. A summons; the calling of a person to give testimony before an ecclesiastical court or judge, usually by letter in which the time and place is given; all ecclesiastical citations must be obeyed or a penalty is imposed.

**Civil marriage** (sĭv′ĭl), n.; L., Fr. The contract of marriage entered into before an authorized civil authority and bearing force in civil law.

**Civory** (sĭv′ō·rĭ), n.; also, cibory (sĭb′ō·rĭ), L., A.S. The *ciborium magnum*. The canopy of wood, stone, or metal supported by columns which covers the altar and platform. Sometimes referred to as a baldachin.

**Clandestine** (klăn·dĕs′tĭn), adj.; L., Fr. That marriage which is null and void because of the lack of the matrimonial form prescribed by canon law. Said of a marriage of a baptized person which is not performed before one's proper pastor or a priest delegated by him, and before at least two witnesses.

**Claretians** (klă·rā′shănz), n. pl.; L. Members of the Missionary Sons of the Immaculate Heart of Mary, a society founded for missionary work by St. A. Maria Claret in 1849 at Vich, Spain.

**Classics** (klăs′ĭks), n. pl.; L., Fr. A term denoting the great writings of Greece and Rome which have survived; in Catholic circles this refers to the writings of the patristic ages, the time of the monastic schools, or the time of the universities in the twelfth and thirteenth centuries when the classical studies had begun a decline. The literature of the classical Christian writers.

**Clausura** (klô·zū′rá), n.; L. The enclosure. (1) That

part of a monastery or convent which has been canonically set apart as the place of residence of the religious and which may not be transgressed by an outsider. (2) The rule separating members of a convent from the world by forbidding them to commune with those outside the walls. (Cf. Enclosure; also Cloister.)

**Clementine** (klĕm′ĕn·tĭn), adj.; Gr., L. (1) Apocryphal writings attributed to St. Clement of Rome. (2) Also used of an edition of the Vulgate; the Clementine edition.

**Clementine Instruction,** n. The book containing the regulations for the Forty Hours' Prayer as given by Pope Clement VIII in 1592 and modified and reissued by Pope Pius X in 1914. The *Instructio Clementina.*

**Clergy** (klûr′jĭ), n.; L., O.Fr. Persons who have received tonsure or Holy Orders; those elevated to a higher rank than the laity and given a special duty in the divine service or in administering to the Church. Sometimes the use of the word includes all religious, even sisters and lay brothers.

**Cleric** (klĕr′ĭk), n.; L. One belonging to the clergy; one raised to the clerical state; applied to those who have received tonsure or the minor or major orders preparatory to ordination.

**Clerical** (klĕr′ĭ·kăl), adj.; L. Of or pertaining to a cleric or an ecclesiastic.

**Clerk** (klûrk), n.; Gr., L., A.S. A name generally applied to the inferior ranks of the secular clergy;

sometimes applied to all those entitled to clerical privileges. (Obs.)

**Clinical (Baptism)** (klĭn′ĭ·kăl), adj.; Gr., L. In the early ages of the Church this was reception on the bed of sickness of the sacrament of Baptism. (Obs.)

**Cloister** (klois′tẽr), n.; L., O.Fr. (1) The canonically enclosed living quarters of a convent or monastery. (2) The close. An enclosed space, square or oblong in shape, with covered passages around the outer wall and pillars on the inner side; the covered passageway around the inner square or garden often found in monasteries.

**Clothing** (klōth′ĭng), n.; A.S. An investiture; the ceremony at which the habit of a religious order is given to one of a religious community of women who has completed her postulancy.

**Coadjutor** (kō·ăj′ōō·tẽr), n.; L., O.Fr. One who helps a bishop in performing the duties of the diocese. An administrator bishop. (Cf. Bishop.)

**Coat (the holy)** (kōt), n.; O.Fr. The relic kept in the cathedral of Treves which tradition holds to be the seamless coat worn by our Lord at His Passion.

**Coats of arms** (kōts-ŏv-ärmz), n. pl.; Fr. An escutcheon. The hierarchy of the Church, that is, the Pope, cardinals, archbishops, and bishops have coats of arms. These are heraldic emblems, usually consisting of a shield surmounted by the tiara or ecclesiastical hat from

A papal coat of arms

which cords with tassels descend. Usually a motto is also attached. The coat of arms of a cardinal is distinguished by a scarlet ecclesiastical hat from which drop two cords, each having fifteen tassels; the archbishop's has a green hat and ten tassels on each descending cord; the bishop's has a green hat also, but only six tassels on each cord. The right (from the viewpoint of the bearer) side of the shield represents the diocese; the left side the family arms of the prelate.

**Co-consecrators** (kō-kŏn′sē·krā′tērz), n. pl.; L. The two bishops assisting the presiding bishop in an episcopal consecration.

**Code** (kōd), n.; L., Fr. The collection of laws known as canon law; the codex. The Church law. The name applied to the collection of laws promulgated on May 27, 1917. The code binds Catholics of the Latin rite only. (Canon 1.) (Cf. Canon Law.)

**Codex** (kō′dĕks), n.; L. (1) A manuscript of a part or the whole of the Bible, usually forming a book. (2) A collection of writings which have authority. (3) When used alone it usually refers to the code of canon law.

**Coenobite** (sē′nō·bīt), n.; Gr. In the early eastern Church, one who lived in a community, religious in nature; a word equivalent in the eastern Church to monk. Also cenobite.

**Collarium**, n.; L. The name sometimes applied to the large, stiffly starched linen collar worn by the members of some religious orders of sisters or nuns.

**Collateral** (kǒ·lăt′ēr·ăl), adj.; L. Term applied to the

line of descent of indirect blood relationship, the bond between persons descending from the same stock; brother or sister, uncle or aunt, nephew or niece, first or second cousin. This is opposed to the direct line of descent, that of grandparent and grandchild.

**Collation** (kŏ·lā′shŭn), n.; L., O.Fr. (1) The light meal taken on days of fast; a meal of eight to ten ounces. (2) The act of an ecclesiastical authority in appointing a suitable person to a vacant benefice.

**Collect** (kŏl′ĕkt), n.; L. The prayer said during the Mass between the *Gloria* and the Epistle.

**Collection** (kŏ·lĕk′shŭn), n.; L. Offering, usually made in money, taken up during services in the church; an alms offered during Mass.

**College** (kŏl′ĕj), n.; L., O.Fr. (1) A corporation of persons joined in a common pursuit. The colleges of the different nationalities at Rome for the training of theological students. (2) An institution of higher learning of a general rather than a professional character. It may also be applied to a particular branch of a university, e.g., the college of journalism. (3) The collective name used in regard to the cardinals who form the advisory body of the Pope: "the college of Cardinals."

**Collegiate Church** (kŏ·lē′jĭ·ĭt), adj.; L., O.Fr. Church other than the cathedral church served by a body of secular canons. Chiefly an English term.

**Colobium** (kŏ·lō′bĭ·ŭm), n.; Gr., L. A long sleeveless garment of royalty in which Christ is often pictured.

**Color (liturgical)** (kŭl'ēr), n.; L. The colors which may be used in the vestments of the Church. They are: white, red, green, purple, black, and old rose for use on the third Sunday of Advent and the fourth Sunday of Lent. Sometimes sky blue is permitted. Cloth of gold may be substituted for white, red, or green; silver for white only.

**Comb** (kōm), n.; A.S. An ivory comb required by the rubrics for the consecration of a bishop, used to smooth the hair of the consecrated bishop after the application of the chrism.

**Comes,** n.; L. The lectionary. (Cf. Lectionary.)

**Commandments (of God)** (kŏ·mȧnd'mĕnts), n. pl.; L. The commandments or laws given by God to Moses on Mount Sinai; the decalogue; the ten commandments.

**Commandments (of the Church),** n. pl. Laws binding under conscience, which the Church by lawful authority has made and imposed on the faithful. The laws, usually six in number, for the spiritual good of the faithful impose obligations under pain of sin. They are: (1) To hear Mass on Sundays and Holydays of obligation; (2) to fast and abstain on all days appointed; (3) to receive holy Communion during the Easter season; (4) to receive the Sacrament of Penance at least once a year; (5) to contribute toward the support of our priests; (6) to refrain from marrying within the fourth degree of kindred, or to solemnize marriage during the forbidden times.

**Commemoration** (kŏ·mĕm″ō·rā'shŭn), n.; L. Act of

remembrance; a prayer of the Mass. All commemorations of the Mass are made up of Collect, Secret, and Post-communion. There are four kinds of added prayers: (*a*) those of feasts occurring on the same day; (*b*) prescribed anniversary prayers or prayers prescribed for definite occasions, during exposition, etc.; (*c*) prayers added to fill up a required number demanded by the rubrics (*orationes de tempore* or *orationes votivae*); (*d*) a prayer or prayers added to the Mass by local episcopal direction (*orationes imperatae*).

**Commendation (of the soul)** (kŏm'ĕn·dā'shŭn), n.; L. A prayer for the dying, found in the Roman ritual.

**Commendatory letters** (kŏ·mĕn'dȧ·tō'rĭ, n. pl.; L. Letters given by the bishop as introductions to members of the faithful who travel to a foreign country and wish to be identified as being in communion with the Church. Such letters are now given to clerics who go from one diocese to another, testifying that they are duly ordained and free of canonical censure. (Cf. Celebret.)

**Commission** (kŏ·mĭsh'ŭn), n.; L., Fr. The doing of something; applied to an act of sin which consists in the doing of something forbidden, as distinguished from a sin of omission which consists in the neglect to do something commanded. (Cf. Omission.)

**Commission,** n.; L., Fr. A group of ecclesiastics appointed to perform special duties or to carry out certain work; the group may be papal or diocesan.

**Common** (kŏm'ŭn), n.; L. (1) The ordinary of the

Mass, especially the sung parts. (2) The part of the Missal or Breviary wherein are found the Masses and offices of all saints who are not assigned special Masses or offices.

**Communicate** (kŏ·mū′nĭ·kāt), v.t.; L. To receive the Eucharist; to partake of communion.

**Communion** (kŏ·mūn′yŭn), n.; L. *a.* (1) A word often applied to the Eucharist, derived from the time of the Mass when the Eucharist is received; the name designating the Sacred Host and Wine in which the Body, Blood, Soul, and Divinity of Christ are present. (2) The reception of the Sacred Species of wine and bread by the priest in Mass. (3) The Sacred Species received by one communicating. (4) The antiphon said by the priest after the ablutions of the Mass. (5) Spiritual Communion: the earnest desire to communicate and the spiritual uniting of oneself with our Lord in the Eucharist through appropriate prayers or acts of Love and Thanksgiving. *b.* Frequent Communion: the term by which daily Communion, or Communion received on many days other than Sundays or Holydays, is known.

**Communion of Saints,** n.; L. The sharing of spiritual goods between the faithful on earth, the Church Triumphant in heaven, and the Church Suffering in purgatory; the three states of the faithful. (Cf. Church Militant; Church Suffering; Church Triumphant.)

**Commutation** (kŏm′ū·tā′shŭn), n.; L. The substitution of another work for the fulfillment of an obligation; particularly with reference to the obligation assumed by one in making a vow. (Cf. Vow.)

**Compensation (occult)** (kŏm′pĕn·sā′shŭn), n.; L. The act of a creditor compensating himself for a debt justly due to him from the goods of the debtor without the latter's knowledge.

**Compline** (kŏm′plĭn), n.; L., O.Fr. The last hour of the Holy Office; the final prayer in the hours of the breviary.

**Concelebration** (kŏn·sĕl′ē·brā′shŭn), n.; L. The joint celebration of Mass by a priest and his assistants; in the Latin Church such celebration of Mass is made by the priests only on the day of ordination or by bishops on the day of their consecration.

**Conclave** (kŏn′klāv), n.; L., Fr. The place of assembly for the cardinals at the electing of a new Pope; also the assembly itself.

**Concomitance** (kŏn·kŏm′ĭ·tăns), n.; L. The presence of Christ's Body and Blood, under either consecrated bread or wine, by "concomitance" or by virtue of the fact that a glorified living body cannot be divided; the presence of the Body of Christ in the Eucharistic bread, together with the Blood, Soul, and Divinity, because these are inseparable from the Body; the presence of Christ, whole and entire, in both species of the Sacrament.

**Concordance** (kŏn·kôr′dăns), n.; L., O.Fr. An alphabetical index to the Bible, arranged according to the principal words in each text.

**Concordat** (kŏn·kôr′dăt), n.; L., Fr. A treaty drawn

up between the Holy See and a secular state or government concerning the interests of religion in that particular country.

**Concupiscence** (kŏn·kū′pĭ·sĕns), n.; L. The appetite tending to the gratification of the senses; in itself it may be either good or bad, depending on whether or not its object is conformable to right reason. Most frequently it refers to the immoderate desires of the flesh due to original sin, an inordinate sensual appetite for sinful pleasures of sense.

**Concurrence** (kŏn·kûr′ĕns), n.; L. Term applied to the joining in vespers of two offices which follow one upon the other.

**Concursus** (kŏn·kûr′sŭs), n.; L. (1) The examination of candidates to be raised to ecclesiastical benefices. (2) Divine—the providence of God which permits man to exist, and because of which God concurs in man's acts, and by which God coacts with His creature.

**Conditional** (kŏn·dĭsh′ŭn·ăl), adj.; L. Depending upon conditions. Applied to the intentions of the minister in administering the sacraments when he doubts if all the requisites for validity are present; may be expressed orally by the clause: "If" with the statement of the particular doubt, placed before the essential words of the form. (Cf. Intention.)

**Confession (Sacramental)** (kŏn·fĕsh′un), n.; L. The telling of our sins to a duly ordained priest who has the authority to give absolution; the receiving of the sacrament of Penance; the confessing of sins vocally. All mortal sins, sincerely and clearly told;

concerning faith and morals; (*b*)—of the Consistory, regulating the affairs of dioceses; (*c*)—of the Sacraments, caring for the discipline and validity of the sacraments; (*d*)—of the Council, having care of the discipline of the clergy and laity; (*e*)—of Religious, which exercises jurisdiction over religious communities; (*f*)—of the Propaganda, which has jurisdiction over missionary regions; (*g*)—of Rites, regulating the liturgical ceremonies of the Latin rite; (*h*)—of Ceremonies, which has charge of Papal functions; (*i*)—of Extraordinary Affairs, for the discharge of international transactions; (*j*)—of Seminaries and Universities, which has charge of Catholic institutions of higher education; (*k*)—for the Oriental Church, which may discharge the duties of all the above except the first in matters pertaining to the Eastern Rites. (4) Congregations of general councils: groups of bishops appointed at the meeting of a council of the Church for the carrying out of particular matters of business to be handled in the council.

**Congress** (kŏng'grĕs), n.; L. A mass gathering of the Catholic faithful and clergy for the advancement of spiritual, social, and intellectual activities. The most common of these today are the National or International Eucharistic Congresses.

**Congruism** (kŏng'grōō·ĭz'm), n.; L. A theory of grace expounded by the theologian, Suarez. The grace is given in accordance with the circumstances in which God foresees that it will be accepted and used; it is thus termed "congruous."

**Conopaeum** (kō'nŏ·pē'ŭm), n.; L. Also: conopeum or conopium. A canopy. (Cf. Canopy, 3.)

**Consanguinity** (kŏn'săng·gwĭn'ĭ·tĭ), n.; L. In the natural sense, the bond between persons descending from the same stock; blood relationship. In canon law, consanguinity makes marriage invalid in the direct line of descent in all degrees and to the third degree inclusive of the collateral line. (Cf. Collateral.)

**Conscience** (kŏn'shĕns), n.; L., O.Fr. Judgment of reason concerning the goodness or badness of an act, which one is contemplating performing, according to the principles of moral law. A person is bound to follow his conscience even though it be inculpably erroneous and, also, one is bound to form a right conscience.

**Consecration** (kŏn'sē·krā'shŭn), n.; L. (1) The solemn blessing dedicating a person, a place, or a thing to the service of God. (2)—of Mass. The *action* of the Mass; that part of the Canon of the Mass at which the celebrant changes the bread and wine into the Body and Blood of Christ. This occurs when he takes the bread and says, "This is My Body, etc.," and the wine, saying, "This is the chalice of My Blood, etc." (3)—of altars. The consecrating or blessing by the bishop of altars and altar stones by an anointing with chrism and the placing of relics within the altar stone. Such consecration lasts until the altar stone is broken or the seal of the relics is broken. Chalices and churches are also consecrated.

**Consistory** (kŏn·sĭs'tō·rĭ), n.; L. A meeting or the place of meeting where official business is transacted. The term is applied to a papal consistory which is a group of cardinals presided over by the Pope and deliberating upon matters of ecclesiastical importance.

**Constitutions** (kŏn'stĭ·tū'shŭnz), n. pl.; L. (1) An ordinance in canon law, of an ecclesiastical authority, either by letter or decree. (2) The particular regulations governing the life of members of a religious institute.

**Consubstantial** (kŏn'sŭb·stăn'shăl), adj.; L. The term used to denote the oneness of the nature of Christ with that of the Father and the Holy Ghost, and the oneness of Christ's substance with God. Through this oneness of substance we also confess the equality of God the Father, God the Son, and God the Holy Ghost, and their co-eternity.

**Consubstantiation** (kŏn'sŭb·stăn·shĭ·ā'shŭn), n.; L. The heretical doctrine which holds that the substance of the bread and wine merely exists together with the substance of the Body and Blood of our Lord after consecration.

**Consultors** (kŏn·sŭl'tĕrz), n. pl.; L. Men of special knowledge who serve to advise the Roman Congregations. Also, in America, the advisors of a bishop.

**Contemplation** (kŏn'tĕm·plā'shŭn), n.; L. A high state of interior union with God. A term applied to the manner of life of religious who devote themselves to prayer and meditation rather than to active works, such as teaching, etc.

**Continence** (kŏn′tĭ·nĕns), n.; L. (1) Abstinence from the indulgence of sexual actions and desires. (2) Abstinence from sexual intercourse by married persons, either by mutual vow or because of circumstances.

**Contract** (kŏn′trăkt), n.; L. An agreement in which one or more persons are bound to another person or persons to perform or not to perform a stated act.

**Contrition** (kŏn·trĭsh′ŭn), n.; L., O.Fr. Sorrow and detestation of sin which has been committed together with the purpose of sinning no more. It is perfect contrition if it is based on love of God, imperfect contrition (attrition) if based on a lower motive. (Cf. Attrition.)

**Convent** (kŏn′vĕnt), n.; L. The community living quarters of sisters or brothers. It may include all the accessory buildings which form a part of the community property. Likened to a monastery.

**Conventual** (kŏn·vĕn′tū·ăl), adj.; L., A.S. (1) Pertaining to a convent or to the monastic life; opposed to life in the world. (2)—church. A church attached to a monastery or convent of religious.

**Conversion** (kŏn·vûr′shŭn), n.; L. (1) The technical term used in theology to express the mode of the passage of the entire substance, both matter and form, of the bread and wine, in the transubstantiation of the Holy Eucharist. (Cf. Transubstantiation.) (2) The turning toward the Church by acceptance of her teachings; becoming a member of the Church. (3) "Conversion of manners": literally, a change. The overcoming of vices and the practice of virtue.

**Conversus** (kŏn·vûr′sŭs), n.; L. A lay brother; one who seeks a conversion of manners.

**Convert** (kŏn′vûrt), n.; L. A person who has not been baptized or one baptized as a non-Catholic who becomes a Catholic by reception of Baptism or by profession of faith and abjuration of errors; one who becomes an active, participating member of the Catholic Church.

**Cooperation** (kō·ŏp′ēr·ā′shŭn), n.; L. The formal or material assistance given another in the commission of a sin. *Formal* cooperation is the concurrence with the will of the sinner or a partaking in his sinful act; this is never permitted. *Material* cooperation is the providing of means or material which the sinner himself uses for the commission of the sin against the will of the one cooperating. For a sufficient reason, material cooperation is sometimes lawful.

**Cope** (kōp), n.; L. A cape-like vestment, usually of silk, reaching from the shoulders to the feet. It is fastened with a clasp in front called the morse and usually has a smaller cape resting on the shoulders. It is the external vestment worn for liturgical services as Exposition or processions and the absolution of the dead, and yet is not a vestment limited to the use of priests alone but may be worn by a cantor, even if a layman.

**Copts** (kŏpts), n. pl.; Gr., L. (1) The Christian Egyptians who adhered to Monophysism and are governed by the Patriarch of Alexandria. (2) Catholic Copts, using the coptic rite, who were purged of doctrinal error and had restored to them their Patriarch of Alexandria by Pope Leo XIII.

**Cornette** (kôr·nĕt′), n.; Fr. Also cornet. The large tri-cornered white headdress worn by certain sisters, e.g., the Sisters of Charity of St. Vincent de Paul.

**Corona** (kŏ·rō′na), n.; L. (1) Eive mysteries of the rosary. (2) Candles or vigil lights arranged in a circle. (3) The circlet of hair on the head of a tonsured cleric.

**Corporal** (kôr′pŏ·ral), n.; L. The square linen cloth which is carried to the altar in the burse and placed on the table of the altar before the tabernacle and on which the chalice is placed; it symbolizes the winding sheet in which the body of Christ was buried.

Monk with corona.
(1) The tonsure. (Cf. 3 of def.).

**Corporal (works of mercy)**, n.; L. Seven forms of charity or mercy directed to the physical well-being of a needy person; the seven works of mercy are: to feed the hungry, to clothe the naked, to give drink to the thirsty, to visit the sick, to visit prisoners, to give shelter to strangers, and to bury the dead.

**Corpus Christi** (kôr′pŭs krĭstĭ′), n.; L. Literally, "the body of Christ." The name of the Feast of the Blessed Sacrament celebrated on the Thursday following the first Sunday after Pentecost.

**Costume (clerical)** (kŏs'tūm), n.; L., Fr. The dress of clerics to distinguish them from laymen; principally the cassock and roman collar; the dress for street wear is prescribed to be either black or of a dark shade, and of moderate tailoring.

**Cotta** (kŏt'à), n.; L., It. Originally a garment worn by laymen; it is now the short surplice.

**Council** (koun'sĭl), n.; L. An assembly of higher ecclesiastics and rulers in the Church to discuss and decide upon ecclesiastical matters, either of legislation or doctrine. Councils may be either for the Church in general or for a particular country or for an ecclesiastical province or a particular diocese. A diocesan council is called a synod. (Cf. Ecumenical.)

**Counsel** (koun'sĕl), n.; L. A gift of the Holy Ghost; prudence in recognizing and doing what is right, especially in difficult circumstances.

**Covetousness** (kŭv'ĕ·tŭs·nĕs), n.; O.Fr. Avarice. Excessive love of temporal things, usually riches; desire for things of the world. The desire becomes excessive when not guided by reason; it is reasonable when directed toward moderation, e.g., the desire for sufficient means for one's family. It becomes a grievous sin when it is not reasonable and leads to other grievous sins such as injustice, neglect to pay just debts, dishonesty, etc. Covetousness is one of the capital sins because it easily leads to other sins. Its contrary virtue is liberality. (Cf. Capital sins.)

**Cowl** (koul), n.; L., A.S. A hood usually attached to the upper part of a monk's habit which may be pulled up to cover the head.

**Create** (krē·āt'), v.t.; L. To make a thing from nothing; to cause to exist.

**Creation** (krē·ā'shŭn), n.; L. The act of God causing something to be made out of nothing; the calling of a thing into existence; the causing of a thing's existence. Also applied to all created things together.

**Crèche** (krāsh), n.; Fr. See Crib. Sometimes used as a name for lying-in hospitals for the poor and for public day nurseries.

**Credence** (krē'dĕns), n.; L., O.Fr. The table placed in the sanctuary near the Epistle side of the altar on which the cruets containing wine and water are placed. During a solemn high Mass the chalice and burse and humeral veil for the subdeacon are placed upon it when not in use at the altar.

**Creed** (krēd), n.; L. A listing of the principal articles of faith; a prayer in which the articles of faith are contained and which may be said as a profession of faith. The creeds in the Catholic Church are four: The Apostles' Creed, the Nicene Creed, the Athanasian, and the Creed of Pius the Fourth.

**Cremation** (krē·mā'shŭn), n.; L. The act of burning the mortal remains of a person. Because this was not in keeping with the rite of Christian burial which reverences the body that in life was the temple of the Holy Ghost, and because historically the practice originated among unbelievers as a means of expressing scorn for the doctrine of the resurrection of the body, it is condemned by the Church.

**Crib** (krĭb), n.; L., A.S. The place wherein Jesus is said to have been laid after His birth at Bethlehem; a representation of the stable, together with Jesus, the Blessed Virgin, and St. Joseph, erected at Christmas time in churches. Also called crèche.

**Crosier** (krō'zhēr), n.; L., O.Fr. Crozier. A staff with a curved top or a crook at the top and pointed at the lower end, about the height of a man (5 ft. 10 in.), which is a symbol of authority for the bishop; sometimes called pastoral staff. It is presented to a bishop at his consecration.

*The top of the Crosier*

**Cross** (krŏs), n.; L. (1) The chief implement of execution used at the death of Christ; a single upright with a slightly shorter crossbar bisecting the upright toward the upper part. (*a*) Greek—the equilateral cross, the four arms being equal in length. (*b*) Latin—the cross in which the transverse beam is shorter than the upright and the headpiece projects above the transverse bar. (2) The sign of the cross is a

*Two types of crosses. (1) Greek; (2) Latin*

sacramental which represents the cross of Christ through the making of the form by touching the forehead, breast, and each shoulder and repeating the words "In the name of the Father and of the Son and of the Holy Ghost."

**Crotalum** (krŏt'*a*·lŭm), n.; L. The wooden clapper used during Holy Week in place of bells; a tabula. (Cf. Tabula.)

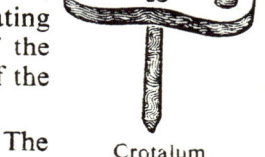
Crotalum

**Crucifix** (kroo'sĭ·fĭks), n.; L., O.Fr. A representation of the cross of crucifixion together with the figure of Christ. The crucifix differs from the cross in that it has affixed to it the body or corpus or a representation of Christ.

Crucifix

**Cruet** (kroo'ĕt), n.; O.Fr. Vessel with a long neck and a handle in which the wine or water to be used at Mass is contained. A vaselike vessel with a stopper.

**Crypt** (krĭpt), n.; Gr., L. Originally this was an underground place used for concealing persons or things. It was used during the persecutions. A place of burial beneath a church. A basementlike place beneath a church sometimes used for services when fitted with an altar.

Cruets

**Cuculla** (kū·kŭl'*a*), n.; L., It. A cowl; an ample choir cloak to which a cowl is attached.

**Culdees** (kŭl'dēz), n. pl.; Celt. A celtic word applied

to those who devote themselves to divine service either as monks or secular priests. (Obs.)

**Culpa** (kŭl′pȧ), n.; L. A fault; a transgression.

**Cultus** (kŭl′tŭs), n.; L. The term which means either veneration or worship; it embraces all the acts of adoration, direct or indirect, by which honor is given to God. The Church distinguishes three kinds of cultus: (*a*) *Latria*, the worship which is due to God alone and which cannot be given to any creature without sinning by idolatry. (*b*) *Dulia*, that veneration given to saints and angels. (*c*) *Hyperdulia*, that veneration given to the Blessed Virgin because of her exalted nature.

**Curate** (kū′rāt), n.; L. A priest assisting a pastor in caring for souls; an assistant to a pastor.

**Cure of Souls** (kūr), n.; L., O.Fr. The responsibility resting upon the parish priest in regard to the souls of those within his district or jurisdiction, which is the administering of the sacraments, the giving of necessary instruction, and the other cares which may be necessary for the spiritual welfare of the parishioners.

**Curia** (kū′rĭ·ȧ), n.; L. The Roman Curia, the Pope's court or cabinet. The entire group of organized bodies and their personnel which assists the Pope in the government and ministration of the Church; namely, the congregations, tribunals, and the curial offices. The diocesan curia is the court and personnel of a diocesan bishop which assists in the administration of the diocese.

**Curialia,** n. pl.; L. The duties and functions of one

attached to the Roman Curia, or to the ecclesiastical court.

**Cursing** (kûrs′ĭng), n.; A.S. The expression of a desire that some evil will befall a person, place, or thing. The act of calling down evil upon God or His creatures; if calling down evil on God or on creatures as connected with God, it is a form of blasphemy. (Cf. Blasphemy.)

**Cursus** (kûr′sŭs), n.; L. The order in which the psalms are arranged in the breviary; sometimes applied to the Divine Office alone.

**Custodial** (kŭs·tō′dĭ·ăl), n.; L. The round metal case in which the lunette is kept; the luna. (Cf. Pyx.)

**Custom** (kŭs′tŭm), n.; L., O.Fr. An action or practice repeated under similar circumstances. A long established practice which may have the force of law if it is good and useful and is performed by the majority of people with the intention of binding themselves to it. Furthermore, in Church law, custom must have the consent of a competent superior before it can obtain the force of law.

**Cycle** (sī′k'l), n.; Gr., L. A series of numbers or letters standing for numbers or parts in a series which are counted again in the same order after the first counting has been completed, e.g., counting from one to ten and then starting again with one. A time for fixing dates, i.e., a system of measuring the time elapsed between dates. The lunar cycle has nineteen years, so after nineteen years the full moon reoccurs on nearly the same day. The solar cycle is of twenty-eight years, after which Sundays and week days fall on the same days of the month. Both cycles are necessary for the determination of the Church calendar.

**C.Y.O.,** abbre. The abbreviation of the title of the "Catholic Youth Organization," a group of young Catholics having a definite program of athletics, religion, and social life forming a program of Catholic Action. The program may vary with different groups.

## ✠ D ✠

---

**Dalmatic** (dăl·măt'ĭk), n.; L., Fr. A vestment open at the sides, with wide open sleeves with an opening for the head, and having two stripes running from hem to hem; the external garment worn by a deacon in solemn functions, or worn by bishops underneath the chasuble during the celebration of Pontifical Mass.

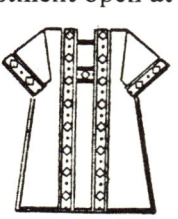
Dalmatic

**Damnation** (dăm·nā'shŭn), n.; L. Eternal separation of a human being from God; condemnation to hell in punishment of mortal sin.

**Damnum** (dăm'nŭm), n.; L. In canon law that loss or harm received by one through the crime of another.

**Daniel** (dăn'yĕl), n.; Heb.; Bib. Name of an historical and prophetical book of the Old Testament of the Bible, named after its traditional author.

**Darnel** (där′nĕl), n.; Fr. Cockle; a fast-growing weed. (Matt. 13:24–30.)

**Dataria** (da·tā′rĭ·a), n.; L. A papal curial office for examining the candidates for papal benefices, drawing up the documents of the appointment, exacting the fees, and looking after all claims and pensions.

**Deacon** (dē′kŭn), n.; Gr., L. (1) The word in early ages for a minister or servant. One who has received subdeaconship and deaconship. The duties of the deacon are to assist the priest in celebrating solemn Mass and sometimes to preach and baptize. (2) Deacons of Honor: the two clerics in the vestments of a deacon who assist the bishop at Pontifical Mass and Vespers or who sit beside him when he attends a solemn Mass in cope.

**Deaconess** (dē′kŭn·ĕs), n.; Gr., L. In the early ages, women who assisted at the baptism of other women; women who assisted a deacon in the early ages. (Obs.)

**Dead (Mass for)** (dĕd), n.; A.S. A requiem Mass; a Mass offered for the purpose of gaining suffrage for or lessening the temporal punishment due the soul of a deceased person.

**Dean** (dēn), n.; L., O.Fr. (1) The head of a cathedral or collegiate chapter; (2) rural dean, a senior priest entrusted with vigilance over Church discipline in the several parishes which constitute the deanery; he has the power of summoning and presiding at meetings of the clergy of this district. A vicar forane.

**Deanery** (dēn′ēr·ĭ), n.; L., O.Fr. A territory consisting of several parishes, under the disciplinary vigilance of a dean.

**Decade** (dĕk′ād), n.; Gr., L. The fifteenth part of a rosary; one part of a rosary consisting of an *Our Father*, ten *Hail Marys*, and one *Glory be to the Father*; one mystery or the meditation on one mystery while saying the above prayers.

**Decalogue** (dĕk′*a*·lŏg), n.; Gr.; Bib. A familiar name applied to the Ten Commandments of God. (Cf. Commandments.)

**Decree** (dē·krē′), n.; L., O.Fr. Any legislative act of a superior; a pronouncement of law regarding faith or discipline made by the Pope or by one of the Roman congregations or by a bishop.

**Decretal** (dē·krē′tăl), n. pl.; L. A letter containing a pontifical decision; the formal reply of the pope concerning a question of discipline. Collection of such laws or decisions.

**Dedication (of churches)** (dĕd′ĭ·kā′shŭn), n.; L. The act whereby a church is solemnly declared to be set apart for the worship of God. Today, it is often said that a church is dedicated to some particular saint, but this arises from a popular devotion to the saint carried on in that church or the name given to the particular church.

**Definitors** (dĕf′ĭ·nī′tērz), n. pl.; L. The counselors or advisers to the general or provincial of a religious order.

**Degradation** (dĕg′r*a*·dā′shŭn), n.; L. Deposition of a cleric from clerical orders or from the performing of the functions of his office, together with the deprivation of his benefice; the act perpetually reducing one to the state of a layman.

**Degree** (dē·grē′), n. pl.; L., O.Fr. Title of scholarship conferred by universities as a mark of having completed certain prescribed studies, such as the degrees of bachelor, master and doctor, e.g., A.B.; A.M.; and Ph.D.

**Delation** (dē·lā′shŭn), n.; L. The reporting of a person or thing—such as a book—to an ecclesiastical superior for the purpose of securing judgment and condemnation.

**Delegation** (děl′ē·gā′shŭn), n.; L. The delegating or the turning over of jurisdiction or power to the exercise of another.

**Demon** (dē′mŭn), n.; Gr., L. Evil spirit; an angel who was cast out of heaven with Lucifer; an inhabitant of hell.

**Demoniac** (dē·mō′nĭ·ăk), n.; L. One possessed by a devil or evil spirit.

**Denudation** (děn′ū·dā′shŭn), n.; L. A term applied to the stripping of the altar on Holy Thursday; removal of coverings.

**Denunciation** (dē·nŭn′sĭ·ā′shŭn), n.; L. An edict of the seventeenth century inquisition ordering the faithful under obedience to denounce or to give the names of persons known to be heretics. The word today is considered practically obsolete in the sense that the obligation of so denouncing a heretic does not rest upon a person when it might revert to the detriment of the person denouncing. In the code of canon law today Catholics are ordered to "denounce" certain major crimes committed by ecclesiastics.

**Deontology** (dē'ŏn·tŏl'ō·jĭ), n.; Gr. That part of the study of moral philosophy or ethics which treats of duty or moral obligation; the study of man's obligation to do good.

**Deposit of Faith** (dē·pŏz'ĭt), n.; L. The sum total of revealed truths given by Christ to His Church; truths guarded by the Church and taught infallibly. The truth of Christ said by the Council of Trent to exist in both written books (SS.) and in unwritten traditions.

**Deposition** (dĕp'ō·zĭsh'ŭn), n.; L. (1) Withholding from a cleric for life the right to exercise his office or jurisdiction or to accept the fruits of his benefice; an ecclesiastical punishment for grave crime imposed upon clerics. (2) In an ecclesiastical court, a formal statement of evidence.

**Deposition (day of),** n.; L. The day of the death of a saint or the anniversary of his death. The day on which a Christian is buried.

**Deputatrix** (dē'pū·tā'trĭks), n.; L. The lay person employed by a religious community for small tasks of shopping or otherwise which must be performed outside of the convent.

**Derogation** (dĕr'ō·gā'shŭn), n.; L. The partial revoking of a law; doing away with a part of a law as distinct from abrogation which is the total revocation of a law.

**Desecration** (dĕs'ē·krā'shŭn), n.; L. The act by which

a thing which has been consecrated is made unfit for sacred use; after desecration a thing must be consecrated again. This may also be taken in the sense of the degrading or insulting use of something sacred.

**Despair** (dē·spâr′), n.; L., O.Fr. The contrary of hope; the state of being hopeless; deliberate act of the will by which one turns away from salvation, considering it as impossible of attainment.

**Determinism** (dē·tûr′mĭn·ĭz'm), n.; L. The denial of free will; the assertion that the acts of man are determined by a set rule or formula over which he has no power of choice.

**Detraction** (dē·trăk′shŭn), n.; L. The sin of telling the true but hidden faults of another and thereby injuring his reputation. (Cf. Calumny, Slander.)

**Deuterocanonical Books** (dū′tēr·ō·k*a*·nŏn′ĭ·k*a*l), adj.; Gr. Books of the Bible which are not found in the Hebrew Bible but which are found in the Septuagint Greek translation; later their canonicity was established by the Church. (Cf. Canon of Scripture, Canonicity.)

**Deuteronomy** (dū′tēr·ŏn′ō·mĭ), n.; Gr., L. Bib. The fifth book of the Old Testament of the Bible.

**Development (of Doctrine)** (dē·vĕl′*ŭ*p·mĕnt), n.; L., Fr. The more clear or more explicit formulation or expression of a belief contained in the deposit of faith; a clarification or defining of some tenet of belief.

**Devil** (dĕv″l), n.; Gr., L., A.S. An evil spirit. Name

applied to Satan as the prince of darkness or of hell; or commonly to all evil spirits.

**Devil's Advocate** (ăd'vŏ·kāt), n.; L. The official whose duty it is to bring objections against the beatification and canonization of a saint. Also called *Promotor Fidei*. (Cf. *Advocatus Diaboli*.)

**Devolution** (dĕv'ŏ·lū'shŭn), n.; L. The right of presentation of a benefice exercised by an ecclesiastical superior. This superior has the right of devolution only after the proper patron has failed to exercise or exercised uncanonically his right of presentation.

**Devotion** (dē·vō'shŭn), n.; L. (1) A manner of reverence and piety; devoutness. (2) A formula of prayer or a pious exercise. (3) Feasts of—feasts which formerly were holydays of obligation, but which no longer bear the precept of hearing Mass but are merely days to be observed according to the spiritual intention of the faithful.

**Diaconate** (dī·ăk'ŏ·nāt), n.; Gr., L. The order of deaconship. The state of one who has received two of the Major Orders. (Cf. Deacon.)

**Diaconicum** (dī'*a*·kō'nĭ·kŭm), n.; Gr., L. A building adjoining a basilica and resembling somewhat the sacristy of the present day. Sometimes applied to the sacristy.

**Dialogue Mass** (dī'*a*·lŏg măs), n.; Gr., L. A low Mass at which the responses are made aloud with the server by those present. Sometimes the parts which are sung in High Mass are also recited aloud with the celebrant in this Mass. A *Missa recitata*.

**Diaspora** (dĭ·ăs′pō·rȧ), n.; Gr. The dispersion of the Jews by their conquerors; the places to which they were dispersed.

**Diatessaron** (dī′ȧ·tĕs′ȧ·rŏn), n.; Gr. A narrative made up from the four Gospels, first made by Tatian, a convert; a harmonized account from the Gospels.

**Dicastery** (dĭ·kăs′tēr·ĭ), n.; Gr. A term applied to any one of the congregations, tribunals, and offices which make up the Roman Curia.

**Didache** (dĭd′ȧ·kē), n.; Gr. A writing of the first century, valuable because of its testimony of the doctrine and teaching of the early Church.

**Dignitary** (dĭg′nĭ·tĕr′ĭ), n.; L. Fr. A member of a chapter who has a precedence of honor over the other canons; the dean, the precentor.

**Dilati**, n. pl., L. Literally, "the deferred." Name applied to the forty-four English martyrs of the late sixteenth and early part of the seventeenth centuries who have not yet been declared venerable.

**Dimissorial** (dĭm′ĭ·sō′rĭ·ăl), n.; L. A letter testifying to the fitness of a person to be ordained; a license proclaiming one worthy of receiving ordination. This may be granted by popes, bishops, abbots, or by delegated vicars, or by major superiors of exempt religious.

**Diocese** (dī′ō·sēs), n.; Gr., L. That portion of a country together with its population which are under the pastoral jurisdiction of a Christian bishop. The territory ruled over by a bishop.

**Diptych** (dĭp′tĭk), n. pl.; Gr. Originally the word meant anything folded double. Two tablets or sheets of metal, ivory or wood or, later, of vellum which were bound together. Upon one the names of the living and on the other the names of the dead to be commemorated at the Mass were inscribed. They were read aloud from the ambo. The use of diptychs ceased in the twelfth century.

**Directorium** (dĭ·rĕk′tō′rĭ·ŭm), n.; L. The directions arranged and set down by competent authority concerning the Mass and office to be read on each day of the year. It is also called ordo and gives the various commemorations attached to each feast day in the Church calendar; it is published each year, usually on the Feast of Epiphany. (Cf. Ordo.)

**Dirge** (dûrj), n.; L. In its literary sense, a poem dedicated to a departed person or referring to death; sometimes applied to an antiphon read in the Office of the Dead. Sometimes applied to the Office of the Dead.

**Diriment (impediment)** (dĭr′ĭ·mĕnt), adj.; L. A condition arising from either the natural law or the law of the Church which prohibits and prevents marriage between persons so affected; it makes the marriage impossible or nullifies it. (Cf. Impediments.)

**Discalced** (dĭs·kălst′), adj.; L. Unshod or barefooted; referred to those branches of religious orders who observe the austerity of not wearing shoes.

**Disciple** (dĭ·sī′p'l), n.; L., O.Fr. A pupil, a student; name sometimes applied to one of the Apostles, more frequently one of the early followers of Jesus, one of the seventy-two.

**Discipline** (dĭs′ĭ·plĭn), n.; L. (1) In its first meaning it is instruction; or also that which is taught; it ordinarily means the rules or order observed in a community or by a group of persons. In Church legislation it is used to refer to the laws which govern the faithful in their actions. (2) It has also come to be applied to acts of mortification, such as scourging, which one voluntarily inflicts upon himself; used in the sense "to take the discipline." (3) In recent years it is being substituted in Roman usage for the term "rite" as applied, for example, to the terms "The Roman discipline"—"The Oriental discipline."

**Disparity (of worship or cult)** (dĭs·păr′ĭ·tĭ), n.; L. The difference of religion or worship existing between a baptized person and an unbaptized person. Two such persons are not permitted to marry without a dispensation; an impediment to marriage.

**Dispensation** (dĭs′pĕn·sā′shŭn), n.; L. The loosening or freeing from a law in a particular case; the relaxing of the binding force of a law for a certain purpose or for certain persons; release from an obligation; it must be granted by someone in authority and may be recalled.

**Dissident** (dĭs′ĭ·dĕnt), adj.; L. Name applied to Churches of the East, either schismatic or heretical, to distinguish them from Catholic groups. (Cf. Eastern Churches.)

**Distraction** (dĭs·trăk′shŭn), n.; L. The voluntary or

involuntary taking of the mind away from one course of thought to another; a diversion of attention. In regard to prayer it is applied to the failure on the part of the person praying to be mindful of God or of the object of his prayer; willful distractions are sinful.

**Divination** (dĭv′ĭ·nā′shŭn), n.; L., O.Fr. The practice of seeking out hidden things or events of the future by unlawful means, such as cards or the lines of the hand; always sinful, because it is equivalent to seeking information from the devil.

**Divorce** (dĭ·vōrs′), n.; L., O.Fr. The legal unbinding of the marriage bond with permission to marry again; the grant of a separation by lawful authority. In the ecclesiastical law no one may dissolve the marriage bond consummated between baptized persons; the only grant of a separation with permission to marry between baptized persons is a declaration of nullity, which is a declaration that no marriage existed validly in the first instance. The Pauline privilege grants the unbaptized permission to remarry under proper conditions. (Cf. Pauline Privilege.)

**Docetae** (dŏ·sē′tē), n. pl.; Gr., L. The name commonly applied to followers of early heresies which denied that Christ is true man, because they held that He had only an apparent, not a real, human body.

**Doctor** (dŏk′tēr), n.; L., O.Fr. One of great theological learning and holiness; a title given to one for his learned defense of Christian doctrine; that person who because of eminent learning, heroic sanctity, and declaration made by the pope or general council is thus constituted a doctor of the Church.

**Doctrine** (dŏk′trĭn), n.; L. That which is taught; a collection of dogmas of some truth of faith.

**Dogma** (dŏg′ma), n.; Gr., L. In religion a truth found in the word of God, either written or unwritten, and proclaimed by the Church for the belief of the faithful; a revealed truth.

**Dogmatic Theology** (dŏg·măt′ĭk), adj.; Gr., L. The science of Christian dogma; the system of teaching or propounding the doctrines of the Church as a whole or individually as they stand in relation to one another. The systematic teaching of the doctrines of faith; the application of philosophy to religious tenets. The scientific treatment of the relationship between faith and reason.

**Dolor** (dō′lẽr), n.; L. A sorrow; grief. It is a poetical form. In the plural, the name applied to the seven sorrows experienced by the Blessed Virgin in her role of Mother of God. There are two Feasts of the seven dolors—the Friday after Passion Sunday and September 15.

**Dom** (dŏm), n.; L. (1) A contraction of the Latin word *dominus*, which is applied as a title to Benedictine monks, and also to the monks in some other monastic orders. The form is spelled *don* in Italy. (2) The term applied to cathedrals in Germany.

**Domestic Prelate** (dō·měs′tĭk prĕl′ĭt), n.; L. An honor

conferred upon a priest and raising him to membership in the Pontifical household with the title of Right Reverend Monsignor. (Cf. Monsignor.)

**Domicile** (dŏm′ĭ·sil), n.; L., Fr. A person's legal residence in virtue of which he becomes subject to authority (bishop, pastor) and is entitled to certain rights. It can be acquired either by taking up residence in a place with the intention of remaining there, or by actual residence in a place for the period of ten years without any specified intention. Quasi-domicile, which is similar to domicile, is acquired by actual residence in a place with the intention of remaining there for the greater part of the year, or by actually remaining there for more than six months without any intention.

**Dominations** (dŏm′ĭ·nā′shŭnz), n. pl.; L. See dominions.

**Dominica,** n.; L. Latin for Sunday, frequently used in liturgical writings.

**Dominicans** (dō·mĭn′ĭ·kănz), n. pl.; L. Members of the religious order who follow the rule established by St. Dominic; the order arose in the year 1216. The Order of Preachers.

**Dominions** (dō·mĭn′yŭnz), n. pl.; L. One of the choirs of angels; usually called Dominations. (Cf. Angels.)

**Donatists** (dŏn′ȧ·tĭsts), n. pl.; L. Heretics and schismatics who held that the validity of the sacraments was dependent upon the moral character of the one ministering and that sinners could not belong to the Church and were refused membership unless their sins were secret.

**Doorkeeper** (dōr′kēp·ēr), n.; A.S. The name applied to the lowest of the minor orders; most generally known as ostiary; a porter. (Cf. Ostiary.)

**Dormition** (dôr·mĭsh′ŭn), n.; L. A name given to the Assumption of the Blessed Virgin into heaven, derived from the Latin word *dormire*, to sleep. Literally it is a "sleeping." The word is used today by the Greek Church.

**Dossal** (dŏs′ăl), n.; L., Fr. A curtain hung behind the altar or suspended from the canopy. Also called dorsal.

**Douay Bible** (dōō′ā′), n.; Fr. The most common and well-known complete translation of the Sacred Scriptures in use by English speaking Catholics. The translation was begun at Douay, France, and a part of it was published there, hence its name. Also, Douai. (Cf. Bible, Canon of the Scripture.)

**Double** (dŭb′'l), n.; L. (1) The name applied to the feast days of the Church on which the antiphons in the holy office are double or fully repeated at the beginning and end of a psalm. These feasts may be doubles of the first class (the most solemn), the second class (those of some Apostles), greater doubles, or ordinary doubles to distinguish their preference in the event that two feasts fall on the same day. (2) Semidouble feasts are less important than those of the double class, and are so called because the antiphon before each psalm in the holy office is not read in full.

**Dove** (dŭv), n.; A.S. A symbol of the Holy Ghost; also a symbol of peace.

**Dowry** (dou'rĭ), n.; Fr. As used in regard to one entering a religious community, it is the sum of money or personal property that a person seeking profession in a religious order brings to the community; such a religious dowry varies with the different religious orders and may or may not be demanded.

**Dowry of Mary,** n.; O.Fr. Name applied to the Engglish people; members of the Catholic Church of England.

**Doxology** (dŏks·ŏl'ō·jĭ), n.; Gr. A prayer of glory: (1) the greater doxology is the *Gloria in Excelsis* which is recited during the Mass. (2) The lesser doxology is the prayer beginning "Glory be to the Father."

**Dream** (drēm), n.; O.E. Images or phantasms of the mind appearing during sleep. Dreams have no religious significance but may be used by God in in His providence to reveal some truth or course of action to a person.

**Duel** (dū'ĕl), n.; Fr., It. A fight or combat with deadly weapons between two persons at a given place and time before witnesses; usually a fight to death or to the mortal wounding of one of the parties. Condemned by the Church as sinful under the fifth commandment; it incurs the penalty of excommunication.

**Dulia** (dū·lĭ'à), n.; L. Worship given to saints and angels whereby we honor them as friends of God and recognize their superior sanctity. The kind of worship which is given to saints and angels. (Cf. Cultus, Veneration.)

**Duplication** (dū'pl*i*·kā'sh*u*n), n.; L. Celebration of two Masses by a priest on the same day. (Cf. Bination.)

## ✟ E ✟

**Easter** (ēs′tēr), n.; A.S. The feast commemorating the Resurrection of our Lord. In the western Church the Feast is celebrated on the Sunday following the first full moon after the spring equinox, which is March 21.

**Easter water,** n.; A.S. Water drawn from the baptismal font or from an adjacent vessel after the solemn blessing of the baptismal font on Holy Saturday has been performed partially, or before the holy oils have been poured in. It is used in the Church from Holy Saturday until the Sunday after Easter.

**Eastern Church** (ēs′tērn), n.; A.S., Gr. Official name used at Rome for Catholics of eastern rites considered collectively. In the plural it refers to the Eastern rites. These may be either Catholic, that is, united with and under the authority of the Pope, or dissident, that is, non-Catholic. The latter may be schismatical or heretical, separated from the Holy See and having other errors. They all teach the real Presence, the Mass, confession, veneration of the Blessed Virgin and the saints, etc., and so must be distinguished from Protestant churches.

**Ebionites** (ē′bĭ·ŏ·nīts), n. pl.; Gr., L. Those who became Christians and wished to retain Jewish custom and ceremony and held that the Jewish law was binding on Christians.

**Ecclesia** (ĕ·klē′zhĭ·å), n.; Gr., L. The Church of Christ; a church; a word borrowed from the Latin and Greek languages and applied to a church.

**Ecclesiastes** (ĕ·klē′zĭ·ăs′tēz), n.; Gr.; Bib. A book of the Old Testament supposedly written by King Solomon.

**Ecclesiastic** (ĕ·klē′zĭ·ăs′tĭk), n.; Gr., L. A member of the clergy; name applied to one in Holy Orders.

**Ecclesiastical** (ĕ·klē′zĭ·ăs′tĭ·kăl), adj.; Gr., L. Of or pertaining to the Church.

**Ecclesiasticus** (ĕ·klē′zĭ·ăs′tĭ·kŭs), n.; Gr., L.; Bib. A deuterocanonical book of the Old Testament; it is rejected in Protestant versions of the Bible but contained in their Apocrypha.

**Ecstasy** (ĕk′stå·sĭ), n.; Gr. A state of trance or rapture in which one is not in his usual mental state; the suspension of the activity of the senses while the mind is absorbed in God.

**Ecumenical** (ĕk′ū·mĕn′ĭ·kăl), adj.; Gr., L. Also Oecumenical. A council for the universal Church to which all bishops and others entitled to vote are called from the entire world to gather under the

Pope or his legates to determine the interpretation of doctrines or laws for the Church. The decrees of such a council, after papal sanction, apply to the universal Church and bind in conscience. (Cf. Ecumenical Councils in the Appendix.)

**Education** (ĕd'ū·kā'shŭn), n.; L. The training of the moral and intellectual faculties of a human being for the purpose of achieving a more perfect degree of knowledge and character; religious education is training in the doctrines and moral laws of the Church. Education must be directed to definite ends; the principal ends are three and they follow in this order of importance: first, religious, for man must be directed toward God; second, civil, for man is a social being and must be trained in his relations to the State and society; third, domestic, for man must be trained as a member of a family so that he may fulfill in society his responsibilities.

**Ejaculation** (ē·jăk'ū·lā'shŭn), n.; L. A short prayer; a few prayerlike words or pious aspirations which one can make at any time or in any place.

**Election** (ē·lĕk'shŭn), n.; L. (1) In Canon Law, the choosing of a person suited for a vacant position. (2) In theology, the decreeing of God that a chosen person is to receive a special grace.

**Eleemosynary** (ĕl'ē·mŏs'ĭ·nĕr'ĭ), n.; L. One collecting alms or one dispensing alms; one dependent on alms. *adj.* Pertaining to alms; supported by charity.

**Elevation** (ĕl'ē·vā'shŭn), n.; L. The raising of the consecrated species of bread and wine after the Consecration of the Mass for the adoration of the faithful.

**Elias** (ē·lī′ăs), n.; Heb.; Bib. A prophet of the Old Testament.

**Elijah** (ē·lī′jà), n.; Heb.; Bib. Hebrew for the name Elias, used in Protestant versions of the Bible.

**Eliseus** (ĕl′ĭ·sē′ŭs), n.; Heb., L.; Bib. A prophet, successor to Elias.

**Elisha** (ē·lī′shà), n.; Heb.; Bib. Hebrew for the name Eliseus, used in Protestant versions of the Bible.

**Ember Days** (ĕm′bēr), n. (adj.) pl.; A.S. Days of fast and partial abstinence which are the Wed., Fri., and Saturdays which follow Dec. 13, the first Sunday of Lent, Pentecost and Sept. 14. (Cf. Abstinence; Fasting.)

**Embolism** (ĕm′bō·lĭz′m), n.; Gr., L. An added prayer. It usually refers to the prayer appended to the last clause of the Lord's Prayer in the Mass, beginning with the word *Libera*. A memento prayer.

**Eminence** (ĕm′ĭ·nĕns), n.; L. Title of address given to cardinals of the Church. This is the official title of a cardinal since 1630 and thus a cardinal must be addressed as "Most Eminent" or "Your Eminence."

**Emmanuel** (ĕ·măn′ū·ĕl), n.; Heb.; Bib. The name given to the Messias in prophecy, which means "God with us."

**Enclosure** (ĕn·klō′zhēr), n.; O.Fr. (1) The rule separating a convent from the world by forbidding those within to commune with those outside the walls; a measure for protecting the spirituality of religious. (2) That part of the religious house reserved for religious to the exclusion of externs or at least to certain externs. (Cf. Cloister.)

**Encratites** (ĕn′krȧ·tīts), n. pl.; Gr. An heretical sect begun in the second century by Tatian; they denied the divine origin of the Mosaic law and taught a false asceticism.

**Encyclical** (ĕn·sī′klĭ·kăl), n.; Gr., L. A letter addressed by the Holy Father to all bishops in communion with the Holy See to inform them of certain measures or for the general instruction of the faithful under their care.

**Endowment** (ĕn·dou′mĕnt), n.; L., O.Fr. In the Church, property that has been set apart for the support of a church or some religious institution.

**Energumen** (ĕn′ĕr·gū′mĕn), n.; Gr. One possessed by the devil; one to be exorcised.

**Envy** (ĕn′vĭ), n.; L., Fr. Willful grieving because of another's temporal or spiritual good, thus lessening one's own seeking of spiritual good; malicious begrudging of another's good by which one is sad or broods on it. It is one of the seven capital sins because it easily leads to other sins. Its contrary virtue is charity toward one's neighbor. (Cf. Capital sins.)

**Epact** (ē′păkt), n.; Gr., L. Name applied to the difference in duration between the lunar and solar years, the lunar year being eleven days shorter than the solar year; by this we are able to determine the days in the month of the civil calendar.

**Eparchy** (ĕp′är·kĭ), n.; Gr., L. A diocese in the Eastern and Russian Churches.

**Epiclesis** (ĕp'ĭ·klē'sĭs), n.; Gr. Also epiklesis. A form of prayer said after the consecration of the Mass in the oriental liturgies and considered by some schismatic Greeks to be necessary for consecration.

**Epigonation** (ĕp'ĭ·gō·nā'shĭ·ŏn), n.; Gr. A vestment worn by priests of the Greek and other oriental Churches which is a square cloth hanging from the girdle; an apronlike vestment; also worn by the Pope in the West.

**Epikeia** (ĕp'ĭ·kī'a), n.; Gr. Also epieikeia. An interpretation of a law whereby it is considered not to bind in a particular case because of some special circumstances; an interpretation of the law in a particular instance against the letter of the law but in keeping with its spirit; an interpretation of the mind of the lawmaker which reasons that he, knowing the conditions, would not wish his law to bind in this particular case.

**Epiphany** (ĕ·pĭf'a·nĭ), n.; Gr., L. Literally, a manifestation; the feast celebrated on January 6; the feast commemorating the manifestations of our Lord, first, to the Magi, or wise men; second, of His divinity made at His Baptism in the Jordan; third, of His power by His miracle at Cana.

**Episcopacy** (ĕ·pĭs'kō·pa·sĭ), n.; L., Fr. The office of bishop; the body of the bishops collectively. (Cf. Bishops.)

**Episcopate** (ĕ·pĭs'kō·pāt), n.; L., Fr. (1) Collectively, the body of ruling bishops. (2) The active term of office of a bishop.

**Epistle** (ê·pĭs″l), n.; Gr., L. The lesson from Scripture read during the Mass between the collects and the Gospel. These are usually taken from epistles or letters of the Apostles which are writings of Scripture addressed to the early Church as instructions.

**Epistolary** (ê·pĭs′tô·lēr′ĭ), n.; Gr., L. Latin: *Epistolarium*. A liturgical book containing the epistles of the Mass; a book used by the subdeacon, containing the pericopes or passages of Sacred Scripture appointed for liturgical use, which are chanted at the Epistle of a solemn high Mass. (Cf. Evangeliarium.)

**Equiprobabilism** (ē′kwĭ·prŏb′a·bĭ·lĭz′m), n.; L. -See Aequiprobabilism.

**Equivocation** (ê·kwĭv′ô·kā′shŭn), n.; L. (1) The use of a word having several different meanings, usually with intent to deceive or give a wrong impression. (2) Mental reservation, and as such it is permissible only on conditions governing such reservation. (Cf. Mental reservation.)

**Erastianism** (ê·răs′chăn·ĭz′m), n.; L. A system under which the Church is subordinate to the state; church authority in the hands of state dignitaries. Said to have arisen with Erastus in the sixteenth century.

**Eschatology** (ĕs′ka·tŏl′ô·jĭ), n.; Gr. Science of the last things; study of death, judgment, hell, purgatory, the renovation of the world by fire, eternal life.

**Esdras** (ĕz′drăs), n.; Heb.; Bib. A priest of early Israel; a book of the Old Testament written by Esdras.

**Esonarthex** (ĕs'ô·nǎr'thĕks), n.; Gr. In the ancient churches, the outdoor vestibule for the three lower classes of public penitents. (Obs.)

**Espousal** (ĕs·pouz'ǎl), n.; L., O.Fr. The engagement to marry; mutual promise to marry made by two persons capable of so contracting; a betrothal.

**Essence** (ĕs'sĕns), n.; L., Fr. Philosophical term applied to the source of all attributes; that which causes a thing to be what it is; that which distinguishes one thing from another. The nature of a thing considered apart from its existence.

**Esther** (ĕs'tēr), n.; Heb.; Bib. (1) The Jewish wife of the Persian King Assuerus (Xerxes I, 485–465 B.C.). (2) An historical book of the Old Testament.

**Eternal** (ē·tûr'nǎl), adj.; L., O.Fr. Existing without beginning or end and without succession or change of any kind. Everlasting, perpetual.

**Eternal Law,** n.; L. The plan and divine will of God manifested and promulgated from all eternity, regulating all created activities. All persons, things, and events are subject to this eternal law.

**Eternity** (ē·tûr'nĭ·tĭ), n.; L., O.Fr. That attribute of God by which He is without beginning or end and without succession or change of any kind. The measure of the duration of a being that is absolutely immutable, .i.e., God.

**Eucharist** (ū'kȧ·rĭst), n.; Gr., L. The Sacrament of the body and blood of Christ truly present under the species of bread or wine; the Sacrament of the real presence. Term denoting the real presence of

Christ in the Sacrament and the Sacrifice under the appearances of bread and wine. The sacrifice of Christ's body and blood.

**Eucharistic Congress** (ū′k*a*·rĭs′tĭk), adj.; Gr., L. A large diocesan, national or international gathering of the faithful to worship our Lord in the Blessed Sacrament. (Cf. Congress.)

**Euchites** (ū′kĭts), n. pl.; Gr., L. An heretical sect which arose in the east and which rejected all practices of religion except prayer.

**Euchology** (û·kŏl′ŏ·jĭ), n.; Gr. The combined missal and ritual book used by the Greek Church for its ceremonies.

**Eulogia** (û·lō′jĭ·*a*), n.; Gr. In the early Church a substitute for communion, merely bread which had been blessed but not consecrated. (Obs.)

**Eutrapely** (û·trāp′lĭ), n.; Gr. Courtesy, urbanity. Part of the virtue of temperance; the moderation in the use of recreation or recreational pastimes; the avoidance of extremes in such pastimes.

**Eutychianism** (û·tĭk′ĭ·*a*n·ĭz′m), n.; Gr. The heretical teaching of Eutyches of the early fifth century. He taught that Christ's human and divine natures are identical.

**Eutychians** (û·tĭk′ĭ·*a*nz), n. pl.; Gr. Heretics who claim that there is identity in the human and divine natures of Christ.

**Evangeliarium**, n.; L. *Evangelistarium*. A book for the use of the deacon, containing the passages which are sung at the Gospel of solemn High Mass; a lector book. (Cf. Epistolary.) The two books, the

the sins must be told with the number of times committed, together with the circumstances which affect the nature of the sin. Also called auricular confession.

**Confession,** n.; L. (1) A profession of faith. (2) In early times the term applied to the tomb of a martyr if an altar had been erected over the grave. (Obs.)

**Confessional** (kŏn·fĕsh′ŭn·ăl), n.; L. The seat or place used by a priest when hearing the confessions of the faithful. The place of confession set aside in the church for this purpose; a place of two compartments separated by a screen in one of which the priest is seated and in the other the penitent kneels. Also a name given to the transverse arms that extend from either side of the nave in a cruciform church building.

One type of confessional. (1) The side for the penitent; (2) where the confessor sits

**Confessor** (kŏn·fĕs′ẽr), n.; L. (1) The name applied to those saints in early times who confessed the Christian faith or Divinity of Christ in times of persecution and suffered torment but not martyrdom for their confession. Later it was applied to those who confessed faith in Christ through their heroic virtue, writing, or preaching. (2) The priest, duly ordained, having received faculties, who hears confessions.

**Confirmation** (kŏn′fẽr·mā′shŭn), n.; L. The sacrament through which grace is bestowed on baptized persons to strengthen them in Christian faith. It increases sanctifying grace and imprints a lasting character or mark on the soul. Through the anointing with chrism on the forehead of the person, the Holy Ghost is received to make one a strong and perfect Christian and a soldier of Jesus Christ. The ordinary minister of this sacrament is the bishop.

**Confiteor** (kŏn·fĭt′ē·ôr), n.; L. The name applied to the prayer beginning with this word in the Latin, meaning "I confess," said at the beginning of Mass during the prayers at the foot of the altar.

**Confraternity** (kŏn′frȧ·tûr′nĭ·tĭ), n.; L., Fr. A corporate fraternal group of the faithful devoted to the furtherance of works of piety or of charity and likewise for the increase of divine worship; for example, the Confraternity of the Blessed Sacrament or the Confraternity of Christian Doctrine. An association of confraternities is called an archconfraternity. (Cf. Sodality.)

**Congregation** (kŏng′grē·gā′shŭn), n.; L. (1) A group of Catholics, usually members of a parish, assembled in church. (2) *Religious*—a religious institute, whether diocesan or papal, bound by a common rule with only simple vows, whether perpetual or temporary. (3) *Papal*—departments of the Roman curia. Eleven groups organized to carry on the business and ecclesiastical affairs of the Holy See. Each congregation has its particular duties and to each is referred the particular business which it is appointed to conduct; groups to give counsel and advice to the Pope. They are: (*a*) the congregation of the Holy Office which guards doctrines epistolary and the evangeliarium are nearly always combined to form the *comes*, or the lectionary.

**Evangelical Counsels** (ē'văn·jĕl'ĭ·kăl), adj.; Gr., L. The holy admonitions of Christ to poverty, chastity, and obedience in the Gospel; they are not absolutely necessary for salvation, but lead to a more perfect life.

**Evangelists** (ē·văn'jĕ·lĭsts), n. pl.; Gr., L. The authors of the four Gospels, namely, Matthew, Mark, Luke, and John.

**Evangelize** (ē·văn'jĕ·līz), v.; Gr., L. To convert; to preach and teach the gospel and the doctrines of the Catholic religion; to catechize.

**Evovae** (ē·vō'vē), n. pl.; L. The final syllables of any psalm or canticle in any chanted sequence which leads into the antiphon.

**Ewer** (ū'ēr), n.; L., O.Fr. The metal pitcher from which water is poured for the washing of the hands of a bishop or other prelate during a Pontifical High Mass.

**Examen** (ĕg·zā'mĕn), n.; L. A particular or general examination of conscience made daily as a devotion. Also referred to the examination of conscience to be made before confession.

Ewer

**Examination of Bishops** (ĕg·zăm'ĭ·nā'shŭn), n.; L. The questionnaire and profession of faith asked of a bishop who is to be consecrated.

**Examination of conscience,** n.; L. The recalling to

mind of past sins so that they may be confessed, repented of, and forgiven. The practice of making a daily check-up of the faults and sins committed during the day. (Cf. Examen.)

**Exarch** (ĕk′särk), n.; Gr., L. A bishop next in rank to a patriarch, or one ruling a province in the Eastern Church.

**Excardination** (ĕks·kär′dĭ·nā′shŭn), n.; L. The act of transferring a person in Holy Orders from the jurisdiction of one bishop to another; the going out from a diocese of a cleric to take up service in another diocese.

**Exclaustration** (ĕks′klô·strā′shŭn), n.; L. Permission granted to a professed religious to live in the world temporarily while still retaining the obligation of the vows; one granted this permission is not allowed to wear the religious garb.

**Excommunication** (ĕks′kŏ·mū′nĭ·kā′shŭn), n.; L. A censure imposed by the authority of the Church depriving one of the sacraments, excluding one from divine services, prayers of the Church, Christian burial, and canonical rights. There are two classes of excommunicates: (1) *Tolerati*, or those whom the faithful are not obliged to avoid; (2) *Vitandi*, or those with whom the faithful are forbidden to commune either in religious or civil matters.

**Exeat** (ĕk′sē·ăt), n.; L. Permission granted a cleric to transfer from one diocese to another; the declaration of excardination.

**Execration** (ĕk′sē·krā′shŭn), n.; L. The loss of consecration on the part of a church, altar, or chalice and paten. (Cf. Desecration.)

**Exegesis** (ĕk'sē·jē'sĭs), n.; Gr. The study and expounding of the meaning of the Scriptures; the scientific interpretation of the sense of Sacred Scripture.

**Exegete** (ĕk'sē·jēt), n.; Gr. One who studies the Sacred Scriptures; one proficient in exegesis.

**Exemption** (ĕg·zĕmp'shŭn), n.; L. The privilege granted to persons or places by which they are placed under the direct jurisdiction of the Holy See and cease to be subject to the jurisdiction of the local bishop.

**Exequatur** (ĕk'sē·kwā'tēr), n.; L. The right claimed by bishops or temporal rulers to examine papal bulls or constitutions in order to decide on their fitness before putting them into force in their territories.

**Exercises (spiritual)** (ĕk'sēr·sīz·ĕs), n. pl.; L. A system of prayers and other religious acts made according to a fixed plan. The title St. Ignatius of Loyola gave to his series of meditations, counsels, and considerations on the religious life and the striving for Christian perfection.

**Exodus** (ĕk'sō·dŭs), n.; Gr.; Bib. (1) The going out of the Israelites from Egypt. (2) Title of the second book of the Old Testament.

**Exomologesis** (ĕk'sō·mŏl'ō·jē'sĭs), n.; Gr., L. A ritual of penance beginning with confession and performed for the lenten season during the early centuries of the Church. (Obs.)

**Exorcism** (ĕk'sôr·sĭz'm), n.; Gr., L. The act and

means of driving out the devil from a possessed person by an ecclesiastically approved series of prayers and fastings. Blessings given to persons or objects are called lesser exorcisms but do not imply a possession.

**Exorcist** (ĕk′sôr·sĭst), n.; Gr., L. One performing the act of exorcism; one having received the sacramental of Exorcist by which he has the power, to be exercised only with permission, of expelling devils.

**Expectative** (ĕks·pĕk′tȧ·tĭv), n.; L. The right to be assigned to a benefice not yet vacant; the right to be collated to a benefice.

**Exposition (of the Blessed Sacrament)** (ĕks′pō·zĭsh′ŭn), n.; L., O.Fr. The placing of the Most Holy Sacrament before the faithful for veneration. A public act of worshiping the Eucharist. (Cf. Benediction.)

**Extravagants** (ĕks·trȧ′vȧ·gănts), n. pl.; L. The fifth and sixth parts of the old canon law; constitutions now incorporated in the body of canon law.

**Extreme Unction** (ĕks·trēm′ŭngk′shŭn), n.; L. The Sacrament of anointing a person in danger of death from sickness or injury, accompanied by prayers from the ritual; it is administered by a priest for the salvation of the soul through grace, and it may give health to the body. The sacrament of the dying.

**Exultet** (ĕg·zŭl′tĕt), n.; L. The name applied to a hymn of praise sung at the blessing of the paschal candle on Holy Saturday.

**Ezechiel** (ē·zēk′yĕl), n.; Heb., Gr.; Bib. A book of the Old Testament named after its author, a prophet of the sixth century B.C.

**Ezra** (ĕz′rȧ), n.; Heb.; Bib. The Hebrew name of Esdras, used in Protestant versions of the Bible.

## ✢ F ✢

**Fabric** (făb′rĭk), n.; L., Fr. The endowment or provision set up for the erection and maintenance of a church building.

**Faculty** (făk′ŭl·tĭ), n.; L., Fr. (1) The group of professors, lecturers, and teachers educating students. (2) The grant of authority from an ecclesiastical superior to perform legally some act of jurisdiction or ceremony. The jurisdiction granted to a duly ordained priest by the bishop of the diocese validly to hear confessions.

**Faith** (fāth), n.; L., O.Fr. The act of spiritual and intellectual assent to a revealed truth of God with the assistance of divine grace. The theological virtue of faith. The assent is of the intellect and is based upon the authority of God, and has for its object every truth revealed by Him.

**Faithful** (fāth′fo͞ol), n. pl.; L., O.Fr. Those persons who profess their faith; all those who are members of the Church by baptism and profession of faith.

**Falda** (făl′dä), n.; L., It. A white silk garment having a train, worn by the Pope over his cassock at solemn occasions.

**Faldstool** (fôld′stōōl′), n.; A.S., O.E. A seat or small bench or portable folding chair with armrests but no back, used by bishops or lesser prelates in the sanctuary when they do not use the throne; a seat constructed so that it may also be used as a prie-dieu or kneeling bench for liturgical functions. Also called genuflexorium.

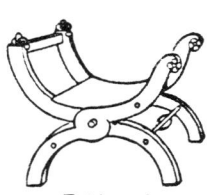
Faldstool

**False Decretals** (fôls dē·krē′tălz), n. pl.; L. A collection of documents anonymously compiled under the name of Isidorus Mercator, containing Apostolic canons and letters of the popes and pronouncements of the councils, and which was published in the ninth century. This collection is in great part a forgery.

**Familiar** (fa·mĭl′yẽr), n.; L. (1) A person serving in the household of a pope or bishop, not as a menial, but rather in a domestic or clerical manner. (2) In pontifical functions, the assistants of a bishop who are vested in the ferriola.

**Fan** (făn), n.; L., A.S. A liturgical instrument used in the early church to drive insects away from sacred vessels. A large flat spread of peacock feathers mounted on a pole and carried in processions of the Pope by an attendant; a puncah, a machine for fanning a room. (Cf. Flabellum.)

**Fanon** (făn′ŭn), n.; O.Fr. The red and gold striped capelike vestment worn only by the Pope when celebrating Pontifical High Mass. It is made of white silk with narrow red and gold stripes and is worn over the alb on the shoulders. In the plural (fanons), the two small flaps which hang down from the back of a mitre; the infulae.

**Fast** (fàst), n.; A.S. (1) The natural fast is the total abstaining from food and drink. (2) Eucharistic fast permits water but food is restricted. (3) The ecclesiastical fast is that which limits the quantity and kind of food, the fast practiced during Lent, on Ember days, and on certain vigils.

**Fasting** (fàs′tĭng), n.; A.S. Limiting one's self in accordance with the law of the Church to but one full meal, two other meatless meals which together should not equal a full meal, not eating between meals except liquids including milk and fruit juices. Meat may be taken at the principal meal on fast days except Fridays, Ash Wed., and vigils of Immaculate Conception and Christmas. The law binds all over 21 and under 60 years of age. (Cf. Abstinence.)

**Father** (fä′thĕr), n.; L., A.S. (1) A title universally given to all priests. (2) The title reverently applied to the first person of the Blessed Trinity, God the Father.

**Fathers (of the Church),** n. pl.; L., A.S. The name by which Christian writers of the first seven centuries are designated. It is commonly agreed that only they can be called "Fathers of the Church" who have the three marks of (*a*) antiquity, (*b*) holiness, (*c*) learning as displayed in teaching or writing in defense of the Church and its doctrines with the approval of the Church. St. John Damascene (died 749) is usually called the last of the Fathers.

**Fear (of God)** (fēr), n.; A.S. (1) Servile fear of God is a dread of the punishment which God inflicts on sinners. (2) Filial fear is the dread of offending God based on love for Him. (3) One of the gifts of the Holy Ghost.

**Feasts (of the Church)** (fēsts), n. pl.; L., O.Fr. The days of the Church calendar which are set aside to commemorate a particular mystery of the faith, or days selected for giving glory to particular saints. These feasts may be holydays with the obligation of hearing Mass imposed on the faithful. Feasts are also divided, in accordance with their rank, into doubles, semidoubles, or simples. The double feasts may be again divided into doubles of the first class (the most solemn) or second class (some of the feast days of the saints) or greater or ordinary doubles. (Cf. Double, Simple.)

**Febronianism** (fē·brō′nǐ·*an*·ĭz′m), n.; O.Fr. The idea propounded by Febronius in the eighteenth century which places the Church and its constitution as subject to the state or to the national mind of the people; a false system of making the Church subservient to the state.

**Fee** (fē), n.; O.Fr. A contribution or tax exacted for services rendered or in support of ecclesiastical undertakings; fees are taken for necessary expenditures. Sometimes inaccurately applied to the voluntary offering for a Mass, called a stipend.

**Feretory** (fĕr′ē·tō′rĭ), n.; L., It. (1) A large portable reliquary. (2) That part of a church set aside for the shrine of a saint.

**Feria** (fē′rĭ·a̯), n.; L. The days of the week, excepting Sunday and Saturday, are so named in the ecclesiastical calendar; the liturgical name for a weekday.

**Ferial** (fẹr′ĭ·a̯l), adj.; L. Pertaining to weekdays.

**Ferriola** (fĕr′ĭ·ō′la̯), n.; It. A short cape, usually attached to any cassock and extending halfway to the elbow. Also ferraiola.

**Ferriolone** (fĕr′ĭ·ō·lō′nã), n.; It. A black cloak or cape worn over the cassock and extending full length; a long narrow cloak, royal purple in color, worn over the cassock by bishops and other prelates on formal nonliturgical occasions. The ferriolone of a cardinal is scarlet; a priest may use a black one.

**Ferula** (fĕr′û·la̯), n.; L. (1) A wand or stick used by priest penitentiaries to strike penitents lightly. (2) A short staff, T-shaped.

**Final perseverance** (fī′na̯l), adj.; L. The gift of God whereby man is taken by death when he is in the state of grace; it can be obtained by sincere, humble, and constant prayer.

**Fire (blessing of)** (fīr), n.; A.S. The first ceremony of Holy Saturday which is the blessing of fire struck by a spark from steel and flint, from which fire the paschal candle and sanctuary lights are lighted.

**Fire (of hell)**, n.; A.S. The punishment of hell which will cause intense suffering but will not consume.

**Firkin** (fûr′kĭn), n.; D. A liquid measure containing about nine gallons; there were two or three firkins in each water jar containing the water which Jesus changed into wine at Cana. (Obs.)

**First fruits** (fûrst froots), n. pl.; L., A.S. In the law of Moses that first part of the harvest which was owed as an offering to the Lord; the first fruits of man, of animals, and of the fruits of the harvest. Sometimes applied to an offering to be given in support of the Church.

**Fisherman's Ring** (fĭsh′ẽr·mănz), n.; A.S. A gold ring used by the Pope to seal papal briefs.

**Fistula** (fĭs′tū·lȧ), n.; L. A tube, usually of gold, through which the faithful drank the consecrated wine from the chalice during the Mass. Now only used in papal Masses when the Pope so receives the consecrated wine.

**Flabellum** (flȧ·bĕl′ŭm), n.; L. (Pl. flabella.) A fan of ostrich feathers carried on either side of the papal chair when the Pope is borne in procession. (Cf. Fan.)

Flabella

**Flag (Papal)** (flăg), n.; L. The official cloth emblem of Vatican State. It is formed of two pieces of cloth sewn together, one yellow which is next to the flagstaff, and the other white on which is a design formed of the pontifical tiara and two crossed golden keys.

**Flagellants** (flăj′ĕ·lănts), n. pl.; L. Certain fanatical groups who made a practice of scourging themselves in common; the group of those practicing the lashing of their bodies in penance. They became heretical and as such last appeared about the fifteenth century. Today some groups still persist in this practice of doing penance publicly and in common, but against the wish and will of the Church.

**Flagellation** (flăj′ĕ·lā′shŭn), n.; L. The scourging of Christ inflicted as a part of His Passion; the punishment given to Christ by the Roman soldiers. This is not to be confused with the acts of mortification of self-inflicted scourging known as the "discipline," yet sometimes this practice is so named.

**Font** (fŏnt), n.; L., A.S. (1) A vessel in which the baptismal water is kept; a vaselike container supported on a pedestal over which the child is held when the baptismal waters are poured on his head. (2) A holy water stoup or basin.

A small font or stoup

**Footpace** (foot′pās′), n.; A.S. The platform on which the altar stands; the predella.

**Forbidden (societies)** (fŏr·bĭd″n), adj.; A.S. All secret societies. (Cf. Secret societies.) Expressly forbidden under pain of excommunication is Free Masonry. Some others forbidden are: The Eastern Star, Odd Fellows, Sons of Temperance, Knights of Pythias.

**Form** (fôrm), n.; L., O.Fr. (1) In philosophy, that intrinsic principle which makes a body to be of this or that kind. (2) A term applied to that part of a sacrament constituted by the words said in applying the matter of the sacrament during administration. (Cf. Matter.)

**Fortitude** (fôr′tĭ·tūd), n.; L., Fr. (1) The cardinal virtue which prompts us to be brave in the face of obstacles to the performance of duty. (2) One of the gifts of the Holy Ghost, giving us strength in difficulties.

**Forty Hours (Devotion)** (fôr′tĭ ourz), n. pl.; Gr., L. A devotion to our Lord in the Blessed Sacrament which continues with exposition of the Blessed Sacrament for forty hours duration. Also referred to as "Forty Hours Prayer" or "Forty Hours Adoration."'

**Forum** (fō′rŭm), n.; L. A place of public assembly, or any public meeting; a tribunal. In canon law, forum refers to the exercise of jurisdiction over the faithful. The *internal forum* or the forum of conscience refers to the private good of the faithful and governs their private actions as individuals in their relation to God, while the *external forum* refers to the common or public good of the faithful, and governs their social actions, in as much as they are members of the Church.

**Fossor** (fŏs′sēr), n.; L. A representation in relief of a gravedigger found in the crypts of the catacombs.

**Foundation** (foun·dā′shŭn), n.; L. A fund established

for the support of a church or a religious institution. (Cf. Endowment.)

**Fraction** (frăk'shŭn), n.; L., O.Fr. The breaking of the host during the Mass at the close of the prayer, *Libera*.

**Fragment** (frăg'mĕnt), n.; L. A piece of host detached from the large host used at Mass or from one of the smaller hosts distributed at communion. (Cf. Altar breads.)

**Franciscans** (frăn·sĭs'kănz), n. pl.; It., Fr. The religious order following the rule of St. Francis of Assisi, established by him in the thirteenth century; friars minor; sometimes referred to as the Seraphic Order. The followers were divided into two groups, conventuals and observantines; at a later date the Capuchins, the Recollects, and Alcantarines were also formed as branches. Among the sisters, the Order of Poor Clares follow the rule which was given to St. Clare by St. Francis as the Second Order. A third order of Franciscans whose membership is composed of the laity or diocesan clergy who wish to dedicate their lives to observances of penance and religious practice was formed; these are known as tertiaries.

**Frankincense** (frăngk'ĭn·sĕns), n.; O.Fr. A resin used in making incense; an incense of fine quality. Incense is used for burning and gives off a sweet-smelling smoke. (Cf. Incense.)

**Fraternal Correction** (frȧ·tûr'năl), adj.; L. The admonition, counsel, or advice which, under certain circumstances, one is obligated out of charity to give his neighbor to correct his faults, to withhold him from sin or to remedy his having fallen into sin.

**Fraticelli** (frăt'ĭ·sĕl'ĭ), n. pl.; It. An heretical sect which branched from the Franciscan order in the thirteenth century; the name means little friars.

**Freedom (of the will)** (frē'dŭm), n.; A.S. The power or faculty of the soul by which the mind of man is able to make a choice in view of the end; the power to act or not to act, to do this or that, in view of the end.

**Friar** (frī'ẽr), n.; L., O.Fr. A member of the so-called mendicant religious orders. The chief mendicant orders are: the Dominicans, Franciscans, Carmelites, and Augustinians.

**Friary** (frī'ẽr·ĭ), n.; L., O.Fr. A name given to a residence for friars.

**Frontal** (frŭn'tăl), n.; L., O.Fr. A colored and embroidered cloth which completely covers the front of the altar. It is suspended from the table (*mensa*) and hangs down to the floor; the color varies according to the liturgical color of the feast or season of the Church calendar; an antependium.

**Fruits (of the Holy Ghost)** (froots), n. pl.; L. Qualities found in the just and bestowed by the Holy Ghost. They are: charity, faith, joy, peace, goodness, patience, benignity, longanimity, mildness, modesty, continence, and chastity.

**Frustulum** (frŭs'tû·lŭm), n.; L. The small breakfast of solid food allowed on days of fast, the quantity and quality of which are determined by local custom. (Cf. Fast, Fasting.)

**Funeral** (fū′nĕr·ăl), adj. & n.; L., O.Fr. The last rites as prescribed in the Roman ritual for the soul of a departed person and the interment of the body.

# ✠ G ✠

**Gabbatha** (găb′ȧ·thȧ), n.; Aram., Heb. The place wherein Pilate tried and condemned Christ.

**Gabriel** (gā′brĭ·ĕl), n.; Heb. The archangel who announced to the Blessed Virgin that she was to be the mother of God; he also announced the birth of St. John the Baptist to Zachary.

**Gallicanism** (găl′ĭ·kȧn·ĭz′m), n.; L. The political belief which held that the national church should have certain powers over and above the authority of the Holy See; it led to the dominance of the State over the Church. It receives its name from some Church leaders of France and arose in the tenth century.

**Gaudete Sunday** (gô·dē′tē), n.; L. The third Sunday of Advent, so named because of the first word of the introit which is the Latin imperative of the verb "rejoice."

**Gehenna** (gĕ·hĕn′ȧ), n.; Heb., Gr. The name applied

to hell, taken from the desolate valley of Hinnon in Palestine.

**Gendarmes (Pontifical)** (zhän-därmz′), n. pl.; Fr. The police force of the Vatican palaces and gardens. The force is made up of ex-service men from the Italian army and all must be of good character. They wear a uniform of white breeches, blue tunic with a white band running from shoulder to waist, and have a high fur helmet. Each carries a sword. There is also a group of men in plain clothes who act as a secret police. (Cf. Guards.)

**General** (jĕn′ẽr-ăl), n.; L., O.Fr. The superior of a religious order who has authority over all his subjects and has spiritual jurisdiction over his subjects in either internal or external forums; it is really an adjective qualifying the nouns provost, superior, or master, but generally used alone to designate the head of the order.

**General Confession**, n.; L., O.Fr. A confession of sins committed since baptism or over some stated period, embracing sins already confessed; necessary for those who have made previous bad confessions, in which case it must include all sins committed since the last good confession; when not necessary, advised as of great spiritual value to some, but dangerous to others because it may lead to scrupulosity.

**Genesis** (jĕn′ĕ-sĭs), n.; Gr., L. The first book of the Bible, written by Moses and telling of the creation of the world and man and the revelation to the chosen people.

**Genuflection** (jĕn′ū·flĕk′shŭn), n.; L. The act of bending the right knee to the floor in adoration and reverence for God in the Blessed Sacrament. A double genuflection, or the bending of both knees to the floor and the bowing of the head, is an act of reverence made before the Blessed Sacrament exposed. The single genuflection is also used to signify an act of homage given to the Pope, a cardinal, or a bishop in his own diocese.

**Genuflexorium** (jĕn′ū·flĕk·sô′rĭ·ŭm), n.; L. A seat or small bench or portable folding chair with armrests but no back. It receives its name from the fact that in ordination the bishop kneels before it while reciting the litany and uses it as a bookrest; a faldstool.

**Gethsemane** (gĕth·sĕm′a·nē), n.; Gr. The garden to the east of the city of Jerusalem beyond the brook of Cedron and at the foot of the Mount of Olives where Christ suffered His agony and was apprehended.

**Ghost, Holy** (gōst), n.; A.S. The third person of the Blessed Trinity proceeding from the Father and the Son, truly God; the Holy Spirit.

**Gifts (of the Holy Ghost)** (gifts), n. pl.; O.E. The gifts, seven in number, bestowed upon the just by the Holy Ghost. They are: Wisdom, Understanding, Counsel, Fortitude, Knowledge, Piety, and Fear of the Lord.

**Girdle** (gûr′d′l), n.; A.S. A cincture or band with which the priest or other cleric encircles his waist in order to bind the alb. (Cf. Cincture.)

**Glebe** (glēb), n.; L. The land surrounding a church or religious building, the cultivation of which may afford maintenance for the church.

**Gloria Patri,** n.; L. The Latin words which are the first two words of the doxology "Glory be to the Father."

**Glory** (glō'rĭ), n.; L. (1) The splendor which attends or accompanies the revelation of the power of God to men. (2) The cloud over the ark of the covenant which represented the presence of God; the *shekinah*. (3) The state of happy existence which the soul enjoys in the presence of the beatific vision. (Cf. Beatific vision.) (4) It is sometimes applied to the aureole.

**Glossator** (glŏ·sā'tēr), n.; L. In the early days of transcribing scriptural writings, the one who wrote the commentaries or notes to the text. (Obs.)

**Gloves** (glŭvz), n. pl.; A.S. The liturgical covering of the hands worn by the bishop or a privileged prelate when reading a Pontifical High Mass (not a requiem); they are worn only until the washing of the hands at the Lavabo. They usually are the same color as the vestments of the feast day. Also called chirothecae.

**Gluttony** (glŭt''n·ĭ), n.; L., O.Fr. Inordinate indulgence in food or drink; the taking of food or drink in excess or in such a manner as to be harmful to the body; eating or drinking for the sole purpose of pleasure.

**Gnosticism** (nŏs'tĭ·sĭz'm), n.; Gr. A philosophico-religious sect of early Christian times whose chief tenet was that its members possessed certain knowledge of natural and supernatural things not given to nor obtainable by others.

**God** (gŏd), n.; A.S. The Supreme Being who owes His existence to no other, who is absolutely and infinitely perfect and who has created all things; the eternal Spirit who created and rules the universe and in whom is every perfection, and who is simple and immutable in His spiritual substance. The three persons of the Blessed Trinity: God the Father, God the Son, God the Holy Ghost—three Persons in one God.

**Godfather** (gŏd′fäthēr), n.; A.S. The male sponsor of an infant at his baptism; the one who makes the profession of faith for the person baptized. He becomes spiritually related to the baptized person and receives the commission in charity to guide him spiritually should necessity arise. (Cf. Sponsor.)

**Godmother** (gŏd′mŭth′ēr), n.; A.S. The female sponsor of an infant at baptism; she makes the profession of faith in the name of the child and assumes a responsibility in the spiritual guidance of the child should the necessity arise. A spiritual relationship is established between the one baptized and the godparent. (Cf. Sponsor.)

**Golden Rose,** adj.; A.S. A replica of a rose and a thorny branch fashioned in gold, sometimes ornamented with precious gems, which the Pope blesses on Laetare Sunday, and which is sent occasionally as an award to Catholic sovereigns or to churches or Catholic cities.

**Golgotha** (gŏl′gō·th*a*), n.; Aram., Heb. The "place of the skull" in Aramaic; the mount of Calvary where Christ was crucified.

**Gong** (gŏng), n.; Jav. An instrument used instead of the small bell during the Mass but condemned as unliturgical by the Congregation of Sacred Rites.

**Good Friday** (good frī′dĭ), n.; A.S. The Friday of Holy Week on which the Church commemorates the Passion and death of Christ.

**Good Works,** n. pl. Actions of a spiritual value by the performance of which one deserves a supernatural reward from God; actions tending toward the perfection of the person performing them; acts which tend toward the increase of grace.

**Gospel** (gŏs′pĕl), n.; A.S. (1) Literally "good news." A recording of the life and works of Jesus written by an evangelist. (2) Collectively, the writings of the four evangelists, Matthew, Mark, Luke, and John, contained in Sacred Scripture. (3) The reading of an extract from Sacred Scripture, taken from the gospel narrative, which takes place in the ceremonies of the Mass just before the Offertory. There is a second Gospel right after the final blessing of the Mass which is of the feast day or vigils, days of special commemoration, and days in Lent when a feast is celebrated, but usually this second gospel is the first fourteen verses of the Gospel of St. John, first chapter.

Chasuble in the Gothic style

**Gothic (vestments)** (gŏth′ĭk), adj.; L., Fr. Vestments

cut to an oblong circular pattern in the chasuble rather than the square Roman pattern and worn over the shoulders and upper part of the arms. A wide variety of full or ample vestments with long and narrow stoles and maniples are usually so designated.

**Grace** (grās), n.; L. Specifically, grace is a supernatural gift freely given by God to rational creatures to enable them to obtain eternal life. Generally, however all that one receives as free gifts from God may be termed graces or favors. Grace may be sanctifying or actual; sanctifying grace is permanent in the soul and elevates the soul by its very presence there and is called habitual grace; all infused virtues accompany habitual grace. Actual grace may be either *exciting* or *helping;* that of exciting stimulates the mind to act and that of helping assists in performing the act which already has been begun. Each person is granted sufficient grace to enable him to save his soul. (Cf. Sanctifying grace.)

**Grace (at meals),** n.; L. A prayer of blessing and thanks to God said over the food which is taken at table. The thanksgiving for food. A prayer to be recited before eating, blessing the food, or said after the meal in thanksgiving for having received the food.

**Gradine** (gra·dēn′), n.; L., It. The back portion of an altar forming a shelf on which are placed the crucifix, candles, or decorations. It is not prescribed by the rubrics, nor is it forbidden. The present tendency is to dispense with it. Also called scabellum.

**Gradual** (grăd'ū·ăl), n.; L. (1) The antiphon sung after the Epistle; it is also called responsory. These antiphons were called "gradual" because they were sung while people marched. (2) The book (Latin: *Graduale Romanum*) containing the ordinary and all the proper parts of the Mass which are to be sung by the choir during the entire liturgical year.

**Gradual Psalms,** n. pl.; L. Psalms 119 to 133 as numbered in the Vulgate which have a somewhat similar theme, namely, joy and trust in the providence of God.

**Graffito** (grȧ·fē'tō), n.; It. A writing or picture scratched or drawn on the walls or stones of ancient monuments or on the walls or tombs of the catacombs.

**Grail** (grāl), n.; O.Fr. An organization for Catholic Action for young girls originated by the religious order, "The Women of Nazareth" or "The Ladies of the Grail."

**Grail (the Holy),** n.; O.Fr. The sacred vessel which according to legend was used by Christ at the Last Supper. The legend has been immortalized by famous writers but has never been given credence by the Church.

**Greater Litanies,** n. pl. Name given to the ceremony including the chanting of the Litany of the Saints and the procession which precedes the Rogation Mass on April 25. The ceremony is in no way connected with the feast of that day.

**Greca** (grā'kȧ), n.; It. A black clerical overcoat worn

by the clergy when the cassock is worn on the street.

**Greek Church** (grēk), adj.; Gr. An independent unit of the Orthodox Eastern Church; the Church which has been separated from the jurisdiction of the Pope and is governed by a synod of nine men of which the Archbishop of Athens is the head.

**Gregorian Altar** (grĕ·gō′rĭ·ăn), adj.; Gr., It. An altar in the church of St. Gregory in Rome which has been given the special privilege of a plenary indulgence applicable to the Poor Souls in Purgatory. The indulgence may be gained by celebrating Mass at the altar and this without any conditions. Also an altar to which has been applied the Gregorian privilege; since legislation of 1912 no further Gregorian altars will be conceded to churches.

**Gregorian Masses,** adj.; Gr., It. Thirty Masses said for the repose of a soul after death and read on successive days.

**Gregorian Music,** adj.; Gr., It. Gregorian chant. The music of the liturgy. The notation and musical form so designated because it was supposed to have been finally developed by St. Gregory in the latter part of the sixth century.

**Gremial** (grē′mĭ·ăl), n.; L. Also gremiale. A rectangular piece of silk cloth decorated with gold or lace and placed upon the lap of the bishop when he sits during the celebration of Pontifical Mass or during the cere-

Gremial

mony of ordination and at other liturgical ceremonies; its original use was as a means of keeping vestments from becoming soiled; also called gremial-veil.

**Grey Friars** (grā), (adj.), n. pl.; A.S., L. The name by which the Franciscan Friars Minor formerly were known in England because their habit was slate gray in color.

**Grille** (grĭl), n.; L., O.Fr. Or Grill. (1) The screen or latticework which is prescribed by canon law to be placed between the priest and penitent in the confessional. (2) The screen separating strictly enclosed nuns from visitors in the visiting parlor or interviewing room. Also the grating or latticework which separates the nuns' choir from the altar of their convent chapel.

**Guadalupe** (gwä′da·lōōp′), n.; Sp. A small town near Mexico City, celebrated for the vision of the Blessed Virgin to a peon, Juan Diego, in 1531; it is the place of the shrine bearing that name. The Feast of our Lady of Guadalupe is on December 12.

**Guardian** (gär′dĭ·an), n.; O.Fr. (1) A person under whose care a child is placed; the one responsible for the bringing up of an orphan child. (2) The superior of a Franciscan friary, elected for a term of three years.

**Guardian Angel,** n.; O.Fr., L. The angel commissioned by God to care for a human being while on earth. (Cf. Angels.)

**Guards (Papal)** (gärdz), n. pl.; L., O.Fr. Protectors.

In Vatican City there are three types of guards: (1) Noble Guards: the personal body-guard of the Holy Father, of which there are seventy-seven, and they are chosen with great care from the Roman nobility. They wear a blue uniform with gold trimmings. On great feasts they wear red tunics and white breeches. When serving as attendants in the papal chambers they are called Chamberlains of the Cape and Sword. (2) Swiss Guards: Members of this group serve as guards of Vatican City, at the doors of the palaces and the Pope's apartments, and are in attendance at all papal functions in the papal chapel. There are one hundred of these and each must be a native Swiss, unmarried, under twenty-five years of age. They have a steel-blue everyday uniform and on solemn occasions wear a costume of red, black, and yellow. All are fully armed. (3) Palatine Guards: These serve as special guards during a conclave and are entrusted with the papal flag. All are Roman citizens and serve without pay. Their uniforms are dark blue with gold buttons. (Cf. Gendarmes.)

**Guimpe** (gămp), n.; Fr. A cloth, usually stiffly starched, worn about and below the neck on the habits of some nuns.

**Gyrovagues** (jĭ′rō-vāgz), n. pl.; Gr., L. The name applied to a group of spurious monks who wandered through the countries of Southern Europe in the early centuries and lived a rambling, unstable life.

# ✠ H ✠

**Habacuc** (hăb′bă·kŭk), n.; Heb.; Bib. A prophet and author of a book of the Old Testament bearing his name.

**Habit** (hăb′ĭt), n.; L. The clothes or garments worn by members of a religious order as mark of their profession in religion; the external garb of nuns or monks.

**Habitual Grace** (há·bĭt′û·ăl), adj. & n.; L. An infused, permanent quality residing in the soul. Since habitual grace is in the soul and sanctifies and makes the soul like to God, it is called sanctifying grace. This perfects the soul, makes one an adopted son of God and the temple of the Holy Ghost, and bestows upon one the title of eternal life. (Cf. Grace; Sanctifying grace.)

**Haceldama** (há·sĕl′dá·má), n.; Heb. Literally, "field of blood"; the burying ground for the poor which was purchased with the money of Judas' betrayal.

It is located to the south of Jerusalem. (Matt. 23: 3–8.)

**Haggai** (hăg′à·ĭ), n.; Heb.; Bib. The Hebrew name of the prophet Aggeus. (Cf. Aggeus.)

**Hagiography** (hăg′ĭ·ŏg′rà·fĭ), n.; Gr., L. The writing of the lives or biographies of the saints.

**Hagiology** (hăg′ĭ·ŏl′ô·jĭ), n.; Gr., L. Study and research leading to knowledge of the lives of the saints.

**Hail Mary** (hāl), adj.; A.S., L. The first words of the prayer known as the Angelic Salutation; the *Ave Maria*.

**Hair shirt** (hâr shûrt), n.; A.S. A garment made of hair, worn next to the skin as a mortification; a cilicium.

**Halo** (hā′lō), n.; Gr., L. The circle of light pictured encircling the head of a saint to denote holiness or sanctity; the nimbus. (Cf. Aureole.)

**Harmonized** (här′mô·nīz′d), adj.; Gr., L. Said of a treatise of the four Gospels to which harmony has been applied; the arrangement of the four Gospels in an historical sequence with a running commentary accompanying the narrative. (Cf. Harmony.)

**Harmony** (här′mô·nĭ), n.; Gr., L. A term used in exegesis to denote the study of the Gospels from the standpoint of explaining the similarities and differences found in the four accounts, developing the continuous narrative, and arranging them in chronological sequence or historical order.

**Hearse** (hûrs), n.; O.Fr. (1) Accepted now to mean the carriage or car in which the coffin bearing the corpse of a deceased person is carried in the funeral procession. (2) Somtimes the multi-candleholder used at Tenebrae services is so called.

**Heart of Jesus** (härt), n.; A.S. The physical heart of Jesus in itself, which as a symbol of His love for us is an object of adoration and devotion. Devotion to the Sacred Heart in its present form dates from the revelations made to St. Margaret Mary Alacoque in 1673–75.

Hearse (Cf. 2 of def.)

**Heart (of Mary Immaculate)**, n.; A.S. The Heart of Mary, the Blessed Virgin, which is venerated as a symbol of Mary's great love and purity. Devotion to the Heart of Mary was begun by St. John Eudes in the seventeenth century.

**Heaven** (hĕv'ĕn), n.; A.S. The place of bliss and happiness where God will manifest His glory to all who are saved and where they will see God; the place and state of perfect happiness. Where it is, is not known, except that it is outside of and beyond the earth.

**Hebdomadary** (hĕb·dŏm'a·dĕr'ĭ), n.; L. Latin: *Hebdomadarius*. Also hebdomadarian. The member of a chapter or convent whose week it is to preside over the recitation of the Divine Office and to celebrate the conventual Mass; the Latin word *hebdomas* means a week. (Cf. Mass, Choir.)

**Hell** (hĕl), n.; A.S. The place and state of eternal

punishment for all who die in mortal sin; the place of the devil and evil spirits. The natural and necessary consequences of the absence of sanctifying grace and the love of God through grievous sin on the soul at death. A place where the damned suffer the pain of loss and of sense.

**Heortology** (hē′ôr·tŏl′ô·jĭ), n.; Gr. The study of the origin, meaning, and development of the feasts of the Church.

**Heptateuch** (hĕp′ta·tūk), n.; Gr. The first seven books of the Old Testament. (Cf. Hexateuch.)

**Heresiarch** (hē·rē′sĭ·ärk), n.; Gr., L. The leader or originator of a heresy.

**Heresy** (hĕr′ĕ·sĭ), n.; Gr., L. Originally a division among Christians; the false doctrine or false interpretation of true doctrine; formal heresy is a grievous sin; it is a rebellion against God.

**Heretic** (hĕr′ĕ·tĭk), n.; Gr., L. One who professes a false doctrine; one who seeks the end of Christian truth but fails in the means because he refuses belief in one or more of the Articles of Faith; one who originates a sect based upon false doctrine.

**Herma** (hûr′mȧ), n.; Gr., L. A reliquary in the form of a bust or replica of the saint whose relics are contained within it.

Herma of St. Thérèse

**Hermas**, n.; Gr., L. The assumed or real name of the writer of a book entitled "The Shepherd."

**Hermeneutics** (hûr′mē·nū′tĭks), n. pl.; Gr. The science

forming the principles upon which the correct interpretation of the Bible is based. Sometimes the study of general Introduction to Sacred Scripture.

**Hermit** (hûr′mĭt), n.; Gr., L. One who lives alone and apart from the world and practices works of prayer and fasting in living in close union with God.

**Heroic** (hē·rō′ĭk), adj.; Gr., L. (1)—Act of Charity: is that act of offering made by a living member of the Church offering to God for the Poor Souls in Purgatory all works of penance and all sufferings to be made for him after his own death; according to the pleasure of the person, these favors may be placed in the hands of the Blessed Virgin to be given by her to the most worthy soul or as she sees fit to give them. The act is heroic because of the willingness of the maker to suffer Purgatory that others may be saved; to it many indulgences have been granted by the Church. The act is not a vow because it may be revoked at any time the maker wishes to do so. (2)—Virtue: excellence in all virtues to such a degree that it is attested to by miracles; the practice of virtue to a degree meriting salvation, either by living as saints or by achieving heroism at the time of martyrdom. It is required in the process for beatification and canonization.

**Hexaemeron** (hĕk′sa·ĕm′ēr·ŏn), n.; Gr., L. Also hexahemeron. The history of the six days of creation which are recorded in the first chapter of Genesis; the time of creation.

**Hexapla** (hĕk′sa·pla), n. (pl. as sing.) Gr. Name applied to Origen's edition of the Old Testament with six texts and versions in parallel columns.

**Hexateuch** (hĕk′sȧ·tūk), n.; Gr. A term designating the first six books of the Old Testament, namely, Genesis, Exodus, Leviticus, Numbers, Deuteronomy, and Josue.

**Hierarchy** (hī′ẽr·är′kĭ), n.; Gr. Collectively it means officials according to their rank and with each rank subordinate to the one above it in order; in the Catholic Church it means collectively the organization of clerics into rank and order of position. In popular usage the bishops of a country as a group.

**Hierurgy** (hī′ẽr·ûr′jĭ), n.; Gr. A sacred rite or function, such as the Mass.

**Holiness** (hō′lĭ·nĕs), n.; A.S. (1) State of being holy; having grace. (2) A mark of the Church. The Church is essentially holy because of its Founder, its doctrine, and its end in the direction and salvation of mankind and because it teaches and cultivates the Christian virtues. (3) A title given to the Holy Father; the title of the Pope denoting his holiness as Vicar of Christ.

**Holocaust** (hŏl′ô·kôst), n.; Gr., L. Burnt offering, a sacrifice wherein the victim is entirely consumed by fire, in use among the Jews and some pagan nations of the early ages. Sometimes, though not properly, used of the Mass.

**Holy** (hō′lĭ), adj. (n.); A.S. (1) As an adj.: sacred; spiritually perfect. One who is of God; one who practices the Christian virtues; one who is in the state of sanctifying grace; something dedicated to

God, or consecrated or devoted to divine service. That which has been blessed. (2) As a noun: an attributed name of God, the Holy (One); also those who have been canonized, more frequently called the blessed.

**Holy Coat,** A.S. The traditional seamless garment worn by Christ at the time of His Passion; the relic kept in the Cathedral of Treves.

**Holydays,** A.S. Days in the calendar of feasts in the Church when the faithful are obliged to cease from servile works and hear Mass; days of obligation. These feasts in the United States are: The Immaculate Conception, Dec. 8; Christmas, Dec. 25; Feast of the Circumcision, Jan. 1; Ascension, movable according to the Church calendar; Assumption of the Blessed Virgin, Aug. 15; and All Saints Day, Nov. 1; and every Sunday. Besides these feasts which are celebrated in the United States, canon law lists the feasts of Jan. 6, March 19, June 29, and Corpus Christi as holydays of obligation to be observed in some countries.

**Holy Ghost** (gōst), adj.; A.S. The third person of the Blessed Trinity, proceeding from the Father and the Son and co-equal with Them; the Spirit of Wisdom; God the Holy Ghost.

**Holy Hour,** A.S. The devotion to the Blessed Sacrament of an hour's duration; it usually consists of exposition, appropriate prayers and hymns, and concludes with Benediction.

**Holy House,** A.S. The home which traditionally housed the Holy Family at Nazareth which is restored and kept under the main dome of the church in the city of Loreto, Italy.

**Holy Name of Jesus,** n. The name of our Lord which in Hebrew means "The Lord is Salvation." The feast of the Holy Name is celebrated on the second Sunday after Epiphany. The society that functions under this name, the Society of Jesus or Jesuits, is distinguished by its devotion to the name of Jesus.

**Holy Office,** n.; L. The most important of the Roman Congregations whose function it is to defend Catholic teaching of faith and morals. Its members are bound to the strictest secrecy, called the secret of the Holy Office. This congregation is the Holy Office. Formerly, the Holy Office was called the Congregation of the Holy Roman and Universal Inquisition. (Cf. Inquisition, Congregations.)

**Holy Oils,** n. pl.; L. The oil of catechumens, the oil of the sick, and chrism consecrated by the bishop at services on Holy Thursday and given to the priests of the parishes. (Cf. Oils, Holy.)

**Holy Orders,** n.; A.S. The sacrament of Holy Orders conferring the power of priesthood and giving grace for the performance of sacred offices. The diaconate, priesthood, and episcopacy are contained in the sacrament and are called major orders. (Cf. Orders, Holy.)

**Holy Places,** A.S. The sites, buildings, and localities which are sacred in the tradition of the Church, such as the place of the birth, of the death, Resurrection, and Ascension of Christ.

**Holy See,** A.S. The Sovereign Pontiff together with

the Roman Congregations, Tribunals, and offices through which he transacts the affairs of the universal Church.

**Holy Thursday,** A.S. The Thursday of Holy Week.

**Holy Water,** A.S. Water in which salt has been mixed and which is exorcised or blessed by the priest. The holy water is a means of grace, a sacramental to promote the spiritual welfare of the faithful; it is one of the most frequently used sacramentals in Church and home.

**Holy Week,** A.S. The last week of Lent; the week properly begins with Palm Sunday and continues through Holy Saturday. It is the time in which the death and burial of Christ are commemorated; a time of particular devotion to the crucified Saviour. The liturgy of this period re-enacts the events of Christ's Passion and Resurrection.

**Homiletics** (hŏm′ĭ-lĕt′ĭks), n.·pl.; Gr. The science or study of the art of preaching; training in the preaching or giving of religious instruction.

**Homiliarium** (hŏm′ĭ-lĭ-âr′ĭ-ŭm), n.; L. A collection of homilies.

**Homily** (hŏm′ĭ-lĭ), n.; Gr. A sermon in which the words of Sacred Scripture are explained and taught; in a sense an oration on passages of Sacred Scripture and exhorting all to follow the teachings presented.

**Homoeans** (hŏ-mē′ănz), n. pl.; Gr., L. A sect which taught that Christ the Son was merely "like" the Father, consequently the followers denied the divinity of Christ.

**Homoousian** (hō'mô-ōō'sĭ-*a*n), n.; Gr. Literally, "of the same substance"; word used at the Council of Nice to express that Christ is one God with the Father; a word denoting the oneness of the Son and Father; opposed to *homoiousian* or "like" to God.

**Hood** (hŏŏd), n.; A.S. Name sometimes applied to the cowl attached to a monk's habit.

**Hope** (hōp), n.; A.S. The theological virtue which is a supernatural gift bestowed by God through which one trusts that God will grant eternal life and the means of obtaining it providing one cooperates. Hope is composed of desire and expectation together with a recognition of the difficulty to be overcome in achieving eternal life.

**Horn (of an altar)** (hôrn), n.; A.S. Any corner of the altar.

**Hosanna** (hŏ-zăn'*a*), interj.; Heb. A word which means "Lord, save us," which was uttered by the Jews at all joyous occasions, hence also a word of joyful greeting or praise.

**Hosea** (hŏ-zē'*a*), n.; Heb. The Hebrew form of the name Osee.

**Hospitallers** (hŏs'pĭt-'l-ẽrz), n. pl.; L. Knights who dedicated their lives to the care of the sick, taking the three major vows of religion; they arose in the eleventh century and had as members laymen who were of noble birth, chaplains or clergy, and brothers who were not of noble birth.

**Host** (hōst), n.; L. A word used to denote: (1) the presence of Christ under the appearances of both bread and wine; (2) the presence of Christ under the form of bread alone, and (3) the unleavened bread before consecration. In its present usage it seems most popular as the bread before consecration; notably, in the Latin Church, the small circular particle which is the usual form under which the Eucharist is received by the faithful.

Altar breads or hosts. (1) The altar bread of the Mass. (2) Types of small altar breads given to the faithful at Communion

**Hours (canonical)** (ourz), n. pl.; L., A.S. (1) The various parts of the Divine Office of the Church which are appointed for different hours of the day; the parts of the breviary. (2) *Little*—a short part of the canonical hours consisting of Prime, Terce, Sext, and None. (Cf. Breviary.)

**Housel** (hou′z′l), n.; A.S. An English name for the Holy Eucharist; it appears in Shakespeare and early writers. (Obs.)

**Huguenot** (hū′gē·nŏt), n. pl.; Fr. The name applied to a French Protestant of the sixteenth and seventeenth centuries; derived from Hugues, a French Protestant leader.

**Humeral Veil** (hū′mĕr·ăl), n.; L. An oblong scarf of the same material and color as the vestment which is worn over the shoulders by the deacon at High Mass when holding the paten, and also worn over the shoulders of the priest when he elevates the Host at Bene-

Humeral veil or velum

diction of the Blessed Sacrament, or when he carries the monstrance and Blessed Sacrament in procession. Also called by its Latin name, the *velum*.

**Humiliati** (hū·mĭl'ĭ·å'tĭ), n. pl.; L. An order devoted to penance which adopted the rule of St. Benedict and was founded in the twelfth century.

**Humility** (hū·mĭl'ĭ·tĭ), n.; L. The moral virtue which promotes us to recognize that of ourselves we are nothing and can do nothing without divine assistance; the reasonable evaluation of ourselves and recognition of our dependence upon God. It is a virtue which is joined to the virtue of temperance in that it moderates the desire for honor, self-glorification, and the esteem of others.

**Hussites** (hŭs'ĭts), n. pl. The name given to the followers of John Huss, a heretic of the fifteenth century.

**Hymn** (hĭm), n.; A.S. A song of praise or honor, sung to give glory to God; psalms and canticles are the most notable. Now applied to any poem of a religious nature adapted for singing.

**Hymnody** (hĭm'nō·dĭ), n.; Gr. Religious lyric poetry; a collective term for all hymns.

**Hymnology** (hĭm·nŏl'ō·jĭ), n.; Gr. The science and study of religious lyric poetry or hymns, usually together with their musical notations.

**Hyperdulia** (hī'pēr·dū·lī'å), n.; Gr., L. The highest kind of saint-worship which is paid to the Blessed Virgin because of her singular privileges of sanctity surpassing all other creatures. (Cf. Cultus.)

**Hypostasis** (hĭ·pŏs′tȧ·sĭs), n.; Gr., L. The subject, the basic thing in which other beings may exist; e.g., the divine Personality is the hypostasis in which the human nature of Christ exists. The Greek equivalent of "person."

**Hypostatic Union** (hĭ′pȯ·stăt′ĭk), adj.; Gr. L. The union of the divine and human natures in the divine person of Christ.

**Hyssop** (hĭs′ŭp), n.; Gr. A branch or leafy twig used for sprinkling water.

☩ **I** ☩

---

**Iconoclast** (ĭ·kŏn′ō·klăst), n.; Gr., L. Literally, "breaker of images"; a follower of the heresy of iconoclasm which in the eighth or ninth centuries protested against statues and pictures in the Church. The heresy rejected both the use and veneration of images as unlawful. The second Council of Nice declared the true teaching on veneration and refuted the heresy.

**Iconography** (ī′kō·nŏg′ra·fĭ), n.; Gr., L. The art of representing God or the saints by pictures, symbols, or statues; images depicting God or the saints.

**Iconology** (ī′kō·nŏ′lō·jĭ), n.; Gr., L. The science treating of the description, history, and interpretation of symbols used in Church art. (Cf. Symbols.)

**Iconostasis** (ī′kō·nŏs′ta·sĭs), n.; Gr., L. The partition separating the apse or choir from the nave in Byzantine churches; sometimes found in Greek and

Russian churches. It is so called because richly ornamented with sacred icons or images.

**Idioms (Communication of)** (ĭd'ĭ·ŭmz), n. pl.; Gr., L. Speaking or appropriating divine attributes to Christ as man and human qualities to Christ as God because the one divine Person is both God and man; human terms of language applied to the God Man.

**Idolatry** (ī·dŏl'åtrĭ), n.; Gr., L. Worship of idols; the giving to a person or thing the divine worship which is due to God alone.

**Ignorance** (ĭg'nō·răns), n.; L. The want of knowledge in one capable of acquiring it; in this sense ignorance may lead to sin because one is obliged to know what is necessary to perform a right action.

**IHS,** abbre. The monogram of the Holy Name of Jesus; first three letters of the Holy Name of Jesus, from a Latinized form of the Greek letters.

**Image (of God)** (ĭm'ĭj), n.; L. Man is made like to God (Gen. 1:26); this likeness is not of bodily shape but is evident in the soul, intellect, and free will of man which distinguish man from the animal, and it is also evident in the body because man was made to rule over all lower creatures.

**Image** n.; L. Replica of Christ, a saint or a holy object which is placed before the faithful to stimulate veneration by calling to their minds the person or object portrayed.

**Imbomon** (ĭm·bo'mŏn), n.; Heb., Gr. A round chapel built on the summit of the Mount of Olives to commemorate the Ascension of Christ.

**Imitation (of Christ)** (ĭm′ĭ·tā′shŭn), n.; L. The title of a book, the greater part of which was most probably written by Thomas à Kempis of Windesheim, Netherlands, and which contains exhortations and admonitions for living a good or spiritual life. It was first published in 1418, and then under the autograph of Thomas à Kempis in 1441. Also known as "The Following of Christ."

**Immaculate Conception** (ĭ·măk′ŭ·lĭt kŏn·sĕp′shŭn), n.; L. The privilege under which the Blessed Virgin was conceived free from the stain of original sin; the gift of God whereby the soul of the Blessed Virgin, because she was to be the Mother of God, was preserved at the time of her conception from the stain of original sin. The feast is celebrated in the Church calendar on the eighth of December. Under the title of the Immaculate Conception the Blessed Virgin is the patroness of the United States of America.

**Immensity** (ĭ·mĕn′sĭ·tĭ), n.; L., Fr. That attribute of God by which God is everywhere in the universe and would be everywhere in any universe. (Cf. Omnipresence.)

**Immunity** (ĭ·mū′nĭ·tĭ), n.; L. In the Church it means the freedom of sacred places or persons from the burden of secular duties or obligations.

**Immutable** (ĭ·mū′tȧ·b'l), adj.; L. Unchangeable; a characteristic of the divine perfection.

**Impanation** (ĭm′pȧ·nā′shŭn), n.; L. The heretical doctrine which states that the substance of bread and wine remain unchanged, that Christ in the Holy

Eucharist is God without a change of the substance of bread and wine.

**Impeccability** (ĭm·pĕk′á·bĭl′ĭ·tĭ), n.; L. The impossibility of sinning; said of Christ, since His human will, being that of a divine Person, could not sin.

**Impediment (of marriage)** (ĭm·pĕd′ĭ·mĕnt), n.; L. A particular condition which either under the natural law or the revealed law of God renders a marriage contract unlawful or invalid; a condition rendering a marriage impossible or illicit. Those conditions which make a marriage impossible or nullify it are called *diriment* impediments; those that make it illicit are called *hindering* impediments. For grave reasons the Church may dispense from impediments, except those of the natural law. (*a*) The *diriment* impediments treated in canon law are: (1) Age; females must be fourteen years old and males sixteen. (2) Impotency. (3) Previous and existing marriage. (4) Disparity of worship. (5) Holy Orders, either subdiaconate, diaconate, or priesthood. (6) Solemn vows. (7) Abduction. (8) Crime. (9) Consanguinity. (10) Affinity. (11) Public decency or propriety. (12) Spiritual relationship between baptized person and minister or baptized person and sponsor. (13) Legal relationship, as adoption. (*b*) The *hindering* impediments are: (1) a simple vow of perfect chastity; (2) mixed religion; (3) special prohibitions.

**Impenitence** (ĭm·pĕn′ĭ·tĕns), n.; L. The absence of repentance in a sinner; when deliberate and absolute, it is one of the sins against the Holy Ghost.

**Impetration** (ĭm′pĕ·trā′shŭn), n.; L. (1) Placing a petition; prayer asking God in His goodness to grant a spiritual or temporal good. One of the four ends of the Mass. (2) A grace following upon good works, especially the Mass.

**Imposition (of hands)** (ĭm′pô·zĭsh′ŭn), n.; L. The act of placing hands upon a person, especially in the sacraments of Baptism, Confirmation, and Holy Orders; it symbolizes the giving of grace and power.

**Imprimatur** (ĭm′prĭ·mā′tēr), n.; L. Literally, "it may be printed." A license required to put in print a Catholic subject, especially one treating of doctrine, morality, canon law, or scripture, and issued by a diocese; approval by the bishop is necessary before a writing bearing teachings of the Church may be printed and presented to the faithful. It is also required for images set up for public devotion.

**Improperia** (ĭm′prô·pē′rĭ·à), n. pl.; L. The reproaches spoken by Christ to the Jews, contained in the Divine Office of Good Friday, sung on that feast by the choir and recited by the celebrant and other ministers during the veneration of the crucifix.

**Incardination** (ĭn·kär′dĭ·nā′shŭn), n.; L. The formal admission of a cleric into a diocese; a term of transference into a new jurisdiction; the opposite of excardination.

**Incarnation** (ĭn′kär·nā′shŭn), n.; L. The fact and doctrine that the Son, the second Person of the Blessed Trinity, became man; God taking human nature, body and soul, for our salvation. This truth is commemorated by the feast of Christmas.

**Incense** (ĭn'sĕns), n.; L. Resin substances which upon being burnt give off aromatic, sweet or spicy smelling smoke. It symbolizes the zeal of the Christian, the odor of Christian virtue, and the rising of prayer to God; used in the liturgy of the Church. *V.t.*, the act of incensing; the motion performed with the thurible, consisting of a rising action and an impelling action; the thurible is raised to the height of the breast and thrust outward toward the object or person to be incensed.

**Incipit** (ĭn·sĭp'ĭt), n.; L. In music, the first few words of a liturgical text sung by a cantor, or in the Mass by the celebrant.

**Inclusi** (ĭn·kloō'sĭ), n. pl.; L. Feminine: *Inclusae*. Monks or nuns who voluntarily, with permission of their superiors, enclose themselves alone in a single cell or room.

**Indefectibility** (ĭn'dē̆·fĕk'tĭ·bĭl'ĭ·tĭ), n.; L. The fact that the Church in its faith and morals and its infallible interpretation will remain unchangeable until the end of time. That attribute of the Church by which it will remain until the end of time essentially the same as it was established by Christ.

**Index (of prohibited books)** (ĭn'dĕks), n.; L. A listing of books by title and author which are judged by the authority of the Church to be harmful to the faith and morals of the faithful. The reading of such books is forbidden under penalty of excommunication.

**Indulgence** (ĭn·dŭl'jĕns), n.; L. The remission in full or in part of the temporal punishment due to sin which already has been forgiven.

**Indult (apostolic)** (ĭn·dŭlt'), n.; L., Fr. A temporary or personal favor granted by the Holy See to a group or to an individual; a dispensation from a law for a particular case.

**Indwelling** (ĭn·dwĕl'ĭng), n.; A.S. The inhabitation of a soul by God because of union with Christ through sanctifying grace.

**Infallibility** (ĭn·făl'ĭ·bĭl'ĭ·tĭ), n.; L. The prerogative of the Church as a teacher by which, being guided by the Holy Ghost, when she actively teaches revealed truths, she is protected from error or the possibility of error; infallibility also extends to those matters which are very closely connected with revealed truths and which the Church also as an authoritative teacher may pronounce upon. It is also a prerogative of the Pope when he speaks as head of the Church on a matter of faith or morals. (Cf. Cathedra, 3.)

**Infamy** (ĭn'fȧ·mĭ), n.; L., Fr. In canon law a mark against the character of a person, arising from some crime or from a penalty.

**Infidel** (ĭn'fĭ·dĕl), n.; L., Fr. One not among the faithful of Christ; one who has not been baptized; one who is ignorant of the true God. Popularly, one who rejects Christianity; or one who has had an opportunity to know revealed religion and yet refuses to accept it.

**Infidelity** (ĭn'fĭ·dĕl'ĭ·tĭ), n.; L. (1) The absence of

faith or belief in the revealed truths of God. The condition of one who has not been baptized, or of one who has rejected Christianity. (2) Failure to fulfill the conditions of a bond, such as that of marriage or of a vow.

**Infula** (ĭn′fû·lȧ—pl. -lē), n.; pl. *infulae*. L. A pendant descending from the back rim of a mitre. (Cf. Vitta, Lappet.)

**Infused (virtue)** (ĭn·fūzd′), n.; L., Fr. A virtue not acquired by repeated acts but gained by being poured into the soul directly by God.

**In Petto** (ĭn pĕt′tô), prep. n.; It., L. Literally, "in the breast." A reservation by the Holy Father by which he does not express or declare to the public the names of newly made cardinals; thus he reserves the information "in his breast."

**In plano** (plā′nō), prep. n.; L. Literally, "on the level." On the floor of the sanctuary, that is, not on the step of the altar.

**Inquisition** (ĭn′kwĭ·zĭsh′ŭn), n.; L., O.Fr. (1) Historically, the establishment of civil powers within ecclesiastical courts that they might protect the message of the Church and repress under civil authority heretics against whom the Church placed censures. Great offenders were referred to the civil courts. It arose in the thirteenth century and was usually administered by the Dominicans. The Spanish—a branch of the Holy Office founded at Seville in 1481 by Ferdinand and Isabella which had for its purpose the punishing with ecclesiastical censure the fraudulent conversions claimed by the

Spanish Jews and Moors. It was bitterly attacked by the nobility and the rich of Spain. It was abolished by the Spanish Revolution of 1820. (2) The present-day Congregation of the Holy Office. (Cf. Holy Office.) (3) In Canon Law, that inquiry which must be made in regard to any accusation brought against a cleric before bringing action against him.

**I.N.R.I.**, abbre. The inscription placed over the head of Christ on the cross. It is composed of the first letters of the Latin words meaning "Jesus of Nazareth, King of the Jews."

**Inspiration (of Scripture)** (ĭn'spĭ·rā'shŭn), n.; L. The supernatural direction or guidance through which a writer of Scripture received matters to be written as God wished; the grace of making record of truths predetermined in the mind of God; that positive divine influence upon the intellect, will, and faculties of the writer of Sacred Scripture whereby he wrote only and all of those things God willed, without fear of substantial error; that impulse and guiding of the writer by the Holy Ghost, said of all Sacred Scripture.

**Installation** (ĭn'stô·lā'shŭn), n.; L. The act whereby an ecclesiastical dignity or benefice is visibly and publicly conferred under the guidance and jurisdiction of a member of the clergy; the enthroning of a bishop; a conferring of spiritual and temporal rights on a priest.

**Institution** (ĭn'stĭ·tū'shŭn), n.; L. The formal ecclesiastical act whereby one having a right to a benefice is actually given possession of it.

**Intention** (ĭn·tĕn'shŭn), n.; L., Fr. (1) In the administration of a sacrament, the purpose or will of the one administering to do what the Church desires and convey to the recipient the grace of the sacrament; the purpose or will of the one administering a sacrament; the habitual or virtual willing to do a thing as it is meant to be done. (2) The purpose or end for which a religious act is performed, e.g., the intention of the celebrant at Mass.

**Intercession** (ĭn'tĕr·sĕsh'ŭn), n.; L., Fr. The prayer of one person on behalf of another; the offering of our prayers to God through saints and thereby gaining a new efficacy for the prayers from the aid of the saints.

**Interdict** (ĭn'tĕr·dĭkt), n.; L., Fr. An ecclesiastical censure which bars people of a place or a person from the use of the sacraments, from all divine offices, and from Christian burial. It may be applied to a place, in which case it is local, and forbids the celebration of the divine offices in that place; it may be attached to a person in which sense it is personal; or it may be mixed, meaning that it is applied to both a place and the persons in that place.

**Interim** (ĭn'tĕr·ĭm), n.; L. A temporary arrangement made with persons outside the Church concerning some religious subject; a concession for a time to promote the greater welfare of the parties concerned.

**Internal forum** (ĭn·tûr'năl), adj.; L. The tribunal for

the administering of the Sacrament of Penance. (Cf. Forum.)

**Internuncio** (ĭn′tēr·nŭn′shĭ·ō), n.; L., It. A legate of the Roman Pontiff of lower rank than a nuncio, but whose duties are the same as those of a nuncio. (Cf. Nuncio.)

**Interpellations** (ĭn·tēr′pĕ·lā′shŭnz), n. pl.; L. The questions or questionnaire which provides evidence and demanded by the bishop or his delegate of the non-Catholic in considering the possible issuance of the Pauline privilege.

**Interstices** (ĭn·tûr′stĭ·sĕz), n. pl.; L. Intervals of time required by canon law to have elapsed between the receptions of degrees of Holy Orders.

**Intinction** (ĭn·tĭngk′shŭn), n.; L. An early method of receiving Holy Communion by which the bread was dipped into the wine before it was received. (Obs.)

**Intoxication** (ĭn·tŏk′sĭ·kā′shŭn), n.; L. The state of being overcome by indulgence in alcoholic drink, accompanied by impairment or loss of the use of reason.

**Introduction (biblical)** (ĭn′trō·dŭk′shŭn), n.; L. The science of the principles underlying the study or interpretation of Sacred Scripture. (Cf. Hermeneutics.)

**Introit** (ĭn·trō′ĭt), n.; L. That prayer of the Mass said when the priest ascends the altar after the prayers at the beginning of Mass; it usually is composed of the words of an antiphon, a psalm verse, the *Gloria Patri*, and the antiphon repeated.

**Investiture (Lay)** (ĭn·vĕs′tĭ·tûr), n.; L. The act and ceremonies by which princes granted to bishops and abbots, besides their spiritual powers, the temporal possessions which constituted their benefices and the political rights which they had to exercise.

**Invitatorium** (ĭn·vī′tă·tōr′ĭ·ŭm), n.; L. Psalm 94 which is said in the office of the Church in the beginning of Matins on all days except Epiphany and the last three days of Holy Week. The invitatory psalm.

**Irregularity** (ĭr-rĕg′ū·lăr′ĭ·tĭ), n.; L., Fr. A canonical impediment forbidding a person from becoming a cleric or from attaining a higher office in clerical rank or from exercising his office. Irregularities may be from *defect* of the individual: (1) Illegitimates; (2) persons bodily deformed; (3) epileptics or insane persons; (4) persons who have been married twice; (5) persons under infamy of law; (6) a judge who has imposed a death sentence or one who has been an executioner. Irregularities may also be from *crime:* (1) Apostates, heretics, and schismatics; (2) those who voluntarily accepted non-Catholic baptism; (3) persons entering a civil marriage while the first marriage still binds or while they are in Holy Orders or under a religious vow; (4) those who have committed voluntary homicide or procured abortion; (5) those who attempt suicide or have mutilated themselves; (6) clerics practicing medicine or surgery when forbidden, should death follow from their practice; (7) persons performing acts reserved to clerics in Holy Orders while not being in that order themselves.

**Irremovability (of pastors)** (ĭr'rẽ·mo͞ov'á·bĭl'ĭ·tĭ), n.; L. The prerogative of certain parish priests whom the bishop can remove from office only for certain grave causes specified in canon law.

**Isaiah** (I·zā'yá), n.; Heb. The name of the prophet Isaias as used in Protestant versions of the Bible.

**Isaias** (I·zā'yás), n.; Heb.; Bib. Prophet and author of a book of the Old Testament who lived about 700 B.C.

**Israel** (ĭz'rā·ĕl), n.; Heb., Gr.; Bib. The original name of the patriarch Jacob; the land inhabited by the Israelites, the descendants of Jacob.

**Itala Vetus,** n.; L. The Bible of the Latin Church down to the time of St. Jerome (d. 420 A.D.). (Cf. Vulgate.)

**Itineraria,** n. pl.; L. Writings telling of the travels of pilgrims to and from the Holy Land.

**Itinerary** (i·tĭn'ēr·ĕr'ĭ), n.; L. A prayer said by clerics before setting out on a journey; it is found at the end of the breviary.

## ✠ J ✠

**J.A.C.,** abbre. Abbreviation of *Jeunesse Agricole Chrétienne*, the Young Christian Farmer, an organization for extended Catholic Action, especially of France and Canada for young people engaged in agriculture.

**Jacist** (jä′sĭst), n.; Fr. The name given to the movement of the J.A.C., an organization for organized Catholic Action to promote the Christianization and salvation of young farmers.

**Jacobins** (jăk′ô·bĭns), n. pl.; Fr. (1) A liberal political group in 1789. (2) Dominicans before the French Revolution in Paris who were sympathetic to the liberalism of the political group. (3) In the singular the title of any liberal.

**Jahweh** (yä′vĕ), n.; Heb. Also Jahveh. The sacred name of God as used by the Jews, and the correct pronunciation of the name which was often mistakenly pronounced Jehovah.

**Jansenism** (jăn′sĕn·ĭz′m), n.; Fr. A heresy which denied the freedom of the will and the possibility of resisting divine grace; it also was intended to be a reform of the Church from within; it arose in the first part of the seventeenth century at Ypres, France, from the religious system of Cornelius Jansen.

**Jeremias** (jĕr′ē·mī′*a*s), n.; Heb.; Bib. The prophet and author of the book of prophecies and lamentations bearing his name and found in the Old Testament.

**Jeronymites** (jĕ·rŏn′ĭ·mĭts), n. pl.; Gr. In the Middle Ages, the name given to various groups of religious men who classed themselves as the hermits of St. Jerome and followed the example of St. Jerome in seeking solitude.

**Jerusalem** (jĕ·rōō′sá·lĕm), n.; Heb.; Bib. A city in Palestine, the center of Jewish political and religious life; it was there that Christ suffered and died. The site of the holy places; the ancient city of the Jews.

**Jesse-window** (jĕs′ē-), n.; Heb. A window of stained glass on which is pictured the genealogical tree of our Lord.

**Jesuit** (jĕz′û·ĭt), n.; L. A member of the society of religious men who follow the way of religious life set down by their founder, St. Ignatius Loyola, in 1534; the society known as the Society of Jesus which is abbreviated, S.J.

**Jesus** (jē′zŭs), n.; Heb., Gr. The name which in Hebrew means "The Lord is Help or Salvation." The name announced to the Blessed Virgin by the angel at the Annunciation and given to God the Son upon becoming man. He is truly God, having one and the same nature with God the Father from all eternity.

**Jews** (jōōs), n. pl.; Heb., Gr. The descendants of Jacob; the people chosen by God to receive His revelation; Israelites.

**Job** (jōb), n.; Heb.; Bib. A character in the book of the same name found in the Old Testament of the Bible; one known to have had great patience in affliction and great trust in the goodness of God.

**J.O.C.,** abbre. *Jeunesse Ouvrière Chrétienne*, the Young Christian Workers. Abbreviation serving as title of an organization for extended Catholic Action for young Belgian and French men and women workers, which was begun by Canon Cardyn in 1924.

**Jocist** (jō′sĭst), n.; Fr. The name given to the movement of the J.O.C., an organization for organized Catholic Action to promote the Christianization and salvation of young workers.

**Joel** (jō′ĕl), n.; Heb.; Bib. The prophet and author of a book of the Bible, the first of the prophets of Juda.

**Jonas** (jō′nɑ̆s), n.; Heb.; Bib. A prophet of Israel who was sent to preach to the Gentiles; the book of the Old Testament recording his prophecies.

**Joseph (Saint)** (jō′zĕf), n.; Heb. The husband of the Blessed Virgin and the foster father of our Lord.

**Josephinism** (jō′zĕf·fĭn′ĭz′m), n.; Heb. The name applied to the erroneous belief and practice of the eighteenth century advocating in principle that the State is completely supreme over the Church, controlling it for the good of all. (Cf. Erastianism, Gallicanism.)

**Joshua** (jŏsh′ū·å), n.; Heb.; Bib. The Hebrew name of Josue as used in Protestant versions of the Bible.

**Josue** (jŏs′ū·ē), n.; Heb.; Bib. The leader of the Israelites after Moses; a book of the Old Testament named after him.

**Jube** (jōō′bē), n.; Fr. The French name for the grill or choir-screen. (Cf. Grill.)

**Jubilate** (jōō′bĭ·lā′tē), n.; L. Literally: shout for joy. Name of the third Sunday after Easter, so named from the first word of the introit of the Mass of that Sunday.

**Jubilee** (jōō′bĭ·lē), n.; Heb., Gr., L. (1) A time of joy and celebration. (2) In the Jewish religion it was the fiftieth year, according to the Levitical Law, which was to be the year of jubilee; the land was to rest, all slaves were to go free, and land and houses in the open country were to revert to the original owners. (3) In the Church a year of jubilee has been adopted as a year of remission from the penal consequences of sin for the faithful, providing they perform certain pious works to gain a plenary indulgence and fulfill conditions of repentance. This jubilee year in the Church is held every twenty-fifth year at Rome, lasting from Christmas to Christmas and is held for the rest of the Church during the following year between the same dates; it may be proclaimed at other times also.

**Jubilee (indulgence),** n.; Heb., Gr., L. A plenary indulgence granted for the time of the Holy Year, or the year of jubilee. It is of a solemn character and attached to certain privileges and special faculties for absolution from reserved cases.

**Jubilus** (jōō′bĭ·lŭs), n.; Heb., Gr., L. The notation to which is sung the final "a" of the second and third alleluias after the gradual of the Mass; a long, melodious group of notes for chanting.

**Juda** (jōō′da), n.; Heb. (1) The son of Jacob. (2) A kingdom in southern Palestine in ancient times.

**Judges** (jŭj′ĕz), n. pl.; L.; Bib. A book of the Old Testament, probably written by the prophet Samuel, relating the history of the governing of Israel by the Judges.

**Judges (Synodal),** n. pl.; Gr., L. Judges appointed by the bishop in synod to decide cases in the diocesan court; if they are appointed outside a synod, they are called prosynodal judges. Their number should not exceed twelve in any diocese.

**Judgment** (jŭj′mĕnt), n.; L. (1) An act of the intellect which compares two ideas and determines whether or not they agree or disagree. It is called a moral judgment when the intellectual act is concerned with the goodness or badness of an action. (2) The passing of sentence by a judge. (3) General—This will take place when Christ will judge all men; the last day when all men will be judged and rewarded with heaven or hell. The manner of this judgment is not known nor the place where it will occur, but theologians hold that the minds of men will be enlightened by God to see their faults and that the sins of all will be declared that God's justice and mercy may be seen. A sentence will be given to each person. The Last Judgment. (4) Particular—The judgment by God of the soul of man immediately after death; the judgment which will declare the soul blessed or damned or confined to Purgatory for a length of time. It is called the particular judgment, but this merely indicates that it will be the individual judgment of the soul by God immediately after death.

**Judica Psalm** (jōō′dĭ·ka), n.; L. Psalm 42 said at the beginning of all Masses, except requiem Masses and those said in Passiontide.

**Judith** (jōō′dĭth), n.; Heb.; Bib. A historical book of the Old Testament, not found in Protestant versions of the Bible. Judith was a widow who killed Holofernes in order to save the city of Bethulia.

**Jurisdiction** (jōōr′ĭs·dĭk′shŭn), n.; L., O.Fr. Jurisdiction in the Church means primarily the public power of the Church to govern the faithful and to direct them to the supernatural end of the Church; it is primarily a power over *persons*, and secondarily over *things;* as such it may be exercised in either the internal or external forum. The power of administration attached by ecclesiastical law itself to some position or office. Jurisdiction may be delegated with limitations of time and broadness of power to another person who is competent of receiving it. (Cf. Forum.)

**Justice** (jŭs′tĭs), n.; L. In its broadest sense the aggregate of all supernatural virtues or the perfection of every virtue; this is the sense used in the saying "Joseph was just." Justice in its particular sense means the virtue moving us to give to each person his due or his right. It is a cardinal virtue.

**Justification** (jŭs′tĭ·fĭ·kā′shŭn), n.; L. The sanctification of the soul of man by God's grace which elevates the perfection of the soul; it normally begins with the grace of faith which leads to repentance. This grace is not merited and assists the free will to dispose itself to the acquiring of perfection, but in adults acts of cooperation such as contrition, faith, etc., are necessary. It is the regaining of sanctifying grace by a soul; the regaining of the friendship of God; the state of never having lost sanctifying grace.

# ✢ K ✢

**Kenosis** (kĕ·nō′sĭs), n.; Gr., L. The heretical theory which considers the Incarnation in the sense that the second Person of the Blessed Trinity took a lower nature, namely, the human nature, discarding His divine nature for a time, or at least foregoing some divine attributes temporarily; the theory of abasement.

**Keys (power of)** (kēs), n. pl.; A.S. A term used to show the superior ecclesiastical authority of the Pope. The keys are the symbol of the office and power of the Pope and also of the Sacrament of Penance. (Matt. 16:19.)

**Kings** (kĭngs), n. pl.; A.S. (1) The four books of the Old Testament dealing principally with the history of the kings of Israel and Juda. The first two are sometimes called the Books of Samuel. (2) The Magi, the three oriental rulers who journeyed to greet the Christ child.

**Kiss** (kĭs), n.; A.S. A gesture of reverence or devotion. The pax or kiss of peace is the ceremonial embrace and kiss given as a sign of fraternal charity during High Mass to all the clergy present and to those serving at the altar. Also the ritual kisses of objects and of the celebrant's hands during a High Mass.

**Knight** (nīt), n.; A.S. (1) A horseman warrior of the Middle Ages who was pledged under oath to fight for just causes only, to be subject to the Church and her priests, and to be a vassal of the Blessed Virgin and thus to protect all women by acts of chivalry. (2) One raised to the dignity of one of the six pontifical orders of knighthood.

**Kyriale** (kĭr′ĭȧ′lē), n.; Gr. A book containing the notation for chanting the ordinary of the Mass; a book of eighteen Masses in plain-chant, used by choirs, each of which is assigned to a particular rank of feast or season.

**Kyrie Eleison** (kĭr′ĭ·ē ĕ·lā′ĭ·sŏn), n.; Gr. The Greek words meaning "Lord, have mercy" used together with the words *Christe Eleison* which mean "Christ have mercy"; it is said immediately after the introit of the Mass.

# ☩ L ☩

**Labarum** (lăb′*a*·rŭm), n.; L. The banner of the cross carried by Constantine in his campaigns. A staff with a banner attached, used as a Christian symbol.

**Lacticinia** (lăk′tĭ·sĭn′ĭ·*a*), n.; L. A word from the Latin meaning milk foods, such as butter and cheese, which are also called "white meats." Formerly the law of the Church obliged those who fasted to abstain from lacticinia; the new code of canon law abolishes this prohibition. (Obs.)

Labarum

**Lady-day** (lā′dĭ-dā), n.; A.S. A name applied to the Feast of the Annunciation, March 25.

**Laetare (Sunday)** (lē·tār′ē), n.; L. The fourth Sunday of Lent, so named because of the first word in the Latin antiphon before the introit.

**Laicization** (lā′ĭ·sĭ·zā′shŭn), n.; L. (1) Reduction of ecclesiastical persons or things to a nonecclesiastical or lay condition by Church authority. (2) The appropriation of Church property by civil authorities contrary to the rights of the Church.

**Laity** (lā′ĭ·tĭ), n.; L. The entire group of lay people, lay men and women. A term distinguishing members of the faithful from the clergy (Cf. Layman.)

**Lamb** (lămb), n.; A.S. A symbol of our Lord as the Eucharistic Victim.

**Lamentabili,** n.; L. Decree of the Holy Office condemning heretical propositions of Modernism, issued in 1907, so called from the first word in the Latin version.

**Lamentations** (lăm′ĕn·tā′shŭnz), n. pl.; L. Parts of the five poems appearing at the end of the prophecies of Jeremias which appear in the breviary at Matins in the last three days of Holy Week, consequently they are a part of the Tenebrae service.

**Lammas-day** (lăm′ăs), n.; A.S. A name applied in the early days of the Church to the Feast of the Chains of St. Peter, celebrated on August 1.

**Lamp** (lămp), n.; Gr., L. A vessel in which a wick soaked in oil burns; a means of giving light by the burning of oil; used in a church to denote the fact that the Blessed Sacrament is reserved there; a sanctuary lamp.

A sanctuary lamp

**Lance (the holy)** (làns), n.; L., Fr. The spear's head now preserved in St. Peter's, Rome, which, according to tradition, was used at the crucifixion of Christ to open His side.

**Lance**, n.; L., Fr. A small knife used in the Greek liturgy to separate the parts to be consecrated from the holy loaf; the knife used to symbolize the piercing of Christ's side.

**Language (of the Church)** (lăng′gwĭj), n.; L., Fr. In general the Church uses dead languages in celebrating the Mass, administering the sacraments, and other services; the Latin language is the most generally used, consequently the Latin language has come to mean in the Roman Church the language of the Church. Other languages used in the liturgies of the Eastern Churches are: Greek, Arabic, Slavonic, Syriac, Roumanian, Armenian, Coptic, and Georgian.

**Lappet** (lăp′ĕt), n.; L., Gr., A.S. One of the flaps or bands of cloth which hang from the back of a mitre.

**Lapsed** (lăpst), n.; L. (*Lapsi*, in Latin.) Under this title were placed all those who gave up the faith under persecution; a special penance was imposed on the lapsed Christians.

**La Salette** (lä sä·lĕt′), n.; Fr. A shrine in Southern France commemorating the appearance of the Blessed Virgin in 1846 to two children.

**Last Day** (làst), adj.; A.S. The day when the created world will come to an end; the day of the general judgment; the day when signs will be given to denote the end of the world, as in Matt. 24 and Luke 21.

**Last Things**, adj.; A.S. Death, judgment, heaven, and hell are said to be the last things; the eschatology. (Cf. Eschatology.)

**Lateran Church** (lăt′ẽr·ăn), n.; L. The church in Rome, called St. John Lateran, so named after the family of Laterani; it is the cathedral church of Rome. The five general councils held in the church are called Lateran Councils. (See Appendix, Ecumenical Councils.)

**Latin** (lăt′ĭn), n.; L. The language of ancient Rome which is the language of the Roman rite of the Church.

**Latria** (là·trī′à), n.; Gr., L. The highest form of worship and which can be offered to God alone; the sacrifice of the Mass is the chief act of latria.

**Latrocinium** (lăt′rō·sĭn′ĭ·ŭm), n.; L. Literally, robbery. The name conferred by Pope Leo I on the heretical council of Ephesus held in 449.

**Latten** (lăt′ĕn), n.; O.Fr. The sheet brass upon which sepulchral memorials were engraved from the thirteenth to the sixteenth centuries.

**Lauda Sion**, n.; L. The first Latin words and title of the sequence in the Mass of Corpus Christi; it was composed by St. Thomas Aquinas on the occasion of the institution of the feast in A.D. 1264.

**Lauds** (lôds), n. pl.; L., O.Fr. The second hour or part of the breviary; literally translated it means praises. It is so called because the Psalms used begin with either of the Latin words *Lauda* or *Laudete*.

**Laura** (lô′rà), n.; L. A group of individual cells or

rooms occupied by monks; it was centered around the church; while living in the laura the monks maintained a community life. The name is still applied to any big monastery of the Byzantine rite.

**Lavabo** (lȧ·vā′bō), n.; L. Literally: I will wash. That part of the Mass at which the server pours water on the thumbs and index fingers of the priest, the parts of his hands that will touch the host; it occurs after the Offertory of the Mass and it derives its name from the first word of verse six of Psalm 25 which is recited by the priest at this time.

**Law** (lô), n.; A.S. The rule of reason by which a person is moved to act or restrained from acting. In the Church this has the meaning of an action which ought to follow upon recognition of a precept, but the action need not always take place, because the person is free and can refuse obedience. In moral theology the necessity which follows upon law is called moral necessity.

**Laxism** (lăk′sĭz′m), n.; L. That system in moral theology which declared that even a slightly probable opinion may be followed in the exercise of one's freedom to act or not act; this system of interpretation has been condemned by the Church.

**Laxist** (lăk′sĭst), n.; L. One who follows a lax interpretation of moral obligation; a person of easy moral conscience.

**Lay Baptism** (lā), adj.; O.Fr., L. The administration of Baptism by a lay person, done out of necessity according to the prescribed form, when no priest is available.

**Lay Brothers and Sisters,** adj.; O.Fr., L. Those who enter religious life, receiving habits and taking vows, but who engage themselves chiefly in manual labor and do not assume the choir duties, study, or other functions of the religious, and who do not receive Holy Orders.

**Lay Communion,** adj.; O.Fr., L. The state to which a cleric is sometimes reduced with the forfeiture of the right to perform his office but without loss of ordinary spiritual privileges of a Catholic. (Obs.)

**Layman** (lā'mǎn), n.; O.Fr., L. A person who has not been admitted to the ranks of the clergy; one having no ecclesiastical title; a member of the faithful.

**Lazarists** (lăz'a·rĭsts), n. pl.; L., Gr., Heb. The congregation of priests of the mission founded by St. Vincent de Paul in 1624, so named from their place of founding, the Priory of St. Lazare. The Vincentian Fathers whose abbreviated title is C.M.

**League (of the Cross)** (lēg), n.; O.Fr., L. The Catholic Total Abstinence League of the Cross which was founded in 1873.

**Lectern** (lĕk'tērn), n.; O.Fr., L. Lacturn, lettern. The reading desk or stand with a slanting top used to support a book before one while reading.

A type of Lectern

**Lection** (lĕk'shǔn), n.; L. Lesson. A reading taken from the Scriptures or from the writings of the early fathers; lections appear in the Mass, e.g., the Gospel and Epistle, and in the Breviary.

**Lectionary** (lĕk'shŭn·ĕr'ĭ), n.; L. (1) A book containing selections from Sacred Scripture to be read at divine services. (2) The portions of Sacred Scripture to be read or chanted by the deacon, subdeacon, or lector. The *comes*. (3) The book containing the lessons for matins. (4) The book containing all the liturgical lessons.

**Lector** (lĕk'tĕr), n.; L. (1) A reader; a cleric whose office it is to read the writings of the Fathers of the Church in public, but not during Mass. He also should sing the epistle in a *missa cantata*. (2) The second of the minor orders, a sacramental.

**Legate** (lĕg'ĭt), n.; L., O.Fr. An ecclesiastical person sent by the Sovereign Pontiff to represent him either for an occasion or by way of a permanent office. (Cf. Nuncio, Delegate Apostolic.)

**Legend (Golden)** (lĕj'ĕnd), n.; L., O.Fr. A book containing the lives of the saints and treatises on feasts of the Church written by Jacopo de Voragine in the late thirteenth century.

**Legitimation** (lē·jĭt'ĭ·mā'shŭn), n.; L. The act both under civil law and the law of the Church which legitimatizes a child born out of wedlock.

**Lent** (lĕnt), n.; A.S. From the Anglo-Saxon word, lencten, meaning *spring*. A time of fast before Easter as penance and preparation for the Feast of the Resurrection; the period of six and one half weeks from Ash Wednesday to Easter.

**Leonine (Prayers)** (lē′ō·nīn), adj.; L. The prayers (three Hail Marys; the Salve Regina, and the Prayer to Michael, the archangel) ordered by Pope Leo XIII to be said after a private Mass.

**Lesser Litanies,** n. pl. The ceremony held on the three rogation days before Ascension Thursday. It is in no way different from the ceremony of the Greater Litanies held on April 25, the term *lesser* merely indicates that this ceremony is not as old as the other. (Cf. Greater Litanies.)

**Lesson** (lĕs′n), n.; L., O.Fr. A reading from Sacred Scripture; a lection, as the epistle read at Mass. (Cf. Lection.)

**Levite** (lē′vīt), n.; Heb. The descendants of the patriarch Levi who were the hereditary ministers to the priests of the Jews; sometimes used today as a name for a cleric.

**Leviticus** (lē·vĭt′ĭ·kŭs), n.; Heb.; Bib. The third book of the Old Testament written by Moses.

**Libellatici,** n. pl.; L. Those who abjured their faith by obtaining a certificate during a time of persecution, denoting that they had offered sacrifice to the pagan gods. (Obs.)

**Liberdiurnus,** n.; L. A collection of formularies used in the early Church and compiled shortly after A.D. 714. (Obs.)

**Libera Me,** n.; L. The response sung by the choir after a Requiem Mass and before the absolution of the corpse or at the catafalque.

**Liceity** (lĭ·sē′ĭt·ĭ), n.; L. In moral and canonical language, the lawfulness of a good or indifferent act.

The term goes further than external legality in the sense that it denotes also the absence of sin or moral guilt in those who perform the act.

**Licentiate** (lĭ·sĕn′shĭ·āt), n.; L., O.Fr. An academic degree conferred by universities for studies in theology, philosophy, Scripture, or canon law.

**Lie** (lī), n.; A.S. An expression of thought contrary to intellectual conviction; a sin against the eighth commandment of God.

**Ligamen** (lĭg′a·mĕn), n.; L. The bond of marriage existing and so prohibiting another marriage; a canonical term meaning the existing previous bond of marriage; an impediment to marriage.

**Ligature** (lĭg′a·tūr), n.; L., Fr. In Gregorian music, a succession of notes which are joined together and are to be sung over one syllable; these may consist of more than one such group of notes. (Cf. Neum.)

**Lights** (līts), n. pl.; A.S. Candles or lamps which are used in the liturgy of the Church; vigil lights are small candles inserted in glass cups which are then burned for an intention or in veneration of some saint.

**Limbo** (lĭm′bō), n.; L. The place where the just who died before man's redemption by Christ were retained. It is also that place wherein the souls of unbaptized infants live a happy eternity. Literally, threshold of the nether world.

*A type of candle holder*

**Litany** (lĭt′a·nĭ), n.; L., O.Fr. A prayer in the form of alternate ejaculations or statements and petitions;

a formula of prayer consisting of a series of supplications and responses; a prayer of petitions in sequence. It may be sung.

**Little Office (of the Blessed Virgin)** (lĭt″l ŏf′ĭs), n.; L., A.S. A short form of breviary in which psalms, lessons, and hymns are recited in honor of the Blessed Virgin; as a prayer it is divided into the seven hours as is the breviary.

**Liturgical (function)** (lĭ·tûr′jĭ·kăl), adj. (n.); Gr. A ceremony which forms part of the official worship of the Church and is, therefore, treated of in one of the official liturgical books.

**Liturgy** (lĭt′ẽr·jĭ), n.; Gr. (1) The worship of God by the Church, comprising the offering of the Sacrifice of the Mass, the recitation of the Divine Office, and the administration of the sacraments. (2) In Eastern Churches, the Mass. Originally, a public service; in the early days it was applied to the solemn service of the Church. The liturgy is: (*a*) all forms of rites and services in any language in the Church in celebrating the Eucharist; (*b*) the rites, official services, ceremonies, prayers, sacraments of the Church, as opposed to private worship.

**L.O.C.,** abbre. Abbreviation for *Ligue Ouvrière Chrétienne*, the Christian Workers' League, begun in 1937 in France as a league of Christian working-class people who carry on a well organized, practical program of Catholic Action and have a truly apostolic spirit. It is an adult group continuing the work of the Jocist groups of France.

**Loci Theologici,** n. pl.; L. Literally, "theological places" or "sources." The sources of theological arguments; the scientific and philosophical arguments used in presenting theology. They are: (1) the authority of Sacred Scripture; (2) the authority of traditions, of both Christ and the Apostles; (3) the authority of the Catholic Church; (4) the authority of the Councils of the Church; (5) the apostolic authority of the Roman Church; (6) the authority of the ancient Fathers; (7) the authority of the scholastic theologians and canonists; (8) of natural reason; (9) the authority of the philosophers; (10) the authority of human history.

**Loculi** (lŏk'ū·lī), n. pl.; L. Literally, places. The receptacles or cavities in the walls of the catacombs for the dead.

**Logothete** (lŏg'ŏ·thēt), n.; Gr. An office resembling that of chancellor in the service of the Patriarch of Constantinople.

**Longanimity** (lŏng'gȧ·nĭm'ĭ·tĭ), n.; L. The virtue whereby one perseveres for a protracted length of time in striving for some good, while resisting the inclinations to yield to sadness; one of the fruits of the Holy Ghost.

**Lord's Prayer** (lôrdz), n.; A.S. The prayer which our Lord taught His disciples (Matt. 6:9-13); the prayer which in Latin is the *Pater Noster* and in English the *Our Father*, and which is said in the Mass. (Cf. *Pater Noster*.)

**Loreto** (lŏ·rĕt'ō), n.; Fr. The city of Loreto, Italy,

whose chief church contains under its central dome the traditional house occupied by our Lord at Nazareth; a celebrated shrine of the Blessed Virgin near Ancona in Italy.

**Loreto (Litany of),** n.; It. The litany which is recited in honor of the Blessed Virgin.

**Lourdes** (lūrd), n.; Fr. A small town in the south of France celebrated because of the apparitions of the Blessed Virgin to Bernadette Soubirous in 1858; the grotto and shrine erected there at the spring which arose at the time of the apparitions and where many miracles have been performed through the intercession of the Blessed Virgin; a place of modern pilgrimage.

**Love** (lŭv), n.; A.S. The theological virtue of charity.

**Low Mass** (lō măs), n.; L., A.S. The common form in which Mass is celebrated, a Mass which is neither a High Mass nor a sung Mass. (Cf. Mass.)

**Low Sunday,** n.; A.S. The first Sunday after Easter is known by this name; it closes the octave of Easter. Also, White Sunday or *quasimodo*.

**Lucernarium** (lū′sûr·năr′ĭ·ŭm), n.; L., Fr. An ancient evening office; name applied to Vespers but no longer used. Referred to sometimes as the blessing of fire on Holy Saturday and the lighting of the Paschal candle.

Luna

**Luna** (lū′nå), n.; L. The small case with a hinged side, into which the lunette is placed; it is the receptacle in which the Host for Benediction of the Blessed Sacrament is reserved. (Cf. Capsula.)

**Lunette** (lû·nĕt), n.; L. A circular case which fits into the enclosed center of the monstrance and in which the Blessed Sacrament is held while being exposed.

Lunette

**Lust** (lŭst), n.; A.S. The excessive appetite for carnal pleasure, especially that experienced in sexual gratification. It is excessive and unreasonable when such pleasure is sought in a way that is not in keeping with the end for which the appetite is given to man, as the procreation of children, or when the appetite is indulged to excess. It is one of the capital sins or vices because it so easily leads to other sins. Its contrary virtue is chastity. (Cf. Capital sins.)

**Lustral (water)** (lŭs′trăl), adj.; L. The hallowed water which is called "blessed" by the Church. Ordinarily called holy water.

# ☩ M ☩

**Macedonians** (măs′ĕ·dō′nĭ·ăns), n. pl.; Gr. A group of heretics in the early fourth century who denied the divinity of the third person of the Blessed Trinity.

**Machabees** (măk′a·bēz), n. pl.; Heb.; Bib. Also Maccabees. (1) Two books of the Old Testament giving the history of Judas Machabeus and his brothers; both are rejected by Protestants. (2) Seven young Jewish nobles and their mother who were martyred in the second century B.C.

**Madonna** (ma·dŏn′a), n.; It. (1) Title given to the Blessed Virgin. (2) The name used in referring to certain pictures of the Blessed Virgin; also used in invocations of the Blessed Virgin.

**Magdalen** (măg′da·lĕn), n.; Gr., L. A name attached to penitent women; also applied to those who themselves are blameless but wish to live a semireligious life in institutions dedicated to reclaiming prostitutes and unfortunate girls.

**Magi** (mā′jī), n. pl.; Gr., L. The three Oriental wise men who visited the Christ Child and presented Him with gifts. The feast is celebrated on Epiphany.

**Magisterium** (măj′ĭs·tē′rĭ·ŭm), n.; L. The authority of the Church, by divine appointment, to teach the truths of religious belief; the commission of the Church to teach; the teaching office of the Church; the teaching and interpreting of the doctrines of faith carried on by the Church through the Pope and bishops and those commissioned by them. It may be *ordinary* when a doctrine is proclaimed throughout the Church as part of divine revelation; or *extraordinary* when a general council defines a doctrine ratified by the Pope or when the Pope speaks as the official teacher of the Church (*ex cathedra*) proclaiming or defining a matter of faith or morals.

**Magistratus,** n.; L. A layman attendant of the bishop at pontifical occasions or at Mass.

**Magnanimity** (măg′nà·nĭm′ĭ·tĭ), n.; L. That virtue which prompts one to exercise every virtue in an excellent degree; one of the virtues connected with the cardinal virtue of fortitude.

**Magnificat** (măg·nĭf′ĭ·kăt), n.; L. The first word of the Canticle or song of the Blessed Virgin recorded in Luke 1:46–55; the first word in the Latin version also used as a title for this canticle.

**Major Orders** (mā′jĕr ôr′dĕrs), n. pl.; L. The highest degrees of the sacrament of Holy Orders, namely those conferred on deacons, priests, and bishops. The episcopacy is a fullness of the sacrament; priesthood a lesser degree, and deaconship a still lesser degree. Subdeaconship became classed as a major order in the twelfth century and is probably not a sacrament although it is necessary for the reception of the sacrament.

**Malabar Rites** (măl′á·bär), adj. The retention of some pagan religious acts by the natives of India, which were permitted by the missionaries and later condemned by the Holy See.

**Malachias** (măl′á·kĭ′ăs), n.; Heb.; Bib. The last prophetical book of the Old Testament, named after the prophet.

**Malediction** (măl′ê·dĭk′shŭn), n.; L. (1) The announcement of loss of a temporal or eternal good as a punishment for sin, made by God Himself. (2) The wishing of evil by a human being to another through a motive of revenge or hatred or in punishment for some offense; in this sense, the same as cursing. (Gf. Cursing.)

**Malice** (măl′ĭs), n.; L., O.Fr. The evil of a conscious and deliberate transgression of the law of God, which constitutes the essential gravity of a sin; contempt for God by actual denial of and contempt for His law.

**Mandatum** (măn·dā′tŭm), n.; L. The ceremony of the washing of feet of thirteen poor men, performed by the bishop at the cathedral on Holy Thursday, in imitation of our Lord who washed the feet of the Apostles.

**Manichees** (măn′ĭ·kēz), n. pl.; L. Also Manichaeans. A sect of Persia and North Africa, more pagan than heretical, of the third century, who under their founder, Manes, taught that good and evil were two positive realities governing the lives of men, and borrowed from gnosticism the idea of the hatefulness of matter.

**Manifestation (of conscience)** (măn′ĭ·fĕs·tā′shŭn), n.; L., Fr. The expression of one's state of conscience for guidance in a spiritual matter; a practice in some religious orders which is not obligatory.

**Maniple** (măn′ĭ·p'l), n.; L., O.Fr. A vestment worn across the left arm between the elbow and the wrist and usually tied or pinned to the sleeve of the alb. The vestment symbolizes penance and sorrow; it is made of the same material and is of the same color as the chasuble.

**Mantelletta** (măn′tĕ·lĕt′à), n.; It. A sleeveless vestment of silk or wool open at the front and fastening at the throat, which reaches about to the knees; it is worn by cardinals, bishops and abbots, and other superior prelates of the Papal court.

**Mantellone** (măn′tĕ·lō′nā), n.; It. A purple, sleeveless coat reaching to the ankles, worn by inferior prelates of the Papal court. (Cf. Mantelletta.)

**Mantum** (măn′tŭm), n.; L. A cape worn only by the Pope; it is either white or red and has a short train.

**Manual Mass,** adj.; L., Fr. A Mass read for the intention of one who gives the offering.

**Manuterge** (măn′ū·tûrg), n.; L. The small linen towel

used during the Mass at the "Lavabo"; a finger towel.

**Mappula** (măp′ū·lá), n.;. L., It. (1) A portable canopy carried over one as a mark of honor. (2) The gremial used by the three ministers of the Dominican Rite when they are seated.

**Mariolatry** (mâr′ĭ·ŏl′á·trĭ), n.; Gr. Forbidden and idolatrous worship of the Blessed Virgin. (Cf. Hyperdulia.)

**Mariology** (mâr′ĭ·ŏl′ŏ·jĭ), n.; Gr. The study of the theology referring to the Blessed Virgin.

**Marists** (măr′ĭsts), n. pl.; Gr. (1) Members of the Society of Mary, a congregation of missionary priests founded in 1824 at Lyons, France, by Ven. John Claude Colin. (2) Members of The Little Brothers of Mary, a teaching brotherhood founded by Ven. B. M. Champagnat in France in 1817.

**Marks (of the Church)** (mărks), n. pl.; A.S. The distinguishing features of the Church, namely, its unity, holiness, catholicity, and apostolicity, which declare it to be the true Church founded by Christ. It is *one*, i.e., it has unity as a whole because all members profess the same faith, practice the same worship, under the Pope as head, according to the will of Christ; it is *holy*, i.e., its purpose with that of Christ Himself is the sanctification of man; it is *catholic*, i.e., universal, for all men and all times; it is *apostolic*, i.e., it was founded by Christ on the Apostles through the Holy Ghost.

**Marriage** (măr′ĭj), n.; L., O.Fr. (1) The natural contract uniting a man and woman in wedlock, which

Christ made a sacrament; the sacrament of Matrimony. (Cf. Matrimony.) (2) Mystical marriage is a permanent consciousness of the presence of God in the soul; mystical union with God.

**Martha** (mär'tha), n.; Bib. (1) The sister of Lazarus and Mary and a friend of Jesus as narrated in Luke 8:40. (2) The name frequently given to a sister or nun who does not teach or do special work, but has care of the tasks about a convent, e.g., the kitchen work, etc.

**Martyr** (mär'tēr), n.; Gr., L., A.S. One who voluntarily suffers death for his religion and thereby gives testimony of Christ; literally a witness for Christ.

**Martyrdom** (mär'tēr·dum), n.; Gr., L., A.S. The suffering of death for the Faith or for Christian virtue; the fullest exercise of the virtue of fortitude. It bestows sanctifying grace and remits all punishment due to sin.

**Martyrology** (mär'tēr·ŏl'ō·jĭ), n.; Gr. A liturgical book containing a list of the martyrs and other saints; it offers a brief biography and the commemoration of each saint for every day in the year.

**Mary** (mâr'ĭ), n.; Gr., Heb. Mary, the daughter of Joachim and Anne, was of the tribe of Juda and of the royal house of David. The Mother of God; the Virgin to whom was born Christ the Son, the Second Person of the Blessed Trinity; the Blessed Virgin, the Queen of Heaven.

**Mass** (măs), n.; L., A.S. The unbloody Sacrifice of Calvary; the Sacrifice of the Eucharist; the highest act of worship in the Catholic Church which is offered up by the priest in the place of Christ Himself. (1) *Capitular* or *Chapter:* The conventual Mass of a cathedral or collegiate chapter. (2) *Conventual:* A Mass celebrated daily in choir at an hour and in a manner determined by the rubrics as the principal part of the daily Sacred Liturgy in cathedral and collegiate churches, and in the conventual churches of such religious as are obliged to recite in choir the canonical hours. (3) *Parochial:* (*a*) The *Missa pro populo*, i.e., the Mass which must be offered on certain days for the members of their parish by those who have the care of souls, or the pastors. (*b*) The chief public Mass celebrated on days of obligation or of special public celebration in a parochial or quasiparochial church for the benefit of the people of the parish. (4) *Public:* (*a*) Mass celebrated in a place open to the public, a church or public oratory. (*b*) A Mass of obligation celebrated for some body of persons who come to take part in the Mass for a public cause, i.e., because of a public obligation or because of a public reason of charity or necessity. Hence Masses (sung or low) in public churches or nonprivate oratories on days of obligation or on special occasions and conventual Masses (sung or low) are "public" Masses. (5) *Private:* (*a*) A Mass celebrated in a private place, private oratory or private house. (*b*) A low Mass, i.e., a Mass which is neither a High Mass nor a sung Mass. (*c*) A nonconventual Mass, whether sung or low. (*d*) A Mass which is neither sung nor conventual. (*e*) A Mass which is not "public" nor "parochial." (*f*) A Mass detached from the liturgy of the day, as a Mass on Palm Sunday at which the palms are not blessed and carried in procession. (*g*) A "private" Mass of the dead is one that is neither sung nor conventual nor "privileged." (6) *Votive:* A Mass celebrated, for a reasonable cause, not in conformity with the office of the day, but according to the wish (*votum*) of the celebrant or of his superior or of the person for whose intention the Mass is being offered.

**Massorah** (ma·sô′ra), n.; Heb. The Jewish comments on the text of the Hebrew Bible compiled from marginal notes which form the body of critical notes and information concerning this text.

**Master of ceremonies,** n.; L. Latin: *Caeremoniarius*. The one who directs the ceremonies in solemn functions; one who directs the liturgy.

**Matellone** (măt′ĕl·lō′nä), n.; It. Variation of mantellone.

**Matins** (măt′ĭnz), n. pl.; L. The first division or hour of the breviary.

**Matricula** (ma·trĭk′ū·la), n.; L. A list of names of the clergy who formally make up the collegiate chapter of a cathedral.

**Matrimony** (măt′rĭ·mō′nĭ), n.; L., O.Fr. The sacrament of marriage; the lawful spiritual and bodily union between man and woman for life; the natural contract uniting a man and woman in wedlock, raised to a sacrament by Christ.

**Matter** (măt′ēr), n.; L., Fr. (1) The term applied to that part of a sacrament made up of the rites and ceremonies and the material used in administering the sacrament. (2) A term applied to that material element of a sacrament, e.g., the water in Baptism, which is essential to a sacrament. (Cf. Form.)

**Maundy Thursday** (môn'dĭ), n.; L. Holy Thursday, the Thursday of Holy Week so named because of the washing of the feet which is a part of the liturgy of that day. The word "Maundy" is derived from the first word, *Mandatum* (commandment), of the first antiphon sung during this ceremony of washing.

**Maurists** (mô'rĭsts), n. pl.; Fr. A Congregation of Benedictine Monks which began as a branch of the Congregation of St. Vannes. It was formed in 1618 as an independent congregation for the reformed houses of France and named after St. Maur, a famous disciple of St. Benedict. It was formally discontinued in 1818.

**Medal** (mĕd″l), n.; L., It. Disk or piece of metal on which has been impressed an emblem or picture representing a particular devotion or object of veneration. Medals are sacramentals of the Church.

A type of medal, views of both sides given.

**Mediana Sunday** (mē'dĭ·ā'nȧ), n.; L. Name sometimes applied to Laetare Sunday, the fourth Sunday of Lent.

**Mediator** (mē'dĭ·ā'tēr), n.; L. One who pleads the cause of another; a person who acts as a link or a go-between between two extremes; Christ is truly the Mediator between God and Man.

**Mediatrix** (mē'dĭ·ā'trĭks), n.; L. Name given to the Blessed Virgin because she, in virtue of her divine motherhood, is the channel through which all graces flow from the merits of Christ to man. The Blessed Virgin is the intercessory mediatrix. Christ alone is the Mediator between God and man.

**Meditation** (mĕd'ĭ·tā'shŭn), n.; L. A wordless prayer of the mind; the act of praying mentally by using the memory, the understanding, and the will in considering a divine truth or in addressing a petition to God. Such mental prayer may lead to contemplation or higher forms of affective (the soul by affection of the will goes direct to God) prayer.

**Melchisedech** (mĕl·kĭz'ĕ·dĕk), n.; Heb.; Bib. The king of Salem and a priest of God mentioned in Gen. 14:18–20 who prefigured Christ.

**Melchites** (mĕl'kīts), n. pl.; Gr. (1) The name attached to those Christians who held to the definition of Chalcedon, namely, the denial of the heretical Monophysite creed that there was only one nature in Christ after the Incarnation. (2) The Arabic-speaking Catholics in Palestine, Syria, and Egypt who are subject to the Patriarch of Antioch and who follow the Byzantine rite.

**Memento** (mĕ·mĕn'tō), n.; L. Either of the two prayers in the Canon of the Mass, one for the living, the other for the dead, beginning with the word *memento*. In these prayers the priest pauses and calls to mind those for whom he especially wishes to pray.

**Memoria** (mē·mō′rĭ·å), n.; L. (1) A reliquary in which relics of the martyrs were kept and which were sometimes carried in processions. (2) A memorial church or chapel built in honor of a martyr or a confessor, which usually contains the relics of the saint who is commemorated. (3) The lowest class feast, just above a feria, in the Benedictine and Dominican calendars.

**Memoriale** (mē·mōr′ĭ·ȧl′lē), n.; L. A liturgical book drawn up by Benedict XIII and extended to all small parish churches of the Roman rite by Pius VII, and made obligatory. The book gives a detailed description of a simpler rite than that of the Missal for carrying out the Sacred Liturgy of Candlemas, Ash Wednesday, Palm Sunday, and the *Triduum Sacrum* or the three days: Maundy Thursday, Good Friday, and Holy Saturday. Its full name in Latin is *Memorialè Rituum*.

**Mendicant Friar** (měn′dĭ·kănt), adj.; L. One who was a mendicant and depended for his livelihood upon begging. Formerly, the Augustinian orders were so named because their rule did not permit them to possess property privately or in common, hence they had to beg. Now, however, the chief mendicant orders are: Order of Preachers, Carmelites, Friars Minor, and Hermits of St. Augustine who still retain the general name and have the begging of alms as part of their vow of poverty.

**Menology** (mĕ·nŏl′ŏ·jĭ), n.; Gr., L. (1) The calendar listing the names of martyrs and later also confessors; a martyrology. (2) In religious orders, a list of eminent deceased members.

**Mensa** (mĕn′sa), n.; L. The flat table-top or stone of an altar; an altar stone. Usually applied to the entire top of the table whereon the Mass is celebrated. Every mensa has five Greek crosses cut into it to indicate the places whereon it was anointed at its consecration. (Cf. Altar.)

**Mensal Fund** (mĕn′săl), adj.; L. The portion of the Church revenue which is set aside for the maintenance of those who serve the Church; the share for the support of a cleric; chiefly an English term.

**Mental (reservation)** (mĕn′tăl), adj.; L. The expression of truth that is likely to be received by the hearer in a different sense or meaning; such restriction is sinful if the manner of expression makes it impossible to perceive the truth.

**Mercy (Sisters of)** (mûr′sĭ), n.; L. An order of nuns founded in 1827 in Dublin by Catherine McAuley whose intention was to perform all works of spiritual and temporal mercy. The sisters are engaged in education, hospital work, the conducting of orphanages and homes for destitute women, and other charitable activities.

**Mercy**, n.; L. Compassion for the sufferings, whether bodily or spiritual, of others, arising from charity; an act of charity bestowed through sympathy. (Cf. Works, of mercy.)

**Meridian** (mĕ·rĭd'ĭ·ăn), n.; L. The name of the midday rest taken at noon by monks in monasteries.

**Merit** (mĕr'ĭt), n.; L. The quality which makes a free moral action deserving of reward; the reward of a morally good action; value attached to morally good actions by God; the eternal value of acts done through the grace of God.

**Messalians** (mĕ·zăl'yăns), n. pl.; Gr. A name attached to an heretical sect of the fourth century who accepted only prayers as rightful acts of religion; Euchites.

**Messias** (mĕ·sī'ăs), n.; Heb. In Hebrew, "the anointed one"; referred to the one who was to come to deliver the people of Israel; rightly used in referring to Christ.

**Messianic** (mĕs'ĭ·ăn'ĭk), adj.; Heb. An adjective applied to those prophecies of Sacred Scripture which refer to man's redemption or to the Redeemer. Any statement made of the Messias.

**Metaphysics** (mĕt'a·fīz'ĭks), n. pl.; Gr. The science which treats of being as such; science treating of that which exists precisely as it is existing. It is divided into: (*a*) general metaphysics or ontology which treats of being and the nature of substance, accidents, quality and quantity; (*b*) special metaphysics which treats of theodicy, the study of God.

**Metropolitan** (mĕt'rô·pŏl'ĭ·tăn), n.; L. Formerly the bishop of the largest city or the place where the government was and who was considered to rank over the bishops of lesser places; at present, the term is applied to archbishops in large cities who have suffragan sees.

**Micah** (mī'kȧ), n.; Heb.; Bib. The name of the prophet Micheas as it appears in the Protestant versions of the Bible.

**Michaelmas** (mĭk'ĕl·mȧs), n.; O.E. Archaic English name for the Feast of St. Michael.

**Micheas** (mĭ·kē'ȧs), n.; Heb.; Bib. The author and prophet who wrote the prophetical book of the Old Testament bearing his name.

**Mildness** (mīld'nĕs), n.; A.S. The virtuous habit which governs the irascible nature of man according to right reason; one of the virtues annexed to temperance; also, one of the fruits of the Holy Ghost.

**Military Orders** (mĭl'ĭ·tĕr·ĭ), adj.; L. Orders of men who combine a semireligious life and a life for the achievement of some particular civic good; knights; templars. (Cf. Knights.)

**Millennium** (mĭ·lĕn'ĭ·ŭm), n.; L. Term applied by some writers to an anticipated age of happiness on earth in the glorious reign of Christ and His saints prior to the end of the world. The hope for this period arises from an erroneous interpretation of Apoc. 20.

**Minims** (mĭn'ĭms), n. pl.; L. An order of mendicant friars founded by St. Francis of Paula at Paola in Italy in 1444.

**Minister** (mĭn'ĭs·tĕr), n.; L., O.Fr. (1) The head of the Franciscan or Capuchin orders, a minister general or minister provincial. The title of the one second in authority in the Society of Jesus. (2) Ordinary—One who acts by right of his office, the lawful person to administer, for example, a sacrament.

**Ministers (of the Sick)**, n. pl.; L., O.Fr. An order founded by St. Camillus of Lellis in 1586 at Rome to serve the sick. The Camillian Fathers; the Fathers of a Good Death.

**Minorites** (mī'nēr·īts), n. pl.; L. Friars minor of the Franciscan order; name also applied to those persons in minor orders.

**Minor Orders** (mī'nēr), adj.; L. The four sacramentals of: doorkeeper, lector, exorcist, and acolyte. These are received preliminary to the reception of the sacrament of Holy Orders.

**Miracle** (mĭr'à·k'l), n.; L. An act or event which is above the natural order. A work or thing of wonder done by God, a fact produced by God alone which is above, beside, or beyond the accustomed order of action of all of created nature.

**Miserere** (mĭz'ĕ·rē'rĕ), n.; L. Literally, "have mercy"; the first word in the Latin version of Psalm 50, which has come to be the title of this psalm; the fourth of the penitential psalms.

**Misericord** (mĭz'ēr·ĭ·kôrd'), n.; L. A dispensation from fasting given to a member of a religious order. Also the room in which persons given such dispensations take their meals.

**Missal** (mĭs'ăl), n.; L. The liturgical book containing the text for all Masses used by the priest in celebrating Mass; the liturgical book used by the priest at the altar in reading Mass; the liturgical prayer-book for all the faithful. (Cf. Ordinary of the Mass; Proper.)

**Missal-stand** (mĭs′ăl-stănd), n.; L. A small wooden or metal support upon which the missal is placed during the Mass for ease in reading.

**Mission** (mĭsh′ŭn), n.; L. A place to which a priest is sent where he has jurisdiction; a place in a country where the majority are not yet converted or have fallen away from the faith. Also said of that place near an organized parish at which services are held for the faithful but at which there is no resident priest.

Missal-stand

**Missions (popular),** n. pl.; L. A number of days set aside in some locality for the practice of religious exercises under the direction of a missionary priest so that the faithful may be instructed and sinners converted; a time of religious pursuit during which meditations, devotions, and addresses are given in a cycle to promote penance and instill the desire to live a more fervent life. Not to be confused with retreats.

**Mitre** (mī′tĕr), n.; Gr., L. A tall double-pointed headdress worn by bishops, abbots, and sometimes by other high-ranking ecclesiastics; the two points of this ornamental headdress symbolize the Old and New Testaments. There are three mitres: Two mitres are used in a Pontifical High Mass:

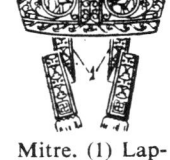

Mitre. (1) Lappets or infulae

(1) the precious mitre which is made of white silk and richly ornamented with gold, jewels and needle-work; (2) the cloth-of-gold mitre of plain gold cloth but without jewels and other rich ornaments. The precious mitre is worn till the Introit; the cloth-of-gold mitre till the Credo inclusive; and finally the precious mitre till the end of Mass. (3) A plain white mitre of silk or linen is used at Requiem Masses.

**Mixed Marriage** (mĭkst), n.; L. Marriage between two persons of different religions; generally a marriage between a Catholic and a person of some other religious affiliation.

**Modernism** (mŏd′ēr·nĭz′m), n.; L. Teachings of a group of thinkers who recognize the reality of the Divine but in so doing depend on their own subjective experience; thus they condemn faith; the seeking by man to find all religion, natural and supernatural, in himself; the theory that religion is of man; men of ultra-liberal thought along scientific lines in the Church are called modernists. Modernism was an outcome of the Reformation, but in the nineteenth century it became drastically liberal and antireligious. Modernism has been condemned by the Church in pronouncements of 1907 and 1910.

**Modesty** (mŏd′ĕs·tĭ), n.; L. (1) The virtue which prompts one to give the proper degree of importance to each act; decorum in all external acts; moderation within reason of all external acts. (2) Today in popular understanding this virtue is chiefly applied to matters of purity or chastity, meaning a proper or decent restraint regarding sex, especially in matters of dress or attire.

**Molinism** (mō′lĭ·nĭz'm), n.; Sp. The theological system originated in Madrid, Spain, under Louis de Molina (1535–1600), which held that grace for its efficacy was dependent on its being accepted by man's will.

**Monarchians** (mō·när′kĭ·ăns), n. pl.; Gr. Heretics of the second century who denied any real distinction between the Persons of the Trinity and later altered their teaching and denied only equality between the Persons of the Trinity. (Cf. Sabellianism.)

**Monastery** (mŏn′ăs·tĕr′ĭ), n.; Gr., L. The place of residence of a group of monks; the building wherein monks have their cells and carry on their religious life; sometimes also applied to convents.

**Monastic** (mō·năs′tĭk), adj.; Gr., L. Of or pertaining to a monastery or to the inmates of a monastery or to their life or work.

**Monk** (mŭngk), n.; Gr., L. Originally a hermit or anchorite. Later a name given to a member of a community of men living apart from the world under the vows of poverty, chastity, and obedience and according to some rule of a religious order. In particular it became associated with those following the Benedictine rule. The title is not to be confused with that given to members of orders of friars, clerks regular, or religious congregations of men.

**Monophysites** (mō·nŏf′ĭ·sīts), n. pl.; Gr. Heretics of the early Church who believed that there was only one nature in Christ; this doctrine was condemned by the Council of Chalcedon.

**Monophysism** (mō·nŏf′ĭ·sĭz′m), n.; Gr. Also monophysitism. The heretical teaching that there is only one nature in Christ, namely, the divine.

**Monothelites** (mō·nŏth′ĕ·līts), n. pl.; Gr. Heretics who believed that Christ has only one will; they held that there are two natures but contended that there is but one person in Christ and consequently only one will or one operation. This heresy was condemned by the sixth general council or the third Council of Constantinople in A.D. 680.

**Monothelitism** (mō·nŏth′ĕ·lē·tĭz′m), n.; Gr. The heresy of the seventh century teaching two natures in Christ but only a divine will. (Cf. Monothelites.)

**Monsignor** (mŏn·sē′nyôr), n.; It. A title or dignity bestowed by the Pope upon a priest entitling him to be called Monsignor; an honorary rank conferred for exceptional service; deserving of this title are: Protonotaries Apostolic, Domestic Prelates, Private Chamberlains, Honorary Chamberlains, and Vicars General. It is abbreviated *Msgr.*

**Mons Pietatis,** n.; L. Latin words meaning a fund for pious purposes; a charitable credit organization from which the poor could borrow money by depositing objects of nominal value as a security. The *montes pietatis* were founded in the fifteenth century to protect the poor from the usurious exactions of the money lenders and traveling bankers of the Middle Ages.

**Monstrance** (mŏn′străns), n.; L., O.Fr. The sacred vessel in which the Blessed Sacrament is usually exposed for veneration at Benediction or in which it is carried during a procession; ostensorium. (Cf. Luna; Lunette.)

**Montanists** (mŏn′tă·nĭsts), n. pl.; Gr. Followers of Montanus of the second century who claimed prophetical powers. They insisted upon individual holiness as against the authority of the Church.

Monstrance or ostensorium

**Month's Mind** (mŭnths mīnd), n.; L. The Requiem Mass said on the thirtieth day after death.

**Moral Theology** (mŏr′ăl), n.; L. The science of the moral laws which regulate the duties of men toward God; the study of moral actions not only in the light of ethical standards but chiefly as they are seen in Christian revelation and in the positive law of the Church.

**Morality** (mŏ·răl′ĭ·tĭ), n.; L. The moral goodness or badness of an act in as far as it is in accordance with the rules of right conduct or opposed to them; nowadays usually refers only to goodness.

**Morganatic** (môr′gă·năt′ĭk), adj.; L. Said of a marriage which is valid but in which the wife is of an inferior social status and in which it is contracted that the wife and children shall not succeed to dignities and benefits of the husband or father;

usually occurs only where a member of royalty marries a commoner.

**Morse** (môrs), n.; L. The ornamental clasp, usually a short chain with a hook and eye attached, used to fasten the cope across the chest.

**Mortal sin** (môr′tăl), adj.; L. A morally bad human act which is grievously offensive to God; that sin which destroys charity, robs the soul of sanctifying grace, and makes it deserving of eternal punishment. (Cf. Sin.)

**Mortification** (môr′tĭ·fĭ·kā′shŭn), n.; L. Acts of fasting or self-imposed corporal punishments performed for a pious intention and for the spiritual good of the soul; acts of temperance; works performed often despite the repugnance of the will which are in themselves good and of spiritual value; acts usually connected with some bodily pain or contrary to the ordinary wishes of a person.

**Motet** (mō·tĕt′), n.; Fr. A vocal musical composition, with Latin words usually taken from the Scriptures, which may be sung during extra-liturgical functions.

**Mozzetta** (mō·zĕt′à), n.; It. A short vestment worn over the shoulders, which can be buttoned down the front and to which a hood is attached behind; it is worn by the Pope, cardinals,

Mozzetta

bishops, abbots, and sometimes by other prelates. It is a state dress rather than a liturgical dress.

**Mundatory** (mŭn′dạ·tôr·ĭ), n.; L. A small unblessed linen cloth with a small cross stitched in the center which is used during the Mass for cleansing the chalice; a purificator.

**Munera** (mū′nēr·ạ), n. pl.; L. Official gifts; the offerings of bread and wine offered in the Holy Sacrifice of the Mass.

**Muratorian Canon** (mū′rạ·tō′rĭ·ăn), adj., n.; L. That canon of the Scriptures which as early as the third century offered a formal list of the New Testament books contained in the Bible.

**Mystery** (mĭs′tēr·ĭ), n.; Gr., L. (1) A truth which cannot be known or understood by human reason. Also a doctrine of faith, acceptance and belief in a doctrine not fully understood, but which is revealed to us through Christ. The theological meaning is a truth which man cannot discover of himself, that is, without teaching or revelation, and which after his becoming informed of it, he cannot fully understand. (2) Sometimes applied to any consideration of a particular doctrine or teaching of faith. (3) The subject of meditation made while saying a decade of the rosary.

**Mystic** (mĭs′tĭk), n.; Gr., L. One who through mental prayer or contemplation is granted a more perfect knowledge of God and thus achieves a greater love of God; one who is granted the gift of wisdom and thereby achieves a high state of perfection; one who understands the mysteries of faith through union with God or by direct revelation. (Cf. Contemplation, Mysticism.)

**Mystical Body** (mĭs′tĭ·kăl), adj., n.; Gr., L. A name of the Roman Catholic Church, derived from the writings of St. Paul; metaphorically it compares the union of Christ and the Church with the union between the human body and its head; it emphasizes the inner life of the Church, vivified by the Holy Spirit, its Soul.

**Mystical (Sense of Scripture)**, adj.; Gr., L. An interpretation of Sacred Scripture which reveals the meaning of certain things as inferred from meanings other than those ordinarily attached to the words. Sometimes God wished that the things signified by the words of Sacred Scripture should also signify other things, and thus we have the mystical or spiritual sense. The mystical sense is subdivided into: (a) allegorical, where the statements of the Old Testament signify the mysteries or teachings of the New Testament; (b) moral, where moral precepts are signified; (c) anagogical, where they denote some aspect of future glory.

**Mystical (theology)**, adj.; Gr., L. Sometimes associated with ascetical theology, but more properly it is that knowledge of God which comes through contemplation and love of God, a close association with God, and direct or semidirect intuitive knowledge of God. The theology of the mysteries of faith.

**Mysticism** (mĭs′tĭ·sĭz′m), n.; Gr., L. The experience

of direct communion with God; the interior union and intercourse of a fervent soul with God; the highest form of mental prayer; the subject of mystical theology; the understanding of the mysteries of faith. (Cf. Mystic; Contemplation.)

# ✣ N ✣

**Nahum** (nā′hŭm), n.; Heb.; Bib. The author of a prophetical book of the Old Testament bearing his name.

**Nails (holy)** (nāls), n. pl.; A.S. The nails with which our Lord was fastened to the cross and which tradition claims were discovered at the finding of the cross by St. Helena. It is not known where they are now.

**Name day** (nām dā), n.; A.S. The day of the feast of the saint whose name one bears, sometimes celebrated rather than one's birthday or in addition to this; the day commemorating one's baptismal name.

**Narthex** (när′thĕks), n.; Gr., L. In ancient basilicas, that space leading from the outer doors to the inner doors; the vestibule in Gothic churches.

**Natal** (nā′tăl), adj.; L. Also, natale; *natalicia*. The day upon which a saint dies, his birthday in heaven which is celebrated in the Church rather than the natural birthday anniversary.

**Nativity** (nă·tĭv′ĭ·tĭ), n.; L. The natural birth of Jesus, who was born of the Blessed Virgin; the Incarnation; the day celebrating the birth of Christ, Christmas.

**Natural Law** (năt′ū·răl), n.; L. Ethical precepts implanted by God in the rational nature of man, by the fulfillment of which man tends to God as his natural end; the rational creature's participation in the eternal law of God.

**Nave** (nāv), n.; L. In cruciform churches, the portion of the building from the crossing to the narthex. That part of the church building in which the laity kneel and assist at Mass.

**Nazarene** (năz′a·rēn′), n.; Gr., L. An inhabitant of the village of Nazareth in Palestine; name referred to Christ because of His residence there.

**Necrology** (ně·krŏl′ŏ·jĭ), n.; Gr. A book in which are listed the names of the dead of a particular place or institution so that they may be prayed for; a list of benefactors or friends so that they may be remembered in the prayers of those living.

**Nehemiah** (nē′hē·mī′a), n.; Heb.; Bib. The Hebrew form of Nehemias, the author of the book of the Old Testament called Second Book of Esdras.

**Neophyte** (nē′ŏ·fīt), n.; Gr. The name by which a newly baptized member of the early Church was known.

**Neo-Scholasticism** (nē′ŏ·skŏ·lăs′tĭ·sĭz'm), n.; Gr., L. Contemporary school of scholastic philosophers who emphasize the close contact philosophy should have with contemporary thought and with recent scientific findings.

**Nestorians** (nĕs·tō′rĭ·ăns), n. pl.; Gr. The followers of Nestorius who held the false doctrine that there were two persons and two natures in Jesus Christ united by a union which was not physical and that the powers of the one person could not be ascribed to the other; they arose in the latter part of the fifth century. There are Nestorians in India today and religious descendants of the Nestorians in Africa.

**Ne Temere,** n.; L. The papal decree of Pius X issued in 1907 regarding the laws of clandestinity of marriage; it states, simply, that a marriage is invalid unless it is contracted before a parish priest in his own parish, or before a bishop in his own diocese, or by a delegate of either, in the presence of at least two witnesses and that it must be registered in the places where the contracting parties were baptized. The first two words of the decree (translated: Lest, rashly—) which form its title.

**Neum** (nūm), n.; L. A group of notes sung to one syllable in plainchant. (Cf. Ligature.)

Neums. (1) Gregorian notation. (2) Modern notation

**New Testament** (nū tĕs′tă·mĕnt), n.; L. The books of the Bible which contain the revelation of God since the coming of Christ; the Gospels, Epistles, Acts of the Apostles, and the

Apocalypse. There are twenty-seven books in the New Testament.

**Nicene** (nī'sēn'), adj.; Gr., L. Of or pertaining to the city of Nice (ancient Nicaea) in Asia Minor where the First Ecumenical Council of the Church was held in A.D. 325; of or pertaining to a Church council held at Nice.

**Nicene Councils** (nī·sēn'), n. pl.; Gr., L. The two general councils of Nicaea, the first in A.D. 325 and the second in A.D. 787. (Cf. Appendix, The Ecumenical Councils.)

**Nicene Creed,** n.; Gr., L. The statement of religious beliefs composed at the first Council of Nice. (Cf. Creed.)

**Nimbus** (nĭm'bŭs), n.; L. A circle of light pictured surrounding the head of a representation of Christ or one of the saints; a halo. (Cf. Aureole.)

**Nocturn** (nŏk'tûrn), n.; L. Also, nocturne. A division of the hour of matins in the breviary.

**Node** (nōd), n.; L. The knob in the stem of a chalice between the base and the cup.

A nimbus about the head of the Madonna

**Noe** (nō'ē), n.; Heb.; Bib. The form of the Hebrew name Noah used in the Douay Bible.

**Nomination** (nŏm'ĭ·nā'shŭn), n.; L. The ordinary manner of appointing clerics to ecclesiastical offices by ecclesiastical superiors. It is opposed to presentation, election, and postulation.

**Nomocanon** (nō·mŏk'à·nŏn), n.; L. A collection of

ecclesiastical law, the elements of which are borrowed from secular and canon law. Found only in Eastern Church law.

**None** (nōn), n.; L., Fr. One of the hours of the Roman Breviary; literally, the ninth.

**Norbertines** (nôr′bĕr·tĭnz), n. pl.; Fr. The name frequently applied to the members of the Order of Premonstratensians, the Order of Canons Regular of Prémontré, founded in 1120 by St. Norbert at Prémontré in France.

**Novatianism** (nō·vā′shăn·ĭz′m), n.; L. The heresy begun by Novatian in the latter part of the third century which held that the Church could not absolve lapsed members.

**Novena** (nō·vē′nà), n.; L. The pious practice of devoting nine days to public or private prayer for gaining special graces.

**Novice** (nŏv′ĭs), n.; L., O.Fr. One who has entered a religious order and is preparing after the time of postulancy to accept the rule of the order; one serving his or her novitiate.

**Novitiate** (nō·vĭsh′ĭ·āt), n.; L. (1) A time of probation, usually of one year, during which the novice prepares to receive the rule of the order he or she has entered; the time in which one prepares for profession in a religious order followed by profession in temporary vows. (2) The residence set aside as living quarters for novices.

**Nullity** (nŭl′ĭ·tĭ), n.; L., Fr. The fact resulting from a diriment impediment which permits a marriage to be declared invalid, which means that no marriage ever existed. The decree of nullity is the declaration of a competent ecclesiastical court that a marriage is invalid, and therefore null.

**Numbers** (nŭm′bĕrz), n. pl.; Bib. The fourth book of the Old Testament written by Moses.

**Nun** (nŭn), n.; L., A.S. A maid or widow consecrated by three major religious vows to God and living in a convent of a religious order; a lady dedicated to serve God in the religious life; one espoused to Christ; commonly called a sister, although in canon law a distinction is made between those having solemn vows, called nuns, and those having simple vows, called sisters.

**Nunc Dimittis** (nŭngk dĭ·mĭt′ĭs), L. Literally, "Now do you dismiss." The first two words in the Latin version of the Canticle of Simeon recorded in Luke 11:29–32 which has come to be the name of this canticle.

**Nuncio** (nŭn′shĭ·ō), n.; L., It. An official prelate representing the Holy See at the seat of a foreign government. His duty is to handle all affairs between the Holy See and the civil government. (Cf. Legate, Internuncio, Delegate.)

**Nuptial Blessing** (nŭp′shăl), adj.; L. The blessing read by the priest after the *Pater Noster* of the Mass (*Pro Sponsis*), called nuptial, which may not be given apart from the Mass except with dispensation. The blessing is directed more to the woman than to the man. It is not given if the woman has received it at a previous marriage, nor during special times or seasons of the Church calendar.

## O

**Oath** (ōth), n.; A.S. The invoking of God to witness the truth of a statement or to bind one's self to the fulfilling of a promise under solemn obligation; oaths may be made more solemn by touching the Gospels or sacred vessels while making the declaration.

**Obadiah** (ō′bȧ·dī′ȧ), n.; Heb.; Bib. The Hebrew name of the prophet Obdias.

**Obedience** (ȯ·bē′dĭ·ĕns), n.; L. (1) The moral virtue by which one submits his will to the will or law of one in authority. (2) The evangelical counsel whereby one renounces his own right to act independently in order to follow Christ. (3) A vow of obedience is that vow made by a cleric or a religious in submitting himself or herself to the authority of an ecclesiastical or religious superior.

**Oblates** (ŏb′lātz), n. pl.; L. A congregation of priests who offer themselves for service in whatever work the bishop may place them; various religious orders, of men or women, bound by simple or solemn vows who are engaged in particular works of an ecclesiastical nature. Chiefly today, those who join with some religious order in order to live in accord with some of its rules but remaining laymen; one who follows a religious rule under the direction of a religious order or its superiors.

**Oblati** (ŏb·lä′tĭ), n. pl.; L. The Latin plural noun given as title originally to those children who were dedicated in early years to a monastic life; in the Middle Ages, those who gave their property and themselves into the keeping of a monastery for their own spiritual good. (Obs.)

**Oblation** (ŏb·lā′shŭn), n.; L., O.Fr. An offering; the victim of a sacrifice offered to God.

**Obligation (Days of)** (ŏb′lĭ·gā′shŭn), n.; L. Holydays or those days when it is required that all Catholics hear Mass. (Cf. Holydays.)

**Obreption** (ŏb·rĕp′shŭn), n.; L. An untrue statement contained in a petition for a papal rescript or dispensation.

**Obsecration** (ŏb′sē·krā′shŭn), n.; L. A prayer in which the appeal is addressed to sacred things or events referring to a person, e.g., "Through Thy death and burial, O Lord, deliver us!"

**Observance** (ŏb·zûr′vǎns), n.; L. The interpretation and manner of keeping the rule established for a religious order, e.g., in a strict or less strict degree.

**Occasion (of sin)** (ŏ·kā′zhŭn), n.; L., O.Fr. An external circumstance or condition which gives one the opportunity and inducement to commit a sin; this may be either a person, a place, or a thing. It is said to be *proximate* when the circumstance or conditions are such that they usually lead to sin. Such a proximate occasion may be *free*, that is, either sought or possible of being avoided; or it may be *necessary*, that is, it cannot be avoided. The occasion is *remote* when the danger of sinning is slight.

**Occult (compensation)** (ŏ·kŭlt′), n. as adj.; L. The secret appropriation of some object to which one has a just claim but which one cannot obtain by ordinary means. The repayment of a creditor from the goods of the debtor without the latter's knowledge.

**Occurrence** (ŏ·kûr′ĕns), n.; L. The happening of two offices on the same day, e.g., a feast falling on a Sunday.

**Octavarium** (ŏk′tȧ·vär′ĭ·ŭm), n.; L. A book containing the breviary readings to be recited within the octaves of feasts.

**Octave** (ŏk′tāv), n.; L. The celebration of a feast to the eighth day after the feast; the time within which a commemoration of the feast is celebrated.

**Octonary** (ŏk′tō·nĕr′ĭ), n.; L. A division of an eight-verse psalm.

**Oecumenical** (ĕk′ū·mĕn′ĭ·kȧl), adj.; Gr. Ecumenical. (Cf. Ecumenical.) (Cf. Appendix, Ecumenical Councils.)

**Offertory** (ŏf′ēr·tō′rĭ), n.; L. That part of the Mass in which the offering of bread and wine or the oblation is made by the priest. That part of the Mass which follows immediately after the Creed.

**Office (Divine)** (ŏf′ĭs), n.; L. The prayer contained in a liturgical book called the Breviary. It is arranged by the Church and ordered to be said daily in her name by all clerics in major orders, by all who hold an ecclesiastical benefice, and by solemnly professed members of certain religious orders of men and women. (Cf. Breviary.)

**Offices (Divine)** (ŏf′ĭs·ĕz), n. pl.; L. (1) Any exercise of public divine worship. (2) The entire daily liturgy, i.e., the canonical hours and the conventual Mass.

**Official** (ŏ·fĭsh′ăl), n.; L. The presiding judge of a diocesan court, appointed by the bishop, with whom he shares ordinary jurisdiction in all court cases which the bishop has not reserved to himself.

**Oils (Holy)** (oils), n. pl.; L. The Holy Oils are blessed annually by the bishop on Holy Thursday. There are three Oils: Chrism, Oil of Catechumens, and Oil of the Sick. The constituent parts of Chrism are olive oil and balsam; the remaining two Oils are pure olive oil. In listing the uses of the Oils it will be observed that each Oil may be used for more than one purpose, and that in some consecrations or blessings more than one Oil is used. (*a*) Chrism is used in the administration of Baptism and Confirmation, in the consecration of a bishop, in the consecration of churches, altars, chalices, patens and in the blessing of church bells and baptismal water. (*b*) Oil of Catechumens is used in Baptism, in the ordination of a priest, the consecration of churches and altars, and in the coronation of Catholic monarchs. (*c*) Oil of the Sick is used in Extreme Unction and in the blessing of church bells. (Cf. Stock.)

**Old Testament** (ōld tĕs′ta·mĕnt), n.; L., Bib. The books of the Bible which relate the history of the chosen people and God's revelation prior to the coming of Christ; the Scripture up to the Gospel accounts in the Bible. There are forty-five books in the Old Testament.

**Olivetans** (ŏl′ĭ·vē′tănz), n. pl.; Gr. A branch of the white monks of St. Benedict founded in the fourteenth century.

**Ombrellino** (ŏm′brĕl·ē′nō), n.; It. A small, flat-topped canopy, usually of white silk, supported on a single staff and borne above the Blessed Sacrament when it is moved from one altar to another for Benediction or taken to sick persons. An umbrella.

**Omission** (ō·mĭsh′ŭn), n.; L. In general, failure to perform a required act or duty. Said of a sin which is committed by neglecting to perform a duty or to keep a law.

**Omnipotence** (ŏm·nĭp′ō·tĕns), n.; L. Power of doing all things. That attribute of God by which He is almighty; God's power to do all things that can be done, i.e., that are not intrinsically impossible.

**Omnipresence** (ŏm′nĭ·prĕz′ĕns), n.; L. Presence in all places and times. An attribute of God arising from the fact that He is above and beyond space and beyond time; without limit of space or time. God is present to everything which He creates as the cause, and because He creates all things He must be present to all things.

**Omniscience** (ŏm·nĭsh'ĕns), n.; L. Knowledge of all things. An attribute of God; the knowing by God of all that is past, present, and future,.even the most hidden thoughts. This knowledge is God's because He created or caused all things, therefore He knows all things as their Maker. (Cf. All-wise.)

**Omophorion** (ŏ'mŏ·fŏ'rĭ·ŏn), n.; Gr. The pallium used by certain Eastern bishops. (Cf. Pallium). A band of silk or velvet worn around the neck, one end of which hangs down short on the front of the left shoulder while the other end hangs far down behind the left shoulder.

**Ontology** (ŏn·tŏl'ŏ·jĭ), n.; Gr. That branch of philosophy which treats of being or reality precisely as such; the science of being; the science of general metaphysics. (Cf. Metaphysics.)

**Ophites** (ŏf'ītz), n. pl.; Gr., L. Followers of the gnostic heresy who worship the serpent or the devil.

**Orale** (ŏ·rā'lē), n.; L. A name sometimes used for the fanon. (Cf. Fanon.)

**Orant** (ŏ'rănt), n.; L. Also *orante* or *orans*. A representation of a female figure, kneeling or standing, with outstretched arms. It was used in the catacombs to symbolize the soul in heaven interceding for the faithful on earth.

**Orarion** (ŏ·rā'rĭ·ŏn), n.; L. Latin: *orarium*. An early name for the long vestment worn by the priest around his neck and crossed in front; a stole. Refers specifically to the diaconal stole. (Cf. Stole.)

**Oratory** (ŏr′*a*·tō′rĭ), n.; L. A chapel which might be public, semipublic, or private wherein Mass may be celebrated; Mass may not be heard validly (i.e., satisfy the obligation of hearing Mass) in a private oratory, except by those having permission. An oratory is public if it is built chiefly for the convenience of some group of persons, even private persons, yet the faithful in general have the right to enter it or at least may enter during divine service. It is semipublic if it is built for the convenience of a certain community or body of the faithful and is not open to everyone, e.g., a college or convent chapel. It is private or domestic if it is erected in a private house for the sole benefit of some family or private person. (Cf. Chapel.)

**Ordeal** (ôr·dē′*ă*l), n.; A.S. The "judgment of God" or the contention that God would give proof which would protect the innocent unjustly accused; a semipagan superstition that an unworthy or a guilty person could not undergo certain trials without his guilt being demonstrated. (Cf. *Judicium Dei* in the Appendix of Foreign Words and Phrases.)

**Orders (Holy)** (ôr′dĕrz), n. pl.; L. The sacrament of Holy Orders by which power and grace is given to a person for the performance of sacred offices. The episcopacy is the fullness of the priestly powers. Priesthood, deaconship, and subdeaconship are called major orders. Acolyte, exorcist, reader, and doorkeeper are called the four minor orders conferred upon clerics. These four are only sacramentals instituted by the Church, but today they are required for the reception of the sacrament of Holy Orders. (Cf. Major Orders; Minor Orders.)

**Orders (Religious),** n. pl.; L. The name which arose in the tenth century to designate certain communities of religious or certain communities following one religious rule; now widely accepted as the term for groups of persons living a religious life according to a rule and receiving solemn vows; groups of religious.

**Ordinal** (ôr′dĭ·năl), n.; L. A form of the prayers, together with the ceremonies, for conferring Holy Orders.

**Ordinary** (ôr′dĭ·nĕr′ĭ), n.; L. A prelate governing a specified territory in the name of the Church, e.g., a residential bishop, vicar, or prefect apostolic, etc., as well as a major superior in an exempt clerical institute in regard to his subjects.

**Ordinary (of the Mass),** n.; L. The unchangeable or practically unchangeable portion of the Mass prayers into which the "Proper" is inserted. The ordinary includes: prayers at the foot of the altar; the *Kyrie Eleison;* the *Gloria;* the prayer before the Gospel; the Creed; the *Lavabo;* the offering of bread and wine; the *Orate, Fratres;* the preface (this changes according to feasts and holy seasons); the *Sanctus;* the canon, with the three prayers of commemoration; the oblation; the consecration; the oblation after the elevation; the commemoration of the dead, sinners, and all nature; the *Pater*

*Noster;* the *Agnus Dei;* the priest's communion; the communion of the people; the ablution; the blessing and the last Gospel.

**Ordination** (ôr′dĭ·nā′shŭn), n.; L. The ceremony in which Holy Orders are conferred upon worthy persons; the act of ordaining; the conferring of the sacrament of Holy Orders.

**Ordo** (ôr′dō), n.; L. (1) The book giving directions for the variant portions of the Mass and office according to the calendar of feasts; it is published annually, and each province, religious order, and congregation has its own particular directions. A directorium. Formerly called a pica, or pie. (2) A ritual book for the administering of the sacraments and other ceremonies.

**Organ** (ôr′găn), n.; L., O.Fr. A wind instrument producing musical notes by forcing air through pipes and played from a keyboard; the customary instrument of accompaniment in church music, or chant. The small electric organ is becoming more widely used at present.

**Orientation** (ō′rĭ ĕn·tā′shŭn), n.; L. (1) The custom of building a church so that it runs lengthwise from east to west with the altar at the eastern end. (2) Also the arrangement or location of the interior space of a building.

**Original Sin** (ō·rĭj′ĭ·năl), adj.; L. The sin which we inherit as natural descendants of our first parents; the privation of sanctifying grace propagated to man by Adam.

**Orphrey** (ôr′frĭ), n.; L., Fr. The ornamental cross

embroidered on the front and back of a chasuble; also the border around a cape or cope.

**Orthodox Church** (ôr′thô·dŏks), adj. & n.; Gr. The name generally applied to the Greek Schismatic Church.

**Osculatory** (ŏs′kû·la·tō′rĭ), n.; L. The pax; the pax-brede; *instrumentum pacis;* the kiss of peace.

**Osee** (ō′sē), n.; Heb.; Bib. The author of a prophetical book of the Old Testament bearing his name.

**Ostensorium** (ŏs′tĕn·sō′rĭ·ŭm), n.; L. The sacred vessel in which the Blessed Sacrament is usually exposed for veneration at Benediction or carried in procession; the monstrance.

**Ostiary** (ŏs′tĭ·ĕr′ĭ), n.; L. A porter, a doorkeeper; one who by his office is declared to be a custodian of the door; that is, the door to divine services. The name comes from the ancient practice of having someone to keep those unqualified from entering divine services. The first of the minor orders, a sacramental. Also the Latin name, *ostiarius*.

**Our Father** (our fä′thĕr), n.; L. The Lord's Prayer; the *Pater Noster;* the prayer taught to the disciples by our Lord. (Matt. 6:9–13; Luke 11:2–4.) (Cf. Lord's Prayer.)

# ☩ P ☩

**Palatine** (păl′a·tĭn), adj.; L. Pertaining to certain high prelates of the papal court; also to the papal guard established by Pius IX in 1850. (Cf. Guards.)

**Palestine** (păl′ĕs·tĭn), n.; L. The land situated at the eastern extremity of the Mediterranean Sea. The land given by God to the chosen people and sanctified by the Life of Christ. The Holy Land. (Lat. 31° n., 31° s.; Long. 34°–36°.)

Pall

**Pall** (pôl), n.; L.; A.S. A square piece of linen usually stiffened with a piece of cardboard which is used to cover the chalice.

**Pallium** (păl′ĭ·ŭm), n.; L. A vestment conferred by the Pope upon an archbishop which consists of a small band of white wool worn around the neck with a short pendant descending on the breast and the back and on which there are six black crosses. Also used as a name for a frontal or antependium.

**Pallottines** (păl′ŏ·tĭnz), n. pl.; It. Members of the religious order known under the title of The Pious Society of the Missions, which was founded at Rome in 1835 by the Ven. Vincent Pallotti. Their work is for the missions and for the preservation of the faith among immigrants.

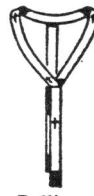
Pallium

**Palm Sunday** (päm), n.; L. The Sunday before Easter; the Sunday celebrating the triumphal entrance of Jesus into Jerusalem.

**Palmatoria**, n.; L. A small candlestick held with a lighted candle at a bishops' Mass; a bugia.

**Papabile** (pà·pá′bĭ·lĕ), n.; It. Colloquial Italian name of a cardinal likely to be elected to succeed a deceased pope.

**Papacy** (pā′pà·sĭ), n.; L. Of or pertaining to the office of the Pope; the rule of a Roman pontiff; the succession of popes.

**Papal Chamberlain**, n. Italian: *Prelate di mantellone*. One upon whom the dignity, either honorary or actual, of attending the person of the Pope has been conferred. A chamberlain is classed as a secondary prelate of the papal court and enjoys the title and honors of a prelate. The title and honor, however, is attached to his office and is usually lost at the death of the reigning Pope. He is addressed Very Reverend Monsignor.

**Parable** (păr′à·b'l), n.; L., O.Fr. An illustrative story pointing to some moral or religious truth; a manner of speaking used by our Lord as related in the Gospel.

**Parabolani,** n. pl.; Gr., It. A name applied in the fourth, fifth, and sixth centuries to those who exposed themselves to danger; for instance, by assisting the priests in caring for the sick or the plague stricken.

**Paraclete** (păr′a·klēt), n.; Gr., L. Literally: a consoler. A name applied in the Gospel of St. John to the Holy Ghost; a name of the Holy Spirit, the third Person of the Blessed Trinity.

**Paradise** (păr′a·dīs), n.; Gr., L. A park or garden; used of that place wherein Adam and Eve lived before their sin; it was later applied to the place known as limbo; in the Gospels it is also applied to heaven.

**Paralipomenon** (păr′a·lĭ·pō′mĕ·nŏn), n.; Gr. The name used in the Catholic version of the Bible for the two books called the first and second Chronicles in Protestant version.

**Parallelism** (păr′a·lĕl·ĭz′m), n.; Gr., L. The most distinctive mark of Hebrew poetry in which one thought is opposed to another or repeats the same idea; it is most frequently found in the Psalms.

**Paraments** (păr′a·mĕntz), n. pl.; L. Vestments; ornamented vestments used in sacred ceremonies.

**Parasceve** (păr′a·sēv), n.; Gr., L. A name used in the missal and designating Good Friday, the Friday of Holy Week; literally, a day preparing for the Sabbath.

**Parish** (păr′ĭsh), n.; Gr., L. A division within a

diocese; a particular district governed by a pastor; the boundaries or limits within which a priest has the serving of a church and the members of the faithful within that territory. There are also: (*a*) *national parishes*, which are erected with the permission of the Holy See and are not divisions of territory but rather divisions according to the nationality and language of the people who are served in these churches; thus a parish established for a certain nationality which is the result of immigration. (Can. 216, sec. 4.) (*b*) *Consistorial parishes*.

**Parish (priest)**, n.; Gr., L. A priest assigned to minister to the faithful within a certain district of a diocese; sometimes called pastor and in French, *curé*.

**Parousia** (på·rōō′zhĭ·å), n.; Gr. The second coming of Christ.

**Particle** (pär′tĭ·k'l), n.; L. Name given to a small altar bread.

**Parvis** (pär′vĭs), n.; L. An enclosed or partly open porch at a church entrance.

**Pasch** (păsk), n.; Heb., Gr. Literally, the Hebrew "passover." A name applied to the Feast of the Resurrection or Easter.

**Paschaltide** (păs′kăl·tīd), n.; Heb., Gr. The season of the liturgical year, extending from Holy Saturday to the Saturday after Pentecost.

**Paschal Candle** (păs′kăl), adj. & n.; Gr., L. The candle blessed on Holy Saturday morning and burned in the sanctuary from Easter to Ascension Thursday, which symbolizes the presence of Christ on earth for forty days after His Resurrection.

**Paschal Precept,** n.; Gr., L. The obligation resting upon all the faithful who have reached the age of reason to receive Holy Communion in the course of the Easter season; also called the Easter duty.

**Passion (of Christ)** (păsh′ŭn), n.; L. The suffering and death of our Lord and the redemption of mankind: in particular, the suffering of our Lord on Good Friday.

**Passion music** (păsh′ŭn mū′zĭk), n.; L. The liturgical singing on Palm Sunday or Good Friday of the Gospel account of our Lord's Passion. It is sung during the Mass by three voices: the *Narrator*, or chronista, who sings the narrative; the *Christus*, who sings the words of our Lord; the *Synagoga*, who sings the words of the other persons in the account. (Cf. Chronista, Christus, and Synagoga.)

**Passion Sunday,** n.; L. The Sunday before Palm Sunday or the second Sunday before Easter.

**Passionists** (păsh′ŭn·ĭsts), n. pl.; L. The religious congregation founded by St. Paul of the Cross in 1720 and first established by him at Monte Argentaro in Tuscany. It is known as the Congregation of the Passion whose full title is: The Congregation of Discalced Clerks of the Most Holy Cross and Passion of Our Lord Jesus Christ. The members are chiefly engaged in missionary work.

**Passiontide** (păsh′ŭn·tīd), n.; L. The time between Passion Sunday and Holy Saturday morning.

**Passover** (pȧs'ō'vēr), n.; L. Easter or the Feast of the Resurrection; the Pasch.

**Pastor** (pȧs'tēr), n.; L. Literally a shepherd; the title by which a parish priest is most generally known in the United States.

**Pastoral** (pȧs'tō·rǎl), n.; L. A letter addressed by a bishop to all the faithful within his diocese for their spiritual good.

**Pastoral Staff** (stȧf), n.; Gr., L. The crosier; the staff with a crook at the top, usually ornamented, which is the symbol of the jurisdiction of a bishop.

**Pastoral Theology,** n.; Gr., L. That branch of theology which is called the science of the care of souls; it really may mean the application of all other branches of theology to the spiritual instruction of the faithful.

**Pastorate** (pȧs'tēr·ĭt), n.; L. The office of a pastor for the period he serves as pastor; the jurisdiction of a pastor.

**Paten** (păt'ĕn), n.; Gr., L. (1) A plate of gold used with the chalice in celebrating Mass; a circular saucerlike dish, usually of gold or gold plated, used in the celebration of Mass to hold the consecrated host. (2) A communion paten, or plate, to be held beneath the chin of the person receiving communion.

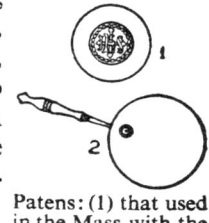

Patens: (1) that used in the Mass with the chalice; (2) the communion paten

**Pater Noster** (pā'tēr nŏs'tēr), n.; L. The first two words of the Latin version of the Lord's Prayer, meaning, Our Father;

the prayer taught to the disciples of our Lord. (Cf. Lord's Prayer.)

**Paternines** (pā'tĕr·nĭnz), n. pl.; L. A group of eleventh-century Manichean heretics who taught that matter was evil, condemned marriage, and denied the authority of the Church; they were condemned by the Council of Lombez in 1165.

**Patience** (pā'shĕns), n.; L. That virtue which moderates within reasonable bounds the feeling of sadness arising from evils or pains.

**Patriarch** (pā'trĭ·ärk), n.; Gr., L. (1) In biblical use, the father or family ruler of a tribe or race. (2) The highest honor next, of course, to the Holy Father in the hierarchy of jurisdiction; a title conferred upon certain leading Church dignitaries of certain countries; the highest rank in the Orthodox Church.

**Patrimony** (păt'rĭ·mō'nĭ), n.; L., O.Fr. The possession of sufficient personal property to secure one a living, which in the early ages was required of a cleric before ordination; an independent fund or personal properties for self-support.

**Patripassians** (pā'trĭ·păs'ĭ·ănz), n. pl.; L. The name given to the earliest followers of the heresy of Sabellianism which held that there was only God the Father and that He became man and suffered and died.

**Patristic** (pa·trĭs'tĭk), adj.; L. Of or pertaining to the Fathers of the Church or their writings; that which is of the study of patrology. (Cf. Patrology.)

**Patrology** (pa·trŏl'ō·jĭ), n.; Gr., L. The study of the

early Fathers of the Church and of their writings; the science of patristic literature. (Cf. Fathers of the Church.)

**Patron** (pā′trŭn), n.; L. (1) A person having a right to present a cleric to a vacant benefice. (2) A saint chosen by a nation, diocese, province, confraternity, religious family as well as by other moral persons and places with the confirmation of the Holy See.

**Patronage** (pā′trŭn·ĭj). n.; L. In canon law, the right or power of naming or presenting a cleric to a vacant benefice.

**Paulicians** (pô·lĭsh′ănz), n. pl.; Gr., L. A quasi-Manichaean or semi-Manichaean sect. They denied the sacraments, the invocation of saints and of the Blessed Virgin, and believed in two powers—one of good and one of evil. They arose in the seventh century, probably near Samosata in Asia Minor.

**Pauline Privilege** (pôl′ĭn), adj. & n.; Gr. The principle based upon "the dispensation of the Apostle" which states that two unbaptized persons having contracted marriage, though it has been consummated, may dissolve the marriage if one of them becomes a Christian and the other refuses to be converted or places obstacles in the way of the other's observance of his religion.

**Paulists** (pôl′ĭsts), n. pl.; Gr. The popular name for the members of the Missionary Society of St. Paul the Apostle which was founded in New York in 1858 by Father Isaac Thomas Hecker. Their chief works are the conducting of missions and the work of the press.

**Pax** (păks), n.; L. Literally, peace. (1) The kiss of peace given in the Mass after the consecration. (2) A tablet given to the people to kiss during the Mass, an osculatorium.

**Pax-brede** (păks-brēd), n.; L., A.S. A tablet or disk of precious metal, ivory, etc., bearing a sacred image and used after the *Agnus Dei* in the Mass to convey the kiss of peace from the celebrant to certain persons.

**Pectoral Cross** (pĕk′tō·răl), adj. & n.; L. A small ornamental cross attached to a chain which the bishop wears about his neck and hanging down on his breast. The pontifical pectoral cross is one that is hollowed out to contain relics. It is usually studded with gems and is suspended on a cord, at the end of which is a gold tassel.

**Peculium** (pē·kū′lĭ·ŭm), n.; L. The money given by a superior to a member of the religious order to be spent for a necessary purpose at his own discretion.

**Pelagianism** (pē·lā′jĭ·ăn·ĭz′m), n.; L. The heresy begun by Pelagius in the fifth century which denied original sin and hence denied the necessity of grace. It was condemned by the third council at Ephesus.

**Penance** (pĕn′ăns), n.; L., O.Fr. (1) The sacrament for the forgiving of sins; the sacrament instituted by Christ for judgment of sins committed after Baptism through which remission is granted by the absolution of a duly authorized priest providing there is sorrow, intent of amendment, and a confession of sins by the penitent. It is necessary that all mortal sins be named. The power of forgiving sins given to the Apostles (John 20:23). (Cf. Absolution, Confession.) (2) Some act of mortification imposed on one confessing his sins as a condition of completely fulfilling the requirements of confession made by the confessor, usually some práyers.

**Penitential Psalms** (pĕn′ĭ·tĕn′shăl), adj. & n. pl.; L. The seven Psalms, numbers 6, 31, 37, 50, 101, 129, and 142, which express the sorrow for sin and the wish of forgiveness.

**Penitentiary** (pĕn′ĭ·tĕn′sha·rĭ), n.; L. Latin: *Penitentiaria*. The Sacred Apostolic Penitentiary is the Roman tribunal of absolutions and dispensations in the internal forum to which matters of conscience may be submitted by anyone without charge, at any time and in any language. It also has charge of the granting and use of indulgences.

**Penitentiary**, n.; L. The Cardinal who presides over the Sacred Penitentiaria.

**Pension** (pĕn′shŭn), n.; L. An amount of money from the diocese for the support of an aged cleric granted with the fulfilling of certain conditions.

**Pentateuch** (pĕn′ta·tūk), n.; Gr.; Bib. The first five books of the Bible, namely, Genesis, Exodus, Leviticus, Numbers, and Deuteronomy.

**Pentecost** (pĕn′tē·kŏst), n.; Gr., L. The feast commemorating the descent of the Holy Ghost upon the Apostles, fifty days after Easter; Whit-Sunday.

**Peplum** (pĕp′lŭm), L. A name formerly applied to the chalice veil. (Obs.)

**Pera** (pĕr′a̦), n.; L. The burse or bursa. (Cf. Burse.)

**Peregrinus** (pĕr′ē·grī′nŭs), n.; L. A traveler; in canon law, one away from his domicile or quasi-domicile.

**Perfection** (pēr·fĕk′shŭn), n.; L. Possession of all attributes without limitation; infinity of all goodness, thus applied to God alone. Also that state of grace toward which all lesser beings are directed.

**Pericope** (pĕ·rĭk′ō·pē), n.; L. A lesson from Sacred Scripture to be sung or read in the liturgy.

**Perjury** (pûr′jēr·ĭ), n.; L. The calling upon God to witness to the truth of a falsehood; a grave sin against the virtue of religion.

**Perpetual Adoration** (pēr·pĕt′ū·a̦l), adj. & n.; L. The adoration of the Blessed Sacrament permitted in some chapels where one or more religious will be continuously kneeling in adoration before the altar.

**Persecution** (pûr′sē·kū′shŭn), n.; L. Penalty of suppression inflicted upon persons or their activities for the purpose of destroying a belief; the bodily harm or death inflicted upon adherents of a religion. The early persecution of the Church and the modern persecution by the civil authorities against members of the Catholic religion.

**Perseverance** (pûr′sē·vēr′a̦ns), n.; L. (1) A moral virtue by which one continues in performing a good act despite difficulties; a virtue connected with fortitude. (2) Final—The grace of continuing to death in the state of sanctifying grace; it may last many years or it may have begun only a short time before death.

**Person** (pûr's'n), n.; L., O.Fr. (1) An intelligent and free being; that which subsists in intellectual nature. (2) A term designating either the Father, Son, or Holy Ghost in the Blessed Trinity.

**Peter's Pence** (pē'tērz), n.; Gr., L. The alms collected from the faithful for the support of the Holy See and the expenses of the Vatican.

**Petrobrusians** (pĕt'rô·brōō'sĭ·ănz), n. pl.; Gr., L. The members of a heresy of the twelfth century which denied the real presence, and rejected infant Baptism, and prayers and Masses for the dead.

**Pew** (pū), n.; L., O.Fr. The bench for seating people in church, usually with a kneeling rack attached; a long bench with a back.

**Pew-rent** (pū-rĕnt), n.; L., A.S. A fee paid for the use of a pew in church.

**Pharisees** (făr'ĭ·sēz), n. pl.; Gr., L. Those Jews who in our Lord's time scrupulously observed the Jewish law and refused to have communication with the gentiles; the proud and self-righteous.

**Philosophy** (fĭ·lŏs'ô·fĭ), n.; Gr., L. The science of knowledge, the science of reasoning in following things from cause to effect and understanding their law of sequence. Philosophy is made up of the four major subdivisions, the particular sciences of logic, metaphysics, physics, and ethics. The development of philosophy in the Church is called scholastic philosophy which is the system of philosophy taught by the great Schoolmen and accepted as the means of applying reason to theological principles and concepts. (Cf. Scholastic, Neo-scholastic.)

**Piarists** (pī·*a*′rĭsts), n. pl.; L. A group of religious founded in 1597 by St. Joseph Calasanctius for the teaching of children. They are still active in Italy, Spain, and Central Europe.

**Pietà** (pyā·tä′), n.; L., It. A sculpture or representation of Christ lying dead in the arms of the Blessed Mother.

**Piety** (pī′ĕ·tĭ), n.; L. (1) The faithful performance of religious exercises; worship, adoration, thanksgiving, and fidelity to God's law are all contained in the true concept of piety. (2) One of the seven gifts of the Holy Ghost. (3) The moral virtue, called filial piety, which aids one to give honor, love, and respect to his parents and to his country in recognition of the benefits received from them.

Pietà in St. Peter's Basilica

**Pileolus** (pī·lē′ō·lŭs), n.; L. A skullcap. (Cf. Zuchetto.)

**Pilgrim** (pĭl′grĭm), n.; L. One making a pilgrimage to a place of religious significance or a shrine of particular devotion; one making a journey to a shrine for the purpose of becoming familiar with the place, in fulfilling a vow, in petition of some special favor, or in penance.

**Pilgrimage** (pĭl′grĭ·mĭj), n.; L. The undertaking of a journey to a place of religious significance or to a shrine. (Cf. Pilgrim, Shrine.)

**Pious Union,** n.; L. Association of the faithful established for the exercise of works of piety or charity; if these associations are organized as a body under a head and rules, they are referred to as a sodality. Sodalities which have, besides the above conditions, the purpose to further public worship are called confraternities.

**Piscina** (pĭ·sī′nȧ; pĭ·sē′nȧ), n.; L. (1) An aperture in the wall of a sanctuary at the epistle side designed to hold the cruets; it is connected by a drain to a cavity in the ground which is the receptacle of water that has been used for any sacred purpose. The aperture, drain, and cavity constitute the piscina. There may be one in connection with a baptismal font. The piscina serves the same purpose as the sacrarium in the sacristy. (2) A water basin; sometimes used as a name for the baptismal font or the holy water font.

**Pity** (pĭt′ĭ), n.; L. The virtue which seeks to relieve another's distress or prompts one to perform acts of mercy in another's behalf.

**Plain Chant** (plān chȧnt), n.; L. The name applied to that system of notation used in the official music of the Church. (Cf. Chant, Gregorian Music, Plain song.)

**Plain song** (plān′sŏng), n.; L., A.S. Unison music in free rhythm; Gregorian music or chant.

**Planeta** (plȧ·nā′tȧ), n.; L. The chasuble.

**Platform** (plăt′fôrm), n.; O.Fr. The footpace; the predella; the suppedaneum. The highest level at the top of the altar steps, or that level on which the celebrant stands during the celebration of Mass. (Cf. Footpace, Predella.)

**Pluvial** (ploō'vĭ-ăl), n.; L. Also *pluviale*. A cope, a capelike vestment.

**Pluvialistae,** n. pl.; L. (1) Chanters and other assistants at solemn functions who are dressed in copes. (2) Cope-bearers.

**Podium** (pō'dĭ-ŭm), n.; L. (1) The portable platform on which the Pope is carried when officiating at processions of the Blessed Sacrament. (2) The screen of open columns between the altar and the nave in early churches. (Obs.)

Pluvial or cope

**Polemics** (pō-lĕm'ĭkz), n. pl.; Gr. Theological argumentation; theological proofs used in apologetics.

**Polygamy** (pō-lĭg'á-mĭ), n.; Gr. The possession of more than one wife by a single husband. This is forbidden by the natural law as well as by the law of the Church.

**Polyphony** (pō-lĭf'ŏ-nĭ), n.; Gr. Counterpart music; four-voice musical arrangement of a melody used in chanting and choir singing. This is the notation referred to in the *Motu Proprio* of Pius X. It is especially applicable to the polyphony of the Roman school of the sixteenth century.

**Pontiff** (pŏn'tĭf), n.; L., Fr. A bishop; usually used in referring to the Pope, the bishop of Rome.

**Pontifical Mass** (pŏn·tĭf'ĭ·kăl), adj. & n.; L. A High Mass celebrated by higher prelates; e.g., bishops, abbots, etc., when they wear pontificals, or the insignia or ceremonial ornaments; High Mass celebrated according to the rite proper to prelates.

**Pontifical,** n.; L. Latin: *Pontificale Romanum*. A book wherein is contained the rites and ceremonies which are performed by the bishop, or the ceremonies which pertain to the office of bishop, such as Confirmation, Ordination, the consecration of churches, altars, etc.

**Pontificals** (pŏn·tĭf′ĭ·kălz), n. pl.; L. The ceremonial ornaments and vestments proper to prelates when celebrating a pontifical Mass.

**Pontificate** (pŏn·tĭf′ĭ·kăt), n.; L. (1) The reign of a pope. (2) v. To celebrate pontifical Mass.

**Poor Clares** (pōōr klărz), n. pl.; L. The order of nuns founded by St. Clare in the thirteenth century under the rule given to her by St. Francis of Assisi.

**Pope** (pōp), n.; Gr., L. The bishop of Rome, the vicar of Christ on earth, and the visible head of the Church; the Holy Father, the Supreme Pontiff; the successor of St. Peter. (See list of Popes in the Appendix.)

**Porteforium** (pôr′tē·fō′rĭ·ŭm), n.; L. A name used in England to designate the breviary. (Obs.)

**Porter** (pōr′tēr), n.; J. The first of the minor orders, the doorkeeper, the ostiarius. (Cf. Minor Orders.)

**Portiuncula,** n.; It. Literally, the little piece. (1) The church containing the original small chapel which was repaired by St. Francis of Assisi at Assisi. (2) The indulgence granted for a pilgrimage to the church of the Portiuncula or for a visit in a church where the Third Order of St. Francis has been canonically established.

**Possession (Demoniacal)** (pŏ·zĕsh′ŭn), n.; L. That condition in which an evil spirit or devil is permitted by God to enter the body of a person. Through this the body of the person is tortured and the senses attacked by the devil, but the possessed person cannot be made to sin, yet may be tempted strongly by such possession. (Cf. Exorcism, Energumen, and Exorcist.)

**Postcommunion** (pōst′kŏ·mūn′yŭn), n.; L. The prayer or prayers, corresponding in form and number with the Collects, that are said or sung before the *Ite 'missa est;* they vary according to the feast. (Cf. Commemoration.)

**Postil** (pōs′tĭl), n.; Fr. A commentary upon some Scripture text; sometimes applied to a short sermon explaining some passage of Scripture.

**Postulancy** (pŏs′tū·lăn·sĭ), n.; L., Fr. A time of probation before a person is permitted to receive the habit of a religious order and to enter the novitiate.

**Postulant** (pŏs′tū·lănt), n.; L., Fr. The one who seeks to enter a religious order and undergoes a time of probation before the novitiate. (Cf. Novitiate.)

**Postulator** (pŏs′tū·lā′tēr), n.; L. The official, always a priest and a resident of Rome, who presents and carries on a cause of beatification or canonization before the Roman Congregation of Rites.

**Poverty** (pŏv′ēr·tĭ), n.; L. The evangelical counsel recommending the renunciation of riches; the vow of poverty, one of the vows of the religious state.

**Power (of Keys)** (pou′ĕr), n.; L., O.Fr. The authority of forgiving sins conferred on the Apostles by Christ; the authority of the Church vested in the Pope.

**Powers** (pou′ĕrz), n. pl.; L., O.Fr. One of the nine choirs of angels. (Cf. Angels.)

**Praetermissi** (prā′tĕr·mĭs′ĭ), n. pl.; L. Literally, those sent before. The more than two hundred English martyrs, those of the *scaffold* and those in *chains*, who have not been canonized, but who died in evidence of their faith in England during the last half of the sixteenth century.

**Prayer** (prâr), n.; L., O.Fr. An act of religion consisting of thinking about God or speaking with God; meditation; vocal prayer; the reciting of prescribed words to elevate the mind and heart to God. The acts of prayer are adoration, thanksgiving, petition, and contrition; dedication of the acts of the day to God may also be prayer.

**Prayer (Apostleship of)**, n.; L., O.Fr. An association founded by the Jesuits in 1844, for the advancement of zeal and piety in prayer whose particular devotion is the Sacred Heart of Jesus.

**Preaching** (prēch′ĭng), n.; L., O.Fr. The oral instruction of the faithful; the speaking of a sermon or homily to the faithful; the oral instruction usually given by a priest in church.

**Preacher** (prēch′ĕr), n.; L., O.Fr. (1) One who gives a sermon or homily; one who instructs orally in public. (2) One of the Order of Preachers, the official title of the Dominicans.

**Prebend** (prĕb′ĕnd), n.; L., O.Fr. That portion of the revenue of a chapter or collegiate church which is given to each canon or member.

**Precentor** (prē·sĕn′tĕr), n.; L. The leader of the choir of a collegiate or monastic church or of monks in choir; it is obsolete except as the name of one making the arrangements for divine service.

**Precept** (prē′sĕpt), n.; L., O.Fr. The command given to a single person or to a few by a duly authorized superior.

**Precepts (of the Church)**, n. pl.; L., O.Fr. The chief commands of the Church given for the spiritual good of the faithful and obliging under pain of sin. (Cf. Commands of the Church.)

**Precious Blood** (prĕsh′ŭs), adj. & n.; L. The blood of Christ; the symbol of the Sacrifice of Calvary; the blood present after Consecration in the Blessed Sacrament together with the Body, Soul, and Divinity of Christ. Feast of the Precious Blood is celebrated on July 1.

**Preconize** (prē′kô·nīz), v.t.; L. The Pope's act of confirming in public consistory an appointment to a higher ecclesiastical office.

**Predella** (prē·dĕl′à), n.; It. The top step of a platform within the sanctuary on which the altar rests; the footpace.

**Predestination** (prē·dĕṣ′tĭ·nā′shŭn), n.; L. (1) In the Catholic sense is either: (*a*) the election to eternal glory by God of all those whom He foresees will fulfill all the unalterable conditions necessary for salvation as determined by God; or (*b*) the election to glory of certain men by God's absolute eternal decree and the conferring of the graces necessary for such eternal salvation. (2) In the heretical sense it includes not only positive election to glory of certain men but also reprobation of others; that the soul is fated or determined by the foreknowledge of God; it is in this sense a denial of free will and the will of God that all men be saved.

**Preface** (prĕ′fĭs), n.; L., O.Fr. A prayer of thanksgiving said during the Mass at the beginning of the canon, consisting of a dialogue and words of thanksgiving concluding with the Sanctus; there are prefaces for special feasts and for special seasons of the ecclesiastical year.

**Prefect** (prē′fĕkt), n.; L., O.Fr. The head of a Roman Congregation, usually a cardinal, in some cases the Pope himself.

**Prelate** (prĕl′ĭt), n.; L., O.Fr. The name generally applied to an ecclesiastical dignitary who has ordinary jurisdiction in the external forum.

**Premonstratensians** (prē·mŏn′strȧ·tĕn′shȧnz), n. pl.; L. The order founded by St. Norbert in the twelfth century, a teaching and preaching order. (Cf. Norbertines.)

**Presanctified (Mass)** (prē·săngk′tĭ·fīd), adj., L. An Eucharistic service without a consecration, the Host having been consecrated at a previous Mass. The Mass of Good Friday.

**Presbytera** (prĕz·bĭ′tēr·ȧ), n.; Gr., L. In the early ages of the Church this referred to the wife of a presbyter; it is sometimes applied to widows who have devoted themselves to the service of the Church; in the Orthodox Church it is a name of the superior of a convent.

**Presbytery** (prĕz'bĭ·tĕr·ĭ), n.; Gr., L. In the early Church the term applied to the gathering of the clergy of a diocese; it came to be a name for that part of the church in which the clergy assisted at divine services; in recent times it is also a name for the parish house or the priest's home.

**Presbyters** (prĕz'bĭ·tĕrz), n. pl.; Gr., L. Priests or bishops of the early Church. Now sometimes applied to assistant priests.

**Prescience** (prē'shĭ·ĕns), n.; L. The foreknowledge of God; the knowledge God has of future events.

**Prescription** (prĕ·skrĭp'shŭn), n.; L. A mode of acquiring title to property or to other rights founded on uninterrupted possession for a definite period of time prescribed by law.

**Presentation Brothers** (prĕz'ĕn·tā'shŭn), n.; L. A religious group founded in Ireland by Edmund Rice in the nineteenth century for the purpose of conducting schools and orphanages.

**Presentation (of the Blessed Virgin),** n.; L. The presenting of Mary, the Mother of God, in the temple at the age of three and her dedication to religion. The feast day is celebrated on the twenty-first of November.

**Presumption** (prĕ·zŭmp'shŭn), n.; L. An unfounded expectation of gaining salvation or the means of obtaining it; an exaggerated reliance upon means of salvation which are contrary to or other than those willed by God. It follows upon pride and leads one to expect certain favors.

**Prevenient** (prē·vēn'yĕnt), adj.; L. Literally, coming before. Said of that grace which precedes the consent of the will, thus moving and disposing the will to act. (Cf. Grace.)

**Pride** (prīd), n.; A.S. The inordinate desire for one's own exaltation; a sin contrary to charity and to the proper subjection of man to God. One of the capital sins. (Cf. Capital sins.)

**Prie-dieu** (prē'-dyû'), n.; Fr. Literally: pray God. A kneeling bench consisting of a rest for the knees and an upright for the support of the elbows.

**Priest** (prēst), n.; Gr., L. One upon whom the sacrament of Holy Orders has been conferred and who is thereby a minister of divine worship; one upon whom the power of offering sacrifice, of blessing, of giving absolution, and of preaching has been conferred. (Cf. Priesthood.)

Prie-dieu

**Priesthood** (prēst'hōōd), n.; Gr., L., A.S. The office of priest; the character marking the soul by the valid reception of the sacrament of Holy Orders. The power to consecrate, thus to offer the Sacrifice of the Mass; the priesthood has the power to administer sacraments, forgive sins, and to bless. Also the entire body of the clergy.

**Primate** (prī'mĭt), n.; L. In the early Church all bishops of importance were so called; now, an honorary title carrying with it the right to precedence over all bishops and archbishops of a country.

**Prime** (prīm), n.; L., A.S. The name of a portion of the Breviary; the first of the canonical hours.

**Principalities** (prĭn'sĭ·păl'ĭ·tĭz), n. pl.; L. One of the nine choirs of angels. (Cf. Angels.)

**Prior** (prī'ēr), n.; L., A.S. The one in charge of an independent monastery or the assistant or coadjutor of the abbot. Some religious orders have three grades of prior.

**Prioress** (prī'ēr·ĕs), n.; L., A.S. The superior of sisters or nuns immediately below an abbess or the one ruling an independent convent of sisters.

**Priory** (prī'ŏ·rĭ), n.; L. Any monastery of men or convent of women governed by a prior or prioress.

**Private Revelation** (prī'vĭt), adj. & n.; L. Revelation or knowledge imparted by God to individuals for some particular purpose or to give some particular instruction.

**Privation** (prī·vā'shŭn), n.; L. A vindictive penalty in Church law depriving a cleric of his benefice or office.

**Privilege** (prĭv'ĭ·lĭj), n.; L. (1) The grant of a benefit or favor against or outside the law given to a particular individual or place. The grant to one person by the Holy See of a law of concession, given in perpetuity; the granting of a private law outside of the law for grave reasons. (2) The granting of special favors to clerics because of their office; e.g., exemption from military service. Privileges may be acquired not only by direct concession but also by their extension to a group, by legitimate custom and prescription.

**Privileged Altar,** n.; L. An altar with the grant of a plenary indulgence attached to a Mass celebrated on it for a departed soul and applied to that soul.

**Probabilism** (prŏb′*a*·bĭ·lĭz`m), n.; L. That system of moral theology which teaches that, in cases of doubt about the lawfulness of an action, if there is a probable opinion that the law does not bind, the law need not be fulfilled. (Cf. Equiprobabilism.)

**Probabiliorism** (prŏb′*a*·bĭl′*i*·ôr·ĭz′m), n.; L. The system of moral theology which holds that in cases of doubt it is wrong to act by following an opinion that favors liberty against the demands of law unless that opinion is more probable than that which favors the law or obligation.

**Pro-cathedral** (prō′k*a*·thē′drăl), n.; Gr., L. The church used temporarily by a bishop for his cathedral.

**Process** (prŏs′ĕs), n.; L. The preliminaries and the procedure in the beatification or canonization of a saint. (Cf. Beatification; Canonization.)

**Procession** (prŏ·sĕsh′*ŭ*n), n.; L. The mode of distinction and unity between the Holy Ghost, the Son and the Father in the Blessed Trinity. Emanation within the Godhead: either of one divine person from another (the Son from the Father), or of one divine person from two divine persons as from one principle (the Holy Ghost from the Father and the Son).

**Processional,** n.; L: Latin: *Processionale*. A book

containing the chants used in liturgical processions.

**Processional (cross)** (prō·sĕsh′ŭn·ăl), n.; L. A crucifix mounted on a staff which is carried at the head of a ceremonial procession; also the archiepiscopal cross carried before an archbishop when he solemnly exercises the functions of his office in his own ecclesiastical province.

**Processions,** n. pl.; L. People marching together in public adoration of God or for a particular spiritual purpose; a procession of the Blessed Sacrament.

**Procurator** (prŏk′û·rā′tēr), n.; L. An official agent authorized to act for another or for a group of persons.

**Procuratrix** (prō′kū·rā′trĭks), n.; L. The sister or nun who has charge of the business affairs of a religious community.

**Profanity** (prō·făn′ĭ·tĭ), n.; L. The reference in speech to sacred persons or things in a vulgar or improper manner; this presupposes that there is no blasphemy intended or directly stated by the words.

**Profession** (prō·fĕsh′ŭn), n.; L. The promise freely made and lawfully accepted of a person upon entering a religious order, after going through a novitiate which has been continuous over the period of time required.

**Profession (of faith),** n.; L. The oral pronouncement of faith in the principal tenets of the Catholic religion; a statement of assent to belief; an expression of faith such as the recitation of one or the other of the creeds.

**Promulgation** (prō′mŭl·gā′shŭn), n.; L. The making known of a law enacted by the authority of the Church; publication sufficient to make widespread the knowledge of a law.

**Prône** (prōn), n.; Fr. A call to prayer made in French and Belgian churches before preaching the sermon.

**Propaganda** (prŏp′a·găn′da), n.; L. (1) The Sacred Congregation of Propaganda, established for dealing with all ecclesiastical affairs in missions of the Latin rite throughout the world and having jurisdiction over all foreign missions. (Cf. Congregations.) (2) The College of Propaganda, a college founded in Rome for the education of mēn, from all nations, to the priesthood for the purpose of carrying on missionary work.

**Proper** (prŏp′ēr), n.; L., O.Fr. Parts of the liturgy of the Mass which vary according to the feast of the day. Also the proper of the season which is the division of the Missal and Breviary according to the Sundays of the season; or the proper of the saints which is the portion of the Missal and Breviary giving the parts for the feasts of our Lord or the saints. The proper of the Mass is the prayers which are variant and inserted into the ordinary of the Mass. These prayers are: the Introit; the Collects; the Epistle; the Gradual; the Tract; the Gospel; the Offertory; the Secrets; the Communion; the Postcommunion. (Cf. Ordinary of the Mass.)

**Prophecy** (prŏf′ē·sĭ), n.; Gr., L. Something foretold; that which is spoken by a prophet; a prediction.

The foretelling of future events which are not known by natural reason; the revelation to one of knowledge existing in the mind of God to be told to others or to be used for the individual's own salvation; the prediction of a future event which cannot be known from natural causes.

**Prophesy** (prŏf'ē·sī), v.; Gr., L. To predict; to foretell the future. (Cf. Prophecy.)

**Prophets** (prŏf'ĕtz), n. pl.; Gr., L. A prophet of the Jews was a messenger of God and a preacher as well as a foreteller of the future which could not be known from natural causes. (1) *Major*—(Because of the greater length of their work) Isaias, Jeremias, Ezechiel, and Daniel. (2) *Minor*—Osee, Joel, Amos, Abdias, Jonas, Micheas, Nahum, Habacuc, Sophonias, Aggeus, Zacharias, and Malachias. Baruch and the Lamentations are generally included under Jeremias.

**Propitiation** (prō·pĭsh'ĭ·ā'shŭn), n.; L. Appeasement, satisfaction. Prayer addressed to the mercy of God for sinners. One of the ends of the Sacrifice of the Mass and of worship generally.

**Proposition** (prŏp'ō·zĭsh'ŭn), n.; L. (1) In philosophy (logic), a statement which is capable of being believed, doubted, or denied. Usually, expression of that which is to be proved. (2) A term used in regard to heresies, usually that part of the heresy which is condemned by the Church.

**Prose** (prōz), n.; L., O.Fr. A name applied to that part of the Mass between the Epistle and the Gospel and so named because it was originally written in rhythmical prose, not in strict meter as hymns are written. It is regarded as a synonym for sequence. (Cf. Sequence.)

**Proselyte** (prŏs′ĕ·līt), n.; Gr., L. A person converted from one religion to another.

**Protestant** (prŏt′ĕs·tănt), n.; L., Fr. The name of those who at the Reformation rejected the authority of the Church; name of a religious adherent or sect which rejects the authority of the Church.

**Protevangelion** (prō′tē·văn·jē′lĭ·ŏn), n.; L. The promise of a Redeemer to come given to Adam and Eve immediately after the fall (Gen. 3:15); the so-called "First Gospel."

**Protocanonical** (prō′tŏ·kă·nŏn′ĭ·kăl), adj.; Gr., L. Said of those books of the Bible about which there was no controversy as to whether or not they were truly Sacred Scripture; genuine books of the canon of Scripture.

**Protomartyr** (prō′tŏ·mär′tēr), n.; Gr. (1) The first martyr, namely, St. Stephen. (2) The first martyr in any land.

**Protonotary** (prō·tŏn′ŏ·tĕr′ĭ), n.; Gr., L. Also prothonotary. Originally a chief notary, later a member of the college of protonotaries Apostolic of the Roman Curia; it may also be an honorary title conferred by the Pope granting certain privileges to the bearer. The highest grade of *monsignori*, those having the title of monsignor.

**Protopresbyter** (prō′tŏ·prĕz′bĭ·tēr), n.; Gr., L. A name used in the early Eastern Church corresponding to arch-priest. (Obs.)

**Proverbs** (prŏv'ûrbz), n. pl.; L.; Bib. Book of the Old Testament containing proverbs and wise counsels, supposedly written for the most part by Solomon.

**Providence** (prŏv'ĭ-dĕns), n.; L. Used with the word "divine" it means the direction by God of all things to their end. The sustaining by God of all creation, the keeping of all things in existence for the time that He wills.

**Province** (prŏv'ĭns), n.; L. (1) That territory made up of several dioceses under the jurisdiction of an archbishop or metropolitan, the archdiocese and at least one suffragan diocese. (2) The territory forming a division of a religious order, made up of all its religious houses within that district.

**Provincial** (prō-vĭn'shăl), n.; L. The member of a religious order appointed by the general who is in authority or the director of a certain territory and all of the religious houses of that order within this territory; the religious superior of a province.

**Provision** (prō-vĭzh'ŭn), n.; L. A term in canon law which means the granting of an ecclesiastical office by a competent ecclesiastical superior according to the norms of the sacred canons.

**Provost** (prŏv'ŭst), n.; L., A.S. The head of a meeting of clergy or the head of a chapter or body of canons; also the one second in authority of a religious order under an abbot.

**Prudence** (proo'dĕns), n.; L., Fr. The cardinal virtue inclining one to the right choice of action in the particular circumstances of life.

**Prymer** (prīm'ēr), n.; L., A.S. Also primer. A book

used in England before the Reformation containing the office of the Blessed Virgin, Psalms and litanies and various other prayers. (Obs.)

**Psalmody** (săl′mō·dĭ), n.; Gr., L. The singing of Psalms; the music for such singing.

**Psalter** (sŏl′tẽr), n.; L., A.S. The book containing the Psalms which are used in liturgical services; sometimes applied to a vesperal.

**Psalterial** (sôl·tēr′ĭ·ăl), adj.; L., A.S. Of or pertaining to the psalter; of or pertaining to the Psalms. Made up of Psalms.

**P.T.**, abbre.; L. First letters of the Latin words *Paschale tempore*, the Easter time or season, the fifty-six days from Holy Saturday to the Saturday following Pentecost.

**Publicans** (pŭb′lĭ·kănz), n. pl.; L. Jews who were tax gatherers for the Romans in the days of our Lord, and as such were held in contempt.

**Pudicity** (pŭ·dĭs′ĭ·tĭ), n.; L. That virtue of temperance closely allied to chastity which moderates all acts which might give rise to an occasion of sin against purity.

**Pulpit** (pŏol′pĭt), n.; L. The raised platform, approached by steps and usually surrounded by a railing, from which the preacher addresses the congregation or members of the faithful.

Pulpit

**Pulpitum** (pŏol′pĭ·tŭm), n.; L. A lectern.

**Punctum** (pŭngk′tŭm), n.; L. A single note in Gregorian music.

**Purgatory** (pûr′gà·tō′rĭ), n.; L. The state and the place of punishment where the temporal punishment due to sins previously forgiven must be endured, and the guilt of unrepented venial sins is cleared away from the soul of the person dying in the state of grace; the place of cleansing and preparation from which the soul goes directly to heaven.

**Purification** (pū′rĭ·fĭ·kā′shŭn), n.; L. (1) The pouring of wine into the chalice after the priest has received communion to cleanse the chalice of remaining particles; the purification is then drunk by the priest. (2) The ancient custom of the Levitical law by which a woman was said to be unclean for seven days after the birth of a male child and needed to be purified by appearing in the temple after forty days and making a sin-offering; the Feast of the Blessed Virgin celebrated on February 2 and commemorating this event in the life of the Blessed Mother.

**Purificator** (pū′rĭ·fĭ·kā′tēr), n.; L. The small white linen cloth used during the Mass to cleanse and dry the chalice; a purifier; also called mundatory. (Cf. Mundatory.)

**Purity** (pū′rĭ·tĭ), n.; L. The state of innocence and freedom from sin maintained for a high motive; freedom from sin and defilement of soul. It is applied in particular to freedom from sins against chastity in thought, word, or deed.

**Pusillanimity** (pū′sĭ·là·nĭm′ĭ·tĭ), n.; L. A smallness of soul which prompts one to shun virtuous actions; fear or spiritual weakness causing one to refrain from doing good; it is contrary to the virtue of hope.

**Putative** (pū′tá·tĭv), adj.; L. Something supposed or thought to be what it is not. Applied to a marriage entered into by two persons before a priest and two witnesses, but which is invalid because of some impediment unknown to at least one of the parties. Children born of a putative marriage are considered legitimate by the Church.

**Pyx** (pĭks), n.; Gr., L. (*a*) A small vessel, usually shaped like a watch, in which the Holy Eucharist is carried to the sick or dying. (*b*) The round metal case which holds the lunette; the custodial. (*c*) The ciborium. In general this may mean any container for consecrated hosts.

Pyx (*a*)

# ✠ Q ✠

**Quadragesima** (kwŏd′rȧ·jĕs′ĭ·mȧ), n.; L. Literally, the fortieth. The name denoting the number of days in Lent; the name sometimes applied to the first Sunday of Lent, or to the first four Sundays of Lent together with their respective designating numbers as I Quadragesima, etc. The word has come to be applied to the entire season of Lent itself.

**Quaestor** (kwĕs′tŏr), n.; L. Title given to one who is commissioned to preach for the collection of alms for a special purpose.

**Quarant' Ore,** n.; It. Forty Hours Devotion.

**Quarantine** (kwŏr′ȧn·tēn), n.; L., It. A period of forty days. The term is applied to a partial indulgence and means the temporal punishment due to sin which the Pope as Vicar of Christ remitted by a public penance performed for forty days. Indulgences are now given in direct terms of years or days and are no longer expressed by quarantines.

**Quarter tenses** (kwôr′tēr), n.; L. A name formerly applied to the Ember days. (Obs.)

**Quasi domicile** (kwā′sī dŏm′ĭ·sĭl), n.; L. The residence of one within a parish or diocese, taken with the intention of remaining there six months but not indefinitely, and which ceases with departure and intent of not returning.

**Quest** (kwĕst), n.; O.Fr. The office of begging for alms by lay-brothers or sisters for their own support.

**Quietism** (kwī′ĕt·ĭz′m), n.; It. A dangerous system which arose in the seventeenth century and which taught that earthly perfection was a passive state of the soul in which it was necessary neither to make acts of faith, hope, or love nor to desire heaven or fear hell.

**Quinquagesima** (kwĭn′kwa·jĕs′ĭ·ma), n.; L. Literally, fiftieth. The name applied to the Sunday before Lent.

**Quire** (kwīr), n.; O.Fr. Old spelling of the word choir.

## ✠ R ✠

**Rabbi** (răb′ĭ), n.; Fr. French: *rabat* (rā·bā′). A small piece of black cloth worn by priests and other religious, attached to the Roman collar and resting on the chest; a white rabbi, divided in the center into two rectangles, is worn by Brothers of the Christian Schools.

**Raccolta** (rȧ·kŏl′tȧ), n.; L., It. A book in which are printed prayers, pious exercises, and ejaculations to which an indulgence has been attached together with the date and extent of the indulgence. It is no longer the official book of indulgenced prayers, being replaced by the more recent *Preces et Pia Opera*. (Cf. Appendix I.)

**Rashness** (răsh′nĕs), n.; O.Fr. A sin opposed to the virtue of prudence; doing something without due deliberation, as passing judgment without having sound basis of judging.

**Reader** (rēd'ēr), n.; A.S. A lector; one whose office it is to read. (Cf. Lector.)

**Real Presence** (rē'ăl), adj. & n.; L., O.Fr. The theological term used for the presence of Christ in the Blessed Sacrament under the appearances of bread and wine. (Cf. Eucharist.)

**Receive** (rē-sēv'), v.t.; L., O.Fr. To take communion; to communicate. (Colloq.)

**Recidivism** (rē-sĭd'ĭ-vĭz'm), n.; L. Repeatedly committing the same sin after confessing it again and again, giving little evidence of improvement and of the purpose of amendment.

**Recluse** (rē-kloos'), n.; L. One living a solitary life apart from the world, often more rigorous than that of a hermit because he confines himself to a single cell or room.

**Recollects** (rĕk'ŏ-lĕkts), n. pl.; L. A branch of the Franciscan Order which arose in France in the fifteenth century, noted for its austerity.

**Reconciliation** (rĕk'ŏn-sĭl'ĭ-ā'shŭn), n.; L. The act of reblessing or reinstating. Said of a church or cemetery which has been violated; it must be "reconciled" by the bishop before it can again be used for sacred services.

**Rector** (rĕk'tēr), n.; L. The ecclesiastical head of a college or seminary; also used to refer to a missionary priest or a priest of a diocese in charge of an outlying church; also used as a title for the priest in charge of any church which is neither a parish church, nor that of a chapter, nor one attached to a religious community.

**Redactor** (rĕ·dăk′tẽr), n.; L. Literally, an editor. Said of the first or original writer who recorded the Scriptures or one who edited or revised the Scriptures after having been given them by the inspired writer.

**Redeemer** (rĕ·dēm′ẽr), n.; L. The title applied to Christ who in His life, passion, and death made satisfaction for mankind. (Cf. Redemption.)

**Redemption** (rĕ·dĕmp′shŭn), n.; L. The act of bringing man out of the bondage of sin and restoring him to the friendship of God; the satisfaction of divine justice. The satisfaction made to God for the fall of man by the Incarnation of the Son and His death for mankind; Christ's atonement for sin and meriting of grace through the justice and holiness of God the Father.

**Redemptorists** (rĕ·dĕmp′tẽr·ĭsts), n. pl.; L. The members of the Congregation of the Most Holy Redeemer, founded by St. Alphonsus Liguori in 1732; also called Liguorians.

**Refectory** (rĕ·fĕk′tŏ·rĭ), n.; L. The dining room in a monastery, a convent, or seminary.

**Reformation** ((rĕf′ŏr·mā′shŭn), n.; L., O.Fr. The rise in the German empire of a pseudo-reform of the Church in the early sixteenth century which resulted in the formation of so-called reformed churches or the Protestant churches of Lutheranism, Calvinism, and Anglicanism; the revolt or revolution which led to Protestantism begun by Martin Luther in the sixteenth century which destroyed the Christian unity and gave rise to various sects. It was religious, social, and political in its effect.

**Regale** (rē·gā′lē), n.; L. (1) The right claimed by kings by which they were to receive the revenue from a vacant bishopric or benefice. (Obs.) (2) In the plural (regalia), vulgarly and wrongly referred to the insignia and ceremonial vesture of a Church dignitary.

**Regeneration** (rē·jěn′ēr·ā′shŭn), n.; L. A term sometimes applied to Baptism; the act of being raised from the state of original sin to the friendship of God and made an heir of heaven.

**Regesta** (rē·jěst′a), n. pl.; L. The copies of papal correspondence and official documents which are filed in the papal chancery.

**Regina Caeli** (rē·gī′na sē′lī), n.; L. Literally translated, "the Queen of Heaven." The Latin words which form the title of the anthem in honor of the Blessed Virgin and which is said in place of the Angelus during the Easter season.

**Regulars** (rěg′û·lērz), n. pl.; L. Those belonging to a religious order and bound by the vows of religion and obeying a particular rule, yet distinguished from monks; they may be of either sex.

**Relics** (rěl′ĭks), n. pl.; L,. O.Fr. The bodies of saints, particles of their bodies, or articles of clothing, vestments, and the like which they used during their lifetimes and which the Church venerates because of the position of the person in sanctity and virtue and because these may bring a person to the imitation of the saint; often miracles are worked by the grace and favor of God through a relic and through the intercession of the saint whose relic is so used. To be genuine, first-class relics must be fully authenticated, that is, be accompanied by papers stating that such an object was actually a part of the body. Relics are commonly divided into three classes. First-class relics are parts of the actual body of the saint. Second-class relics are bits of the clothing and other articles used by the saint in life. Third-class relics are objects that have been touched to the body or tomb of the saint.

**Religion** ((rē·lĭj′ŭn), n.; L., O.Fr. (1) The union of man with God; the active realization of man's relation to God. The doctrines, precepts, and practices by which man joins himself to God. The science treating of all degrees of faith and practice. (2) The virtue by which we give to God the honor which is due Him; the performance of acts honoring God by which we show our love for God. It is of obligation for everyone.

**Religious** (rē·lĭj′ŭs), n.; L., O.Fr. The name frequently applied to a member of an order who has devoted himself to God by the three vows of religion; a member of a religious institution.

**Religious (life)**, adj. & n.; L., O.Fr. A life devoted by a rule to perfection. It is chiefly the voluntary making of and living according to the three vows of poverty, perfect chastity, and perfect obedience. It is the life led by those who are members of various religious orders, congregations, societies, and communities.

**Reliquary** (rĕl′ĭ·kwĕr′ĭ), n.; Fr. A sealed container in which relics are kept; a monstrance-like upright stand supporting a container of relics. (Cf. Herma.)

**Reparation** (rĕp′a·rā′shŭn), n.; L., O.Fr. Making amends for material or spiritual wrongs committed against another; also restitution. An act performed to make satisfaction for the violation of justice.

Reliquary

**Repentance** (rē·pĕn′tăns), n.; L. Contrition or sorrow for sins, including a purpose of amendment.

**Repository** (rē·pŏz′ĭ·tō′rĭ), n.; L. The chapel or side altar in which the Blessed Sacrament, consecrated on Holy Thursday, is kept or reposes until the Mass of Good Friday. (Cf. Reservation, 1.)

**Reprobation** (rĕp′rō·bā′shŭn), n.; L. The state of those who will not cooperate with the grace of God for their salvation; their eternal punishment as foreseen by God who alone will judge.

**Repus Sunday** (rĕp′ŭs), n.; L. Name applied sometimes to Passion Sunday, the fifth Sunday of Lent.

**Requiem** (rē′kwĭ·ĕm), n.; L. A Mass said for the repose of a soul; a funeral Mass; the name is derived from the first word of the Introit of the Mass for the dead. (Cf. Mass.)

**Reredos** (rēr′dŏs), n.; O.E. An ornamental screen or decorative work of wood or stone placed behind an altar which may or may not form a part of the altar; the term is applied to a painting in the same position. (Cf. Altar.)

**Rescripts** (rē′skrĭptz), n. pl.; L. Granted favors of dispensation; they are answers given to different requests obtained from the Holy See and from other Ordinaries in favor of all those who are not explicitly excluded from this right. One may make use of the rescript or not, as he wishes, hence it need not be followed. It may be revoked or become invalid.

**Reservation** (rĕz′ẽr·vā′shŭn), n.; L. (1) The retention of the Blessed Sacrament in the repository which is the tabernacle. (2) The withholding of the power or jurisdiction to absolve from certain sins or censures made by an ecclesiastical authority. (3) A condition or qualification made in one's mind when making an assertion. (Cf. Mental reservation.) (4) The act by which a benefice is said to be due to a certain individual worthy of the benefice; the papal request that a benefice be conferred upon some particular individual.

**Reserved (Case)** (rē·zûrvd′), adj., L. A sin or censure for which the jurisdiction to absolve is withheld or reserved to a certain ecclesiastical superior; e.g., a bishop. Those who have the ordinary power of giving to another faculties to hear confessions or to inflict censures can also reserve some cases to their own tribunal and thus limit the power of absolution given to their priests.

**Residence** (rĕz′ĭ·dĕns), n.; L., Fr. (1) A house where one resides, a dwelling place. (2) The provision of canon law under which a parish priest, or one holding a benefice, may not be absent from his place of jurisdiction for more than a week without the permission of the ordinary.

**Resignation** (rĕz'ĭg·nā'shŭn), n.; L., O.Fr. (1) The giving up or renouncing of a benefice to the lawful superior and its acceptance by him. (2) The acceptance of the will of God by the performance of all necessary acts in submission to the higher laws of God and His Church.

**Responsory** (rē·spŏn'sō·rĭ), n.; L., O.Fr. The verses recited after the Lessons of the Breviary, so named because, when the office is recited in common, the parts of the responsory are usually read by two acolytes, one answering to the other, or by an acolyte and the hebdomadary; it may also be recited by a group. The method of recitation is not prescribed.

**Restitution** (rĕs'tĭ·tū'shŭn), n.; L., O.Fr. The reparation of the violated right or material losses of another. The obligation to make restitution rests on one who has done injury to another's life or body, his wife, his goods, or his good name.

**Resurrection** (rĕz'ŭ·rĕk'shŭn), n.; L., O.Fr. Reanimation of the body by again uniting the soul and body of a person after death. (1) The historical truth and the greatest of Christ's miracles, which is the fact that He died and came to life again and which incontestably proves His divinity. The feast of the Resurrection or Easter. (2) The resurrection of the body of man, which means that the dead shall live again in their bodies after the general resurrection; the uniting of the dead body with the immortal soul after which the person will live in either heaven or hell.

**Retreat** (rē·trēt′), n.; L., O.Fr. A time set aside in which a person places himself under a spiritual director to receive the guidance of spiritual exercises and admonitions and make a confession of his sins for his spiritual good. Such spiritual exercises consist of the consideration of the meaning and purpose of life and the perfection of living.

**Revealed Law,** n.; L. The divine positive law. The doctrinal, moral, and ceremonial law promulgated by Christ the Supreme Lawgiver and contained in the New Testament of the Bible and in divine tradition (sometimes called the New Law). It also includes the power given to the Church by Christ to form ordinances necessary for discipline or divine worship, which are called ecclesiastical laws. (Cf. Eternal law.)

**Revelation** (rĕv′ĕ·lā′shŭn), n.; L. (1) The manifestation of truth to men on the part of God after the manner of a teacher; this may be recorded for all men, e.g., the revelation of Sacred Scriptures; the revealing of certain truths to individuals, called private revelations, for the spiritual good of the individual or for the particular intention of God. (2) Book of—the title of the Apocalypse in Protestant versions of the Bible.

**Reverend** (rĕv′ĕr·ĕnd), n. or adj.; L., O.Fr. One worthy of respect. The title of address accorded to priests and other clerics. Also to choir-nuns and sisters having the title of "Mother."

**Rheims-Douay** (rēmz'-dōō'ā), n.; Fr. The places at which Dr. Gregory Martin and others made the translation of the Bible bearing that name; the most commonly used version of the Bible among English speaking Catholics.

**Riddels** (rĭd'ĕls), n. pl.; A.S. Curtains hung at the sides of the altar. (Cf. Dossal.)

**Rigorism** (rĭg'ĕr·ĭz'm), n.; L., O.Fr. The system of moral theology which says the law must always be followed except when it is certain that one is free to act otherwise; that system of moral theology directly opposed to laxism. It was condemned in the seventeenth century. (Cf. Tutiorism; Equiprobabilism, Probabilism.)

**Ring** (rĭng), n.; A.S. A band of metal, usually gold or silver, worn on the finger. The ring is used in the Church: (*a*) as a part of the insignia of a bishop, an abbot, or abbess; (*b*) by nuns or sisters to denote their consecration to God and their mystical marriage with Christ. (*c*) The wedding ring marks the betrothal and marriage of a man and woman. (*d*) The "ring of the fisherman" is the signet ring or private seal of the Pope. (*e*) A plain gold ring is sometimes conferred on Doctors of Theology, but this is not worn at liturgical functions.

A Bishop's ring

**Rite** (rīt), n.; L. (1) A religious ceremony or function, e.g., the rite of blessing palms. (2) The manner in which services in worship of God are conducted in the Christian Church. (3) An entire liturgy, e.g., the Roman rite. The liturgy comprises the ceremonies, actions, and language. The various languages of the several liturgical rites in which the Mass is said are nine; namely, Latin, Greek, Syrian, Coptic, Armenian, Arabic, Slavonic, Georgian, and Roumanian.

**Rites (Congregation of),** n. pl.; L. The Roman Congregation which (*a*) prescribes the uniformity of manner of divine worship in the Church; (*b*) and has direct charge of the processes of the beatification and canonization of saintly persons. (Cf. Congregations.)

**Ritual** (rĭt′ū·ăl), n.; L. A book containing the forms to be observed by priests for the administration of the sacraments, blessing of objects, etc. In Latin: *Rituale Romanum*.

**Rochet** (rŏch′ĕt), n.; O.Fr. A vestment resembling a surplice worn by bishops and abbots, made of linen, ornamented with lace, and having closely fitting sleeves.

**Rogation Days** (rō·gā′shŭn), n. pl.; Gr., L., O.Fr. The Monday, Tuesday, and Wednesday before Ascension Thursday which are days of supplication and on which the Litany of the Saints is chanted in procession; the name is derived from the Greek word for litany.

**Roman Catholic** (rō′măn), adj. & n.; L., O.Fr. A qualifying name of a Catholic indicating communion with Rome; the Church of Rome includes those of the Latin Rite and the various Eastern Rites.

**Roman Collar,** adj. & n.; L. A stiffly starched upright white collar whose opening is fastened at the back of the neck; a distinctive mark of a cleric or priest as a part of his public attire.

**Roman Missal,** n. The liturgical book written in Latin which contains the rules to be followed, the prayers to be recited, and the acts to be accomplished in the celebration of Mass according to the Roman rite. (Cf. Missal.)

**Roman Rite,** adj. & n.; L. The authentic and prescribed liturgy of the Latin Church; that liturgy practiced by the Holy See.

**Rome** (rōm), n.; L. The capitol city of Italy, commonly called the center of Christianity; the city within which the Vatican State is located.

**Rood** (rōod), n.; A.S. (1) The cross of Christ. (2) A large crucifix, usually with the figures of the Blessed Mother and St. John; a group representation of Calvary.

**Rood-screen** (rōod-skrēn), n.; A.S., O.Fr. The wooden screen or partition which separates the choir from the nave in a church.

**Rorate Sunday** (rō·rā'tĕ), n.; L. The fourth Sunday of Advent, so called from the first word of the Introit of the Mass.

**Rosary** (rō'zȧ·rĭ), n.; L. The chain and numerous beads which form a chaplet or endless chain for reciting prayers in a given sequence. The name applied to the prayer consisting of fifteen decades of "Hail Marys," each decade having an "Our Father" preceding and a "Glory be to the Father" following. This chaplet usually has in addition three small beads for the "Hail Marys" and one bead for the "Our Father" which precede the prayer and to this short chain there is generally attached a crucifix. Mysteries are contemplated during the saying of each decade, which mysteries are the five joyful, the five sorrowful, and the five glorious.

A rosary

**Rose Window** (rōz wĭn′dō), n.; L., A.S. A circular window of stained glass with delicate tracery resembling the petal form of a rose, usually seen in Gothic churches on the façade which forms the rear wall of the nave.

**Rosminians** (rŏz·mĭn′ĭ·ănz), n. pl.; L., It. Members of the congregation known as the Fathers of the Institute of Charity, founded by Antonio Rosmini at Domodossola, Italy, in 1828. The congregation has a twofold purpose; sanctification of its members by interior charity or love of God, and the doing of external acts of charity.

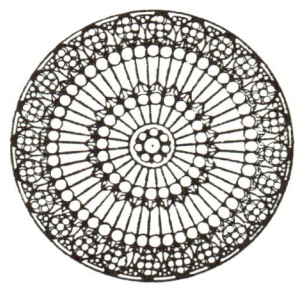

A rose window

**Rota** (rō′tȧ), n.; L. The ordinary tribunal or court of

the Roman Curia; it also serves as a court of appeal for all diocesan courts of the world.

**Rubrics** (roo'briks), n. pl.; L., O.Fr. In liturgical books, the direction or rules of actions to be observed in the celebration of Mass, the recitation of the Divine Office, the administration of the sacraments, etc.; as the name implies, they are printed in red.

**Rule** (rool), n.; L., O.Fr. The order and regulation of life followed by members of particular religious groups. There are four basic rules: (*a*) of St. Basil; (*b*) of St. Augustine; (*c*) of St. Benedict; (*d*) of St. Francis. All other rules are drawn largely from these original four.

**Russicum** (rŭs'ĭ·kŭm), n.; L. The Russian College; an educational institution founded in Rome in 1927 to train priests in the Catholic Russian Rite to work among the Russians.

**Ruth** (rooth), n.; Heb., Bib. An historical book of the Old Testament bearing that name. Named after the wife of the Jew, Booz; she was an ancestor of Christ.

# S

**Sabaoth** (săb′ă·ŏth), n.; Heb., Gr., L. A word found in the Sanctus of the Mass which is taken from the Hebrew and means, literally, hosts.

**Sabbath** (săb′ăth), n.; Heb., L., A.S. In Hebrew the word means rest. In the Jewish law it was the seventh day of the week, or Saturday, and a day of religious worship; among Christians it is recognized as the day of rest and worship or the first day of the week, Sunday.

**Sabellianism** (să·běl′ĭ·ăn·ĭz′m), n.; L. A heresy which arose in the second century with Patripassianism and which denied a distinction between the persons in God; thus it denied the Trinity.

**Sacrament** (săk′kră·měnt), n.; L. The Council of Trent defines sacrament as "a visible sign of invisible grace instituted for our justification." Simply, it is an outward sign instituted by Christ and producing interior grace; the sacrament effects what it symbolizes. There are seven sacraments: Baptism, Confirmation, Penance, Holy Eucharist, Extreme Unction, Holy Orders, Matrimony, all of which are comprised of an outward sign, were instituted by Christ, and give grace.

**Sacramentals** (săk′rȧ·měn′tălz), n. pl.; L. Certain pious practices or objects blessed by the Church. The blessing is attached that these may serve to increase the devotion of the faithful. Scapulars, holy water, etc., are widely used sacramentals.

**Sacramentary** (săk′rȧ·měn′tȧ·rĭ), n.; L. The "book of the sacred mysteries" which was the first complete liturgical book in the Latin rite. This was later incorporated into the Missal. (Obs.)

**Sacrarium** (sȧ·krâr′ĭ·ŭm), n.; L. The piscina; a place connecting directly with the ground where used holy water or relics and ashes of sacred things may be disposed of.

**Sacred (College)** (sā′krĕd), adj. & n.; L., O.Fr. Name given to the college of cardinals; the cardinals officially assembled.

**Sacred Heart,** n.; L. The physical heart of Jesus as the symbol of His love for men, which is an object of devotion in the Church. (Cf. Heart of Jesus.)

**Sacrifice** (săk′rĭ·fĭs), n.; L., O.Fr. (1) An offering to God; an act of external worship recognizing God's supreme dominion and giving honor to God through the offering of a visible creature which is transformed or destroyed. The offering is made only by a qualified minister or priest. (2) It may also be applied to a voluntary act of self-denial.

**Sacrifice (of the Mass),** n.; L., O.Fr. The holy Sacrifice of the Mass is the unbloody re-enactment that makes the Sacrifice of the Cross actually present. It is and must be held to be one and the same sacrifice which is accomplished at Mass and which was accomplished on the cross, because it is the same Victim who is offered and offers, namely, Christ. It is the renewal of Christ's sacrifice of Himself on the cross accomplished in an unbloody manner. It is the sacrifice of the entire Christ, the Mystical Body, for Christ desires to offer Himself for us and with us. The faithful thus participate in the redemptive sacrifice of Christ by offering satisfaction with Christ and in Christ. (Cf. Mass.)

**Sacrilege** (săk′rĭ·lĕj), n.; L., O.Fr. An act violating a sacred person, object, or place; the violation of a vessel set apart for divine services or an act desecrating a place of divine worship. It must be directed against that by which the object is sacred. The administering or reception of sacraments in an unworthy manner is also a sacrilege and merits severe censure by the Church.

**Sacristan** (săk′rĭs·tăn), n.; L. One whose duty it is to care for the church, in particular the altar, vestments, etc.; one who prepares the altar for Mass.

**Sacristy** (săk′rĭs·tĭ), n.; L. A room set aside for the retaining of vestments and in which the priest vests in preparation for Mass; a room off of the sanctuary; the diaconicum.

**Sadducees** (săd′ū·sēs), n. pl.; Heb., Gr., L. A freethinking political party among the Jews which was opposed to the Pharisees and held only to the revelation of Moses.

**Saint** (sānt), n.; L., O.Fr. The person who through a life of heroic virtue or martyrdom has merited the canonization of the Church; a member of the Church triumphant; a person known to be in heaven. One who while on earth exemplified in a special manner not only the keeping of the necessary moral law but also the practice of those counsels left by Christ which are not of strict obligation.

**Salesians** (så·lē′shǎns), n. pl.; L. Fr. The congregation of religious founded by St. John Bosco in the nineteenth century and which is under the patronage of St. Francis de Sales. They are dedicated to the care and education of orphan boys.

**Salic (law)** (săl′ĭk), adj.; Fr. A law derived from Teutonic sources of the fifth century, providing that males should inherit lands in preference to females; also extended to the succession to the throne in France and Spain. (Cf. Morganatic.)

**Salt** (sôlt), n.; A.S. Common salt which is exorcised and blessed and used in administering Baptism and in the blessing of holy water.

**Salut** (så·lū′), n.; Fr. Benediction of the Blessed Sacrament; French term not commonly used.

**Salvation** (săl·vā′shǔn), n.; L., O.Fr. Man's proper end; the attaining of the vision of God in heaven.

**Salvific** (săl·vĭf′ĭk), adj.; L. Having the intent to save; such is the will of God who in creating man wills that he is to be saved provided he cooperates.

**Samaritans** (så·măr'ı·tănz), n. pl.; Heb. The descendants of the Israelites who settled in Samaria and who were rivals of the Orthodox Jews because of a different form of Judaism evolved by them and the erection of a rival temple.

**Sanation** (săn·ā'shŭn), n.; L. (1) The making valid of an act which was invalid because of some impediment; it supposes that the cause of invalidity has ceased and is retroactive. (2) *Sanatio in radice:* a secret validation of an invalid marriage without renewal of consent. The sanation can be granted only by the Holy See, and only in cases in which the marriage was invalid because of some purely ecclesiastical obstacle; it cannot be granted for the validation of a marriage which was invalid because of an impediment of the natural or divine law.

**Sanctifying grace** (săngk'tĭ·fī'ĭng), adj.; L., O.Fr. A divinely produced quality or perfection of the human soul whereby it participates in the nature and life of God and is made to resemble Him as He is; it elevates man's nature to be like God and hence to think as God thinks and to will as He wills. It is absolutely necessary for salvation. (Cf. Grace, Habitual grace.)

**Sanctity** (săngk'tĭ·tĭ) n.; L., O.Fr. Holiness of life; the possession of sanctifying grace; the practice of heroic virtue; the characteristics of a saint.

**Sanctissimum** (săngk'tĭs'sĭ·mŭm), n.; L. In Latin: "The most holy"; the Blessed Sacrament. (Cf. Eucharist; Benediction.)

**Sanctorale** (săngk′tŏr·ăl′ē), n.; L. The section of the Missal or Breviary in which the proper of the Saints is contained. (Cf. *Proprium Sanctorum.*)

**Sanctuary** (săngk′tū·ĕr′ĭ), n.; L. (1) That part of the church embraced by the communion rail and in which the high altar stands; the place in the church reserved for the clergy. Also called *presbyterium.* (2) The right of sanctuary was that right accorded to a holy place wherein a criminal or fugitive from justice might take refuge and have immunity from the law. (Obs.)

**Sanctuary (lamp),** n.; L. The vessel containing olive oil and a lighted floating wick or a candle which is left burning in the sanctuary of a church to indicate that our Lord is within the tabernacle of the altar. It symbolizes the light of faith and of Christ in the world.

**Sanctus** (săngk′tŭs), n.; L. (1) That part of the Mass forming the conclusion of the Preface; also known as the angelic hymn. (2) The Latin title for one who has been canonized, a saint.

**Sandals** (săn′dălz), n. pl.; Gr., L. (1) Footwear which is part of the liturgical dress of bishops. These lightweight shoes or slippers are usually of the color of the vestments worn, and have the top parts made of silk. (2) The footwear of certain religious orders.

**Sanbenito,** n.; It. A scapularlike garment worn by those condemned by the Inquisition. (Obs.)

**Sanpietrini** (săn′pĕ·trĭn′ĭ), n. pl.; It. A group of skilled architects and workmen, about 350 in number, who are permanently employed in repairing and renovating St. Peter's basilica in Rome.

**Satan** (sā′tăn), n.; Heb. The devil; the chief of the devils or Lucifer.

**Satisfaction** (săt′ĭs·făk′shŭn), n.; L., O.Fr. The imposed penance given by the priest as necessary to contrition for sins in the Sacrament of Penance; also the rendering of a just return of a debt. (Cf. Restitution.)

**Scabellum** (skă·bĕl′ŭm), n.; L. The shelf on the back portion of the altar whereon candles, crucifix, or decorations are placed; the gradine. (Cf. Altar, Gradine.)

**Scamnum** (skăm′nŭm), n.; L. The seat or bench upon which the celebrant, deacon, and subdeacon sit during the singing of the Kyrie, Gloria, and Credo in Solemn High Mass.

**Scandal** (skăn′dăl), n.; L., O.Fr. It is defined by St. Thomas as "any word or deed not fully right which is the occasion of sin to another." Scandal may be active, i.e., the giving of the occasion of sin; or passive, i.e., the sin occasioned by another's conduct.

**Scapular** (skăp′ū·lẽr), n.; L., Fr. (1) A dresslike garment covering the shoulders and descending front and back, usually open at the sides, worn as an external part over the habit of certain monks.

A scapular (Cf. [2] of definition)

(2) The most common scapulars of today are made

of two small squares of woolen cloth about two inches wide which are joined by two strings so that one small square may rest upon the back and the other on the breast when placed over one's head; there are eighteen small scapulars now used among Catholics and they may be of various colors.

**Scapular Medal,** n.; L., Fr. A small medallion of metal with a representation of our Lord and His Sacred Heart on one side and that of the Blessed Virgin on the other which is permitted to be worn instead of the small cloth scapular.

**Schism** (sĭz'm), n.; Gr., L. Formal separation from the unity of the Church, a separation from communion with the Church; separation from the head of the Church or from the jurisdiction of the Supreme Pontiff. The movement of any person or group of persons of the Church who refuse to recognize the central authority of the Church; a denial of the authority of the Pope of Rome.

**Schismatic** (sĭz·măt'ĭk), n. & adj.; Gr., L. One who of his own will departs from the unity of the Church and refuses to acknowledge the Pope as the supreme head or to accept his jurisdiction. *Adj.* Of or pertaining to a schism.

**Scholastic** (skô·lăs'tĭk), n. & adj.; Gr., L. (1) A philosopher or theologian teaching according to the system of scholasticism. (2) A Jesuit making studies prior to his ordination. (3) *adj.* pertaining to scholasticism.

**Scholasticism** (skô·lăs'tĭ·sĭz'm), n.; Gr., L. The

thought of Christian philosophers and theologians originating in the ninth century. It developed a characteristic method of investigation and exposition of thought applied to both philosophy and theology, and showed the relationship of philosophy and theology. It reached its height in the thirteenth century, and its greatest propounder was St. Thomas Aquinas. Scholastic theology unfolds and vindicates the conclusions deduced from dogmas by theologians.

**Scholasticus** (skō·lăs′tĭ·kŭs), n.; L. A cleric who was placed in charge of the schools of a diocese; a teacher. (Obs.)

**Scotism** (skō′tĭz′m), n.; L. One of the schools of scholastic philosophy, also called the Franciscan school which followed the interpretation of John Duns Scotus, a Franciscan. This philosophical and theological system insisted upon formal distinctions.

**Scotula** (skō′tū·là), n.; L. A small hand candlestick; a bugia; a palmatoria. (Cf. Bugia.)

**Scribes** (skrībz), n. pl.; L. Professional writers and lawyers among the Jews at the time of our Lord; doctors and teachers of the Law among the Jews.

**Scriptorium** (skrĭp·tō′rĭ·ŭm), n.; L. The room of a monastery where the work of translating and copying manuscripts was carried on.

**Scripture** (skrĭp′tūr), n.; L. The writings of the Bible; the Old and New Testaments as contained in the Bible. (Cf. Bible; Canon of the Scripture.)

**Scruple** (skroo′p'l), n.; L., Fr. Unreasonable fear that a thing is forbidden which is permitted, or that a sin is grave when it is only trivial. An excessively severe judgment on one's own conduct based on an erroneous conscience, an obstacle to spirituality inasmuch as a mental obsession is formed and a right conscience destroyed.

**Scrutiny** (skroo′tĭ·nĭ), n.; L. (1) The examination of an adult person about to receive Baptism concerning his knowledge of the faith. (2) The examination of one presented for Holy Orders. (3) The term is also used for the election by secret ballot, the usual form of electing a pope.

**Seal (of confession)** (sēl), n.; A.S. The obligation resting upon the priest in administering the sacrament of Penance of maintaining absolute secrecy concerning facts learned through sacramental confession; that by which a priest is bound to withhold from the knowledge of others information he has received through sacramental confession.

**Secret** (sē′krĕt), n.; L., O.Fr. The prayer or prayers corresponding in form and number with the Collects, which the priest reads silently between the Offertory and the Preface; they vary according to the feast. (Cf. Commemoration.)

**Secret Society**, n.; L., O.Fr. A secret society is a group which is founded in order to plot against the Church or State, whose members are bound by oath from revealing to lawful authorities the proceedings and must give obedience to the head, and whose ceremonials simulate Christian rites; societies to which a Catholic is forbidden membership, even though they offend in only one of the above.

**Secretarium** (sĕk'rē·tēr'ĭ·ŭm), n.; L. A side chapel or private room in which a cardinal, bishop, or abbot may rest or assist at the recitation of the Divine Office. Name formerly applied to the sacristy.

**Secular (clergy),** n. & adj.; L., O.Fr. Ordained priests who do not belong to any religious order or monastic institution; more properly called diocesan clergy. Their chief work is to conduct parishes and instruct the faithful.

**Secularization** (sĕk'ū·lēr·ĭ·zā'shŭn), n.; L., O.Fr. (1) Permission given to a professed religious to leave his institute permanently; it carries with it a dispensation from the religious vows. (2) The abolishment of the Church's title to property by the giving of that title to the secular authorities.

**Sedia gestatoria,** n.; It. A portable chair; the chair and platform upon which the Pope is carried when making solemn entry into St. Peter's or elsewhere.

**Sediarii,** n. pl.; L., It. The lay porters or men who carry the *sedia gestatoria* of the Pope in processions. (Cf. *Sedia gestatoria*.)

**Sedilia** (sĕ·dĭl'ĭ·à), n.; L., It. The sedile. The bench or seat in the sanctuary on which the celebrant and ministers sit during parts of divine services. The scamnum. (Cf. Scamnum.)

**See (sē),** n.; L., O.Fr. The territory or diocese over which a bishop rules; the extended jurisdiction of a bishop.

**Semidouble** (sĕm′ĭ·dŭb″l), n.; L., O.Fr. One of the classifications under a double in the rank of the feasts of the Church.

**Seminarian** (sĕm′ĭ·nĕr′ĭ·ăn), n.; L. A student studying in a seminary; one preparing for the priesthood.

**Seminary** (sĕm′ĭ·nĕr′ĭ), n.; L. A school for the preparation of young men for the priesthood. A diocesan school under the jurisdiction of the bishop and supported by diocesan funds wherein students are trained for the diocesan clergy.

**Semi-pelagianism,** n.; L. A heresy which arose in the fifth century which denied the proper sphere of the grace of God in the scheme of salvation. It taught especially that grace is not necessary for the beginning of faith, and held a doctrine of predestination. Originally its followers were not considered heretics because they still held a belief in the Catholic doctrine.

**Separation** (sĕp′ȧ·rā′shŭn), n.; L. The discontinuance of co-habitation or the separation of husband and wife from bed and board while both remain under the bond of their marriage; the grant of such separation by the Church for good reasons. However, such separation, in the case of adultery, may be spontaneous and assumed mutually by the two parties; separation may be either permanent or temporary.

**Septuagesima** (sĕp′tū-*a*-jĕs′ĭ-m*a*), n.; L. The third Sunday before Lent; the Sunday which begins the pre-lenten season.

**Septuagint** (sĕp′tū-*a*-jĭnt), n.; L. The first translation of the Bible; the name of the Greek translation of the Old Testament made from the Hebrew between 300 and 130 B.C.

**Sepulcrum** (sĕ-pŭl′kr*u*m), n.; L. Also sepulchre. The square or oblong opening in the altar top or mensa into which the altar relics are placed, or that place where the altar stone is contained in a wooden altar top.

Portion of altar top showing the sepulcrum. (1) The sepulcrum; (2) the altar relic; (3) the altar top

**Sequence** (sē′kwĕns), n.; O.Fr. The hymn sung after the gradual in certain Masses. It is sometimes called a prose because originally it was not written in any particular meter. Formerly sequences were very numerous. Only five are found in the present Roman Missal: for Easter, *Victimae Paschali;* for Pentecost, *Veni Sancte Spiritus;* for Corpus Christi, *Lauda Sion;* for the Seven Sorrows of our Lady, *Stabat Mater;* and the *Dies Irae* in requiem Mass. With the exception of *Victimae Paschali*, the sequences now in the Missal are quite as metrical as the other hymns (Cf. Prose.)

**Seraph** (sĕr′ăf); n.; Heb. An angel; one of the order of seraphim.

**Seraphic** (sĕ-răf′ĭk), adj., Heb. A name applied to St. Bonaventure because of his learned teaching; the seraphic doctor. Also applied to the Franciscan Order.

**Sermon** (sûr′mŭn), n.; L., O.Fr. A discourse preached in church; a homily or an instruction. (Cf. Homily.)

**Server** (sûr′vēr), n.; L., A.S. One who ministers to the priest while he says Mass; an acolyte, usually a boy, who assists the priest by answering the prayers of Mass and completing necessary actions of the Mass; a Mass server.

**Servile** (sûr′vĭl), adj.; L. Work which demands the expenditure of considerable muscular energy and is directed primarily to the bodily welfare of men; originally, work which was performed by a slave or servant.

**Servites** (sûr′vīts), n. pl.; L. The religious order founded in the thirteenth century by seven Florentine merchants and named "Religious Servants of the Holy Virgin."

**Seven Dolors** (sĕv′ĕn), n. & adj., pl.; A.S. The sorrows, seven in number, which the Blessed Virgin suffered by being the Mother of Jesus; namely, the prophecy of Simeon, the flight into Egypt, the three days' loss of Jesus, the meeting with Jesus on the way to Calvary, standing beneath the cross, the descent of Jesus from the cross, and the burial of Jesus. There is a rosary which forms a devotion to the seven mysteries of the Blessed Virgin's sorrows.

**Seven Gifts (of the Holy Ghost),** n. pl. Permanent dispositions in the faculties of the soul, which are received together with sanctifying grace enabling the just man to receive and follow the special enlightenments and inspirations of the Holy Ghost; the seven gifts are: wisdom, understanding, counsel, fortitude, knowledge, piety, and fear of the Lord.

**Sexagesima** (sĕk'sa·jĕs'ĭ·ma), n.; L. The second Sunday before Lent; literally, sixtieth or sixty days before Easter.

**Sext** (sĕkst), n.; L. (1) One of the day hours of the Breviary. (2) In canon law, the abbreviation for the sixth book of the decretals of Boniface VIII.

**Sexton** (sĕks'tŭn), n.; L., O.Fr. The caretaker of the church, or janitor; also the sacristan or the one who rings the bell of the church.

**Shekinah**, n.; Heb. See Glory, 2.

**Shrine** (shrīn), n.; L., A.S. A place of devotion, usually consisting of a grotto or chapel erected to commemorate some event or place of special religious significance; a place to which pilgrimages are made.

**Shroud** (shroud), n.; A.S. (1) A cloth for placing over or binding a corpse; the cloth of death. (2) The holy shroud is the relic of the linen cloth in which, it is claimed, our Lord was wrapped when laid in the tomb. This relic is still preserved in Turin and bears an impression of the body of our Lord. It measures thirteen and one half by four and one fourth feet.

**Shrovetide** (shrōv'tīd), n.; A.S. The Monday and Tuesday immediately following Quinquagesima Sunday. It is so named because people went to confession (shriving) to consult their spiritual directors about fasting.

**Shrove Tuesday** (shrōv), n.; A.S. The day before Ash Wednesday; the day before the beginning of the Lenten fast.

**Sigillator** (sĭj·ĭ·lă′tẽr), n.; L. The title of the person who attaches the seals to the official documents of the Sacred Penitentiary.

**Siglum** (sĭg′lŭm), n.; L. An indicated, abbreviated mark of biblical criticism.

**Sign (of the Cross)** (sīn), n.; L., O.Fr. That sacramental which consists in making the movement with the right hand from the forehead to the breast and to the left and right shoulders in that order. It is erroneously called "blessing one's self."

**Signature** (sĭg′nȧ·tûr), n.; L., Fr. *Segnatura*. One of the three tribunals or courts of the Roman curia; it is both a court of appeal and a court of special cases.

**Simar** (sĭ·mär′), n.; It. The black cassock with a purple cape, sash, buttons, and piping worn in the house by a bishop. Also, zimarra.

**Simony** (sĭm′ô·nĭ), n.; L., O.Fr. The selling or giving in exchange of a temporal thing for a spiritual thing, such as the buying of a blessing; such sale is forbidden by the natural and ecclesiastical law.

**Simple** (sĭm′p'l), n.; L., O.Fr. The third ranking classification of the feasts of the Church, so called because the holy office is in "simple" form with the psalms of three nocturnes recited in one nocturne only. Used of vows: those which are not public.

**Sin** (sĭn), n.; A.S. A transgression of the law of God in thought, word, deed, or omission; broadly, sins are grouped under the headings of either mortal or venial. (Cf. Mortal, Venial, Omission, and Commission.)

**Sinaiticus** (sī'nă·ĭt'ĭ·kŭs), n.; Gr., L. An old Greek manuscript dating back to the fourth or fifth century, containing both the Old and New Testaments.

**Sindon** (sĭn'dŭn), n.; L. The linen winding-sheet wrapped about our Lord when He was placed in the sepulchre. (Cf. Shroud.)

**Sister** (sĭs'tẽr), n.; L., O.E. A member of a religious order of women. (Cf. Nun.)

**Sisterhoods** (sĭs'tẽr·ho͞odz), n. pl.; L., O.E. The name applied to the religious orders of women or to the orders of nuns.

**Sistine** (sĭs'tēn), adj.; It. The chapel of the Pope, the principal chapel of the Vatican Palace. Of or pertaining to one of the popes named Sixtus.

**Slander** (slăn'dẽr), n.; L., O.Fr. The willful detraction by uncharitable words or writings of the good name or reputation of another; malicious statements, whether true or false, which deprive another of his good name, his reputation, or his position in society. Restitution must be made in so far as possible. (Cf. Calumny.)

**Sloth** (slōth), n.; Fr. A spiritual vice which is a heavy sorrow which makes one reluctant to exercise any virtue; sorrow at the spiritual good of any virtue and is contrary to charity which should cause one to rejoice in virtue and easily perform virtuous acts. It is one of the capital sins or vices because it easily leads to other sins such as despair, etc. The contrary virtue is diligence. (Cf. Capital sins.)

**Society** (sō·sī′ĕ·tĭ), n.; L., Fr. (1) A union of men cooperating in attaining an end beneficial to each and all; an association of the laity, either men or women or both, who organize for the purpose of advancing a worthy cause of religion together with the intent of becoming, individually, more perfect. (Cf. Sodality.) (2) A religious society is a group of persons, priests or brothers, following a religious rule and devoted to some apostolic work, yet not living a monastic life as such.

**Socinians** (sō·sĭn′ĭ·ănz), n. pl.; L. Heretics of the sixteenth century who denied the Trinity; in one form or another, theirs is the belief of most extreme modernists.

**Sodality** (sō·dăl′ĭ·tĭ), n.; L. An association of lay persons, male or female or both, who meet for the performing of pious exercises, submitting themselves to the spiritual direction of a leader and following a uniform set of principles or rules for the promotion of a particular devotion or good work. (Cf. Pious Union.)

**Solemn Mass** (sŏl′ĕm), n.; L., O.Fr. A high Mass sung with a celebrant, deacon, and subdeacon.

**Solemnity** (sō·lĕm′nĭ·tĭ), n.; L., O.Fr. Any feast which is celebrated universally or locally with full liturgical observance. Sometimes applied to the title of a feast to indicate its more solemn celebration; e.g. the Solemnity of St. Joseph.

**Solemnization** (sŏl′ĕm·nĭ·zā′shŭn), n.; L., O.Fr. Said of a marriage which is contracted with nuptial Mass and Blessing.

**Solesmes** (sŏl′ê·mā), n.; Fr. Solemn liturgical chant of Gregorian music as derived from the form used and advanced by the Benedictine monks of Solesmes Abbey near Sablé, France.

**Solideo**, n.; L., It. A skullcap; the zucchetto worn by a prelate in Mass except from the beginning of the Preface until after Communion. The Pope's zucchetto is white, a cardinal's red, a bishop's purple, and an abbot's black.

**Solitary** (sŏl′ĭ·tĕr·ĭ), n.; L. A hermit; one living entirely alone to practice mortification and spirituality.

**Son** (sŭn), n.; A.S. The Son of God; the second Person of the Blessed Trinity, the Word, the Only-begotten; Jesus Christ. Also called the Son of Man because His human nature is present with His divine nature.

**Son of Man**, n.; L., O.E. Term frequently used in the Gospels in referring to our Lord.

**Sophonias** (sŏf′ō·nī′ăs), n.; Gr. The Greek word for the Hebrew name Zephaniah; one of the minor prophets.

**Sorbonne** (sôr·bŏn′), n.; Fr. A famous college for the instruction of theological students founded in 1252 in connection with the University of Paris.

**Soteriology** (sō·tēr′ĭ·ŏl′ō·jĭ), n.; Gr. The theology of Christ as the Redeemer of mankind; the study of the Redemption through Christ as Intercessor.

**Soul** (sōl), n.; A.S. The immaterial and immortal principle which is the substantial form of the body and which gives unity to the human being; that infused principle which through God gives life to man and remains for all eternity.

**Spatiamentum,** n.; L. The walk taken once a week by members of a Carthusian community.

**Spiritual Communion** (spĭr′ĭt·û·ăl), adj.; L., O.Fr. The earnest desire to communicate when not actually able to do so, accompanied by appropriate prayers in the form of acts of love, thanksgiving, etc.

**Spiritual (works of mercy),** adj.; L., O.Fr. Acts of love performed for our neighbor by helping him in his needs of body and soul. They are: to counsel the doubtful, to instruct the ignorant, to admonish the sinner, to comfort the sorrowful, to forgive injuries, to bear wrongs patiently, and to pray for the living and the dead.

**Spiritualism** (spĭr′ĭt·û·ăl·ĭz′m), n.; L., O.Fr. A belief in the communication with the dead and the system of doctrines derived from such supposed communication; the practice of individuals, usually called mediums, claiming through exceptional powers to be able to receive messages or manifestations in the form of revelations from the spirit world; condemned by decree of the Holy Office in June, 1856.

**Spirituals** (spĭr′ĭt·û·ălz), n. pl.; L., O.Fr. Things pertaining to the Church or the clergy, either rights, duties, or material possessions intended for religious purposes.

**Sponsors** (spŏn′sērz), n. pl.; L. A person who answers or vouches for another; the spiritual parents or godparents of a baptized person; the two persons who act for the child in making a profession of faith at the reception of Baptism. The spiritual tie formed between the person baptized and the godparents forms an impediment to marriage between a sponsor and the one baptized because it establishes a spiritual relationship; in the case of a sponsor for Confirmation, however, such relationship is not an impediment to marriage.

**Spoon** (spōōn), n.; A.S. A small gold ladle which was used in measuring a few drops of water to be placed in the wine during the Mass; a chalice spoon. This spoon is seldom used today.

**Spy Wednesday** (spī), n.; O.Fr. The name given to the Wednesday of Holy Week because of the betrayal of Christ to Jewish high priests by Judas on this day.

**Staff** (stăf), n.; A.S. A name sometimes given to the crosier or pastoral staff of a bishop.

**Stalls** (stôlz), n. pl.; A.S. The seats in the choir for those who recite the Divine Office in common.

**Stations** (stā′shŭnz), n. pl.; L., O.Fr. (1) The word is still used in the missal on certain feast days and is retained from the old custom of the Roman clergy and people to meet in some church of Rome where the Pope or his delegate sang Mass. Such churches were called Stations. (2) Stations of the Cross are a series of fourteen representations of events in the Passion of Christ; the devotion to the stations or to the particular events which occurred during the Passion of our Lord; such pictures or carved representations on the walls of a church.

The thirteenth of the Stations of the Cross. (Cf. (2) of definition.)

Stigmata (stĭg′mȧ·tȧ), n. pl.; L. The wounds of our Lord, namely, the pierced hands and feet and side, and the marks of the crown of thorns; the miraculous appearance of some or all of these wounds on a person which is permitted so that the person may join in the suffering of our Lord.

Stigmatist (stĭg′mȧ·tĭst), n.; L. A person who through a miracle bears in his body one or all of the wounds of our Lord, e.g., St. Francis of Assisi, St. Catherine of Siena. Also, stigmatic.

Stipend (stī′pĕnd), n.; L., O.Fr. A term applied generally to the support of the clergy or the revenue of a benefice; today it is more commonly applied to the offering made by the faithful when asking that a Mass be said for their particular intentions.

Stipites (stĭp′ĭ·tēz), n. pl.; the plural of stipes (stī′pēz); L. The supports of the *mensa* of a fixed altar; the pillars or posts upon which the mensa rests.

**Stock** (stŏk), n.; A.S. (1) The metal container for the Holy Oils. (2) The piece of cloth (black for priests, purple for prelates) worn on the breast beneath the collar at the opening of a suit coat.

Oil stock in three compartments: (1) O.S. stands for *Oleum Sanctum—Oleum Catechumenorum*, Oil of Catechumens. (2) S.C., *Sanctum Chrisma*, Chrism. (3) O.I., *Oleum Infirmorum*, Oil of the Sick. (Cf. Oils, Holy.)

**Stole** (stōl), n.; Gr., L., A.S. A long narrow vestment of the same material and color as the chasuble, which is worn about the neck; when worn by a deacon it is suspended from the left shoulder, crosses the breast diagonally, and is fastened at the waist; when worn by a priest the ends are crossed on the breast, and when worn by a bishop the two ends hang down from the shoulders in front. It symbolizes immortality and the yoke of obedience assumed by the priest.

Stole

**Stole-fee** (stōl-fē), n. pl.; Gr., L., A.S. An offering made by a lay person to a priest; the customary fee which the laity pays a priest when performing a sacred office such as a marriage or christening.

**Stoup** (stoōp), n.; Scand. A holy water basin or font at the entrances of all Catholic churches.

**Stragulum,** n.; L. See vesperal cloth.

**Stylites** (stī'līt'ēz), n. pl. (sing.); Gr. A solitary or hermit who lived a life of mortification on the top of a pillar; the most famous of such hermits was St. Simeon surnamed Stylites. Also stylite.

**Subcinctorium** (sŭb'sĭngk·tŏr'ĭ·ŭm), n.; L. An ornamental cloth vestment worn by the Pope at Solemn Mass, which hangs from the cincture on the right side and is about a foot square with an embroidered lamb on one side and a cross on the other. Also, succinctorium.

**Subdeacon** (sŭb·dē'kŭn), n.; L. A cleric of the Church who has received the sacramental which is classed as the first of the major orders; his duties in the Latin Church are to prepare the sacred vessels for Mass, to assist at a Solemn Mass by pouring water into the chalice at the Offertory, and to sing the Epistle. (Cf. Major Orders, Holy Orders.)

**Subdelegate** (sŭb·dĕl'ē·gāt), n.; L. The person to whom one who has received delegated ecclesiastical powers transfers his jurisdiction for a particular case.

**Subdiaconate** (sŭb·dī'ă·kŭn·āt), n.; L. State of one who has received the first of the major orders. (Cf. Subdeacon.)

**Submitrale** (sŭb·mĭ·trā'lē), n.; L. A skullcap; the bishop's zucchetto. Meaning literally, worn under the mitre.

**Subreption** (sŭb·rĕp′shŭn), n.; L. The concealment or misstating of truth in statements necessary for the obtaining of a rescript; such a defect in an official ecclesiastical document.

**Substance** (sŭb′stăns), n.; L., O.Fr. A thing which exists in itself and does not need another thing in which to inhere in order to exist; the thing in which accidents exist as in a support; that being which subsists in itself and not in another. (Cf. Accidents.)

**Suburbicarian Diocese** (sŭb′ûr·bĭ·kâr′ĭ·ăn), adj. & n.; L. One of the dioceses immediately surrounding the city of Rome; there are eight such dioceses.

**Succentor** (sŭk·sĕn′tēr), n.; L. The synagoga; the one chanting or singing those portions of the Gospel story of the Passion which are spoken by the crowd or other persons mentioned in the account. (Cf. Passion music.)

**Sudarium** (sū·dâr′ĭ·ŭm), n.; L. The shroud of Christ; sometimes referred to the cloth used by Veronica in wiping the face of Christ. Name sometimes applied to the stole.

**Suffragan (bishop)** (sŭf′ră·găn), n.; L., O.Fr. A bishop of a diocese which forms part of a province.

**Suffrage** (sŭf′rĭj), n.; L., O.Fr. An intercessory prayer generally offered for the poor souls in Purgatory.

**Suicide** (sū′ĭ·sīd), n.; L. The direct ending of one's own life; when fully deliberate, it is punished by the deprivation of ecclesiastical burial. It is a mortal sin, as are also acts dangerous to human life when voluntarily performed without a proportionate necessity.

**Suisse** (swēs), n.; Fr. A soldier in the Pope's Swiss Guard. (Cf. Guards.)

**Sulpicians** (sŭl·pĭsh'ănz), n. pl.; Fr. The society of priests founded in France at the Church of St. Sulpice in Paris by M. Olier in the seventeenth century, which is devoted to teaching in theological seminaries.

**Summa** (sŭm'mȧ), n.; L. Literally, a compendium. A text treating of theology, philosophy, or canon law; a summary of all the findings of reason.

**Sunday** (sŭn'dĭ), n.; A.S. The first day of the week which from apostolic times and from Sacred Scripture (Apoc. 1:10) became known as the "Lord's Day" and is set aside for rest and divine worship. In Latin, *Dominica*.

**Supererogation** (sū'pēr·ĕr'ō·gā'shŭn), n.; L. That which is done over and above duty or obligation. In regard to the saints, those good acts which they performed, which they need not have done, but which were done for a higher motive and usually were to benefit others.

**Superstition** (sū'pēr·stĭsh'ŭn), n.; L., O.Fr. A vice of excess in religion or in worship; the giving to a creature of honor belonging to God alone or the giving to God of a false or undue honor; such excess may be in the object to which it is attached or in the manner of showing religious honor.

**Suppedaneum** (sŭp·pē·dā'nē·ŭm), n.; L. (1) The

predella, the platform on which the altar stands. (2) The small footrest sometimes seen beneath the feet of Christ on a crucifix.

**Suppositum** (sŭ·pŏz′ĭ·tŭm), n.; L. A single complete substance of any kind whatsoever. (Cf. Substance.)

**Suppression** (sŭ·prĕsh′ŭn), n.; L. A word usually used in regard to monasteries or religious houses; it means the confiscation of properties and the disbanding of the communities.

**Surplice** (sûr′plĭs), n.; L., O.Fr. A garment, sometimes called a vestment, made of white linen or of another white cloth which is worn over the cassock by priests in the administration of sacraments; the familiar white garment, about coat length with short sleeves, which is permitted to be worn by altar boys or acolytes in serving Mass. A *superpellicium*.

Surplice

**Suspension** (sŭs·pĕn′shŭn), n.; L., O.Fr. The ecclesiastical penalty or censure imposed upon clerics forbidding them to exercise their orders or perform the functions of their office or to accept the financial support of their benefice.

**Swiss Guard,** n. Soldiers in a group each of whom must be a native Swiss. Their duty is to guard the Vatican City, the doors of the palaces and the Pope's apartments, and to be in attendance at all papal functions in the papal chapel. (Cf. Guards.)

**Syllabus** (sĭl′*à*·bŭs), n.; L. The digest or list of errors which Pope Pius IX condemned and which was printed and circulated at his command in December of 1864; also that of Pius X, entitled "*Lamentabile*," of July 3, 1907, against modernism; the name applied to such a digest made by a Pope and promulgated by him.

**Symbol** (sĭm′bŭl), n.; Gr. (1) An act or representation by which a thing or person is known. (2) The word symbol is also applied to the Creed or to the scientific exposition of doctrinal differences among various religious groups, especially after the sixteenth century.

Early symbol of the Trinity. (Cf. 1 of definition.)

**Symbolism** (sĭm′bŭl·ĭz′m), n.; Gr., L. The picturing of a thing by simile or metaphor rather than by the actual representation of that thing or event; an interior meaning attached to a particular representation of a religious character; visibly representing spiritual things.

**Synagoga** (sĭn′*à*·gō′g*à*), n.; Gr., L. The title of the singer who chants the words of persons other than Christ in Passion music. (Cf. Passion music.)

**Synaxis** (sĭ·năk′sĭs), n.; Gr. The gathering together of the early Christians for worship; any assembly for hearing Mass or praying in common. Also a feast day in the Byzantine rite.

**Syncellus**, n.; L. At one time the name applied to the priest companion of a bishop or one who lived in the bishop's home and served him as secretary.

**Syndic** (sĭn'dĭk), n.; Gr., L. Today this term is applied to an agent or representative of a religious community; one representing a community.

**Synod** (sĭn'ŭd), n.; Gr., L. A gathering of the bishop and priests of a diocese to determine legislation for the diocese or to apply the canon law to the particular needs of the diocese.

**Synodal Examiners** (sĭn'ŭd·ăl), adj. & n. pl.; Gr., L. A group of priests, usually four to twelve in number, appointed at a diocesan synod who test the qualifications of those to be given benefices or other church offices within the diocese.

**Synodal Judges,** n. pl.; Gr., L. See Judges, synodal.

**Synodaticum,** n.; Gr., L. The fee paid by each parish to the bishop of the diocese for his maintenance, so named because it is customary to pay it in synod. More frequently called cathedraticum.

**Synoptics** (sĭ·nŏp'tĭkz), n. pl.; Gr., L. The name given to the first three Gospels, namely the accounts of Matthew, Mark, and Luke, and so named because they all outline the life and teaching of Jesus in a relatively similar manner.

**Synoptists** (sĭ·nŏp'tĭstz), n. pl.; Gr., L. The first three Evangelists, namely, Matthew, Mark, and Luke; the writers of the synoptic Gospels.

**Synteresis** (sĭn'tĕr·ē'sĭs), n.; Gr. Sometimes, synderesis. The natural knowledge of moral law possessed by man; sometimes the interpretation of conscience. In theology, the habitual knowledge of the prime principles of moral actions; knowledge one has naturally of the natural Law of God; the apprehension by the intellect of the general moral principles from which practical reason draws its particular conclusions.

# ✢ T ✢

**Tabernacle** (tăb′ēr·năk″l), n.; L., O.Fr. The small compartment sealed by a door at the center of the main altar wherein the Eucharist is reserved. On a liturgical altar the tabernacle is covered by the canopy. (Cf. Altar.)

**Tabernacle Veil,** n. The conopaeum. The veil prescribed by the Ritual in the strictest terms as a covering for the entire tabernacle in which the Blessed Sacrament is reserved. Its presence is certain indication of the Real Presence.

*Tabernacle*

**Tabula** (tăb′ū·là), n.; L. The wooden clapper, used instead of a bell, to give signals on Holy Thursday and Good Friday; a crotalum.

**Tametsi** (tă·mĕt′sĭ), n.; L. The opening word of the decree of the Council of Trent which declared clandestine marriages invalid; the name by which this decree is usually known. It declared null any marriage attempted other than before the parish priest or bishop or one delegated by either of them, with the exception only of places where priests were not available. It was binding only where the laws of the Council of Trent were promulgated. At present the ruling has been extended to the entire world by the *Ne Temere* decree of Pius X, issued April 19, 1908.

**Tantum Ergo,** L. Literally: "All therefore—" The first two words of the second last stanza of the hymn *Pange Lingua*, the last two stanzas of which form a prescribed Benediction hymn in the Church; the name by which the Benediction hymn is popularly known. (Cf. Foreign phrases in the Appendix.)

**Te Deum** (tē dē′ŭm), n.; L. A hymn of praise and thanksgiving usually sung at the close of the services on occasions of great joy, feast days, etc. (Cf. Foreign phrases in the Appendix.)

**Telaria** (tē·lâr′ĭ·a), n.; L. A rigid form or a crossbar to which the frontal or antependium of the altar is attached.

**Temperance** (tĕm′pēr·ăns), n.; L. The cardinal virtue which helps one to restrain or moderate the desires for what appeals to the senses. The word is particularly applied to total abstinence from strong drink; the movement for moderation or abstinence from intoxicating liquors.

**Templars** (tĕm′plērz), n. pl.; L., O.Fr. The Poor Knights of the Temple, a military religious order founded in the twelfth century for the performing of certain acts of charity; religious knights.

**Temporals** (těm'pō·rălz), n. pl.; L. Those things pertaining to the temporal or secular concern of the Church as support or revenue; the temporalities. (Cf. Spirituals.)

**Temptation** (těmp·tā'shŭn), n.; L. The solicitation to sin from an external or interior cause; the seduction of the will of man to commit a sin, which may come from the devil, from another human being or from man's own concupiscence.

**Tenebrae** (těn'ē·brē), n. pl.; L. The solemn service which is celebrated on the evenings of Wednesday, Thursday, and Friday of Holy Week during which there are chanted the matins and lauds of the Divine Office of Holy Thursday, Good Friday, and Holy Saturday. Literally translated, the word means darkness and the ceremony is symbolical of the sorrow of those days.

**Tepidity** (tē·pĭd'ĭ·tĭ), n.; L. Lack of spiritual fervor; a half-hearted attention to spiritual concerns.

**Terce** (tûrs), n.; L. Tierce. The third of the canonical hours in the Divine Office; an hour of the Breviary.

**Terna** (tûr'nȧ), n.; L., It. The group of three names given by a chapter of canons to the Pope recommending members of the clergy worthy of the episcopate.

**Tertian** (tûr'shăn), n. or adj.; L. A Jesuit after his two years of novitiate, during his third year of probation after he is ordained priest and has completed his studies.

**Tertiaries** (tûr′shĭ·ĕr′ĭz), n. pl.; L. Members of the third order founded by St. Francis of Assisi; lay members who have submitted themselves to the third order rule of St. Francis. Members of any third order group of religious.

**Testament** (tĕs′tá·mĕnt), n.; L., Bib. The old and new divisions of the Bible; a written record of great authority. (Cf. Old and New Testaments.) The word came to be applied to the Bible by a mistranslation of the Greek word διαθ′ηκη, a last will, which was used for rendering the Hebrew word for "covenant."

**Tester** (tĕs′tēr), n.; L. The form of baldaquin found in early English churches which was made of wood, paneled or flat surfaced, with a carved cornice. (Cf. Baldaquin.)

**Thabor** (tā′bēr), n.; Heb. Also Tabor. The traditional "high mountain" where the Transfiguration took place; it is in Palestine a few miles southeast of Nazareth.

**Thaborstand** (tā′bēr·stănd), n.; Heb., A.S. A small movable platform on which the monstrance is placed during exposition of the Blessed Sacrament; a throne.

**Thaumaturgus** (thô′má·tûr′gŭs), n.; Gr. Literally: wonder-worker. A title now given to a saint who performed many miracles during his life. It was first applied to St. Gregory, Bishop of Neocaesarea.

**Theatines** (thē′á·tĭnz), n. pl.; Gr., L. A congregation of regular clerics founded by St. Cajetan in 1528.

**Theism** (thē′ĭz'm), n.; Gr. Acknowledgment of the

existence of a personal and provident God. (Cf. Theodicy.)

**Theocracy** (thē·ŏk′rá·sĭ), n.; Gr. The civil governing of a people directly by God through representatives; a state where civil and religious governance is the same.

**Theodicy** (thē·ŏd′ĭ·sĭ), n.; Gr. The knowledge of God by human reason; natural theology. Natural theology as a branch of philosophy having for its object God, as knowable by reason; special metaphysics. (Cf. Metaphysics.)

**Theological Virtues** (thē′ŏ·lŏj′ĭ·kăl), adj. & n. pl.; Gr. Faith, hope, and charity, so called because they have God for their immediate object; they are supernatural virtues because they tend toward God as man's supernatural end.

**Theologian** (thē′ŏ·lō′jĭ·ăn), n.; Gr. (1) One learned in any particular branch of theology. (2) One learned in the science of theology. (3) A student of theology.

**Theologus** (thē·ŏl′ŏ·gŭs), n.; Gr. (L.) A lecturer in theology or Scripture.

**Theology** (thē·ŏl′ŏ·jĭ), n.; Gr. The science of religious truths which is the systematic presentation of these truths; that science which treats of the revelations of God and man's rational concepts of God and which works toward a more clear expression of these revelations and concepts; it is the science of faith; it is a discipline based on revelation and advancing by means of that revelation; it is a science which, starting from the principles of faith, treats of God and of whatever in any way pertains to Him. Theology proper is divided into dogmatic, moral, mystical, and ascetical theology.

**Theophany** (thē·ŏf′á·nĭ), n.; Gr., L. Appearances or visions of God to man or the direct communication of God with man. The apparitions of God to man, usually as recorded in Genesis where God appeared visibly to man as Lawgiver, Judge, and Prophet. They taught man that there was only one God and that God Himself was speaking to man.

**Theophoric** (thē′ō·fŏr′ĭk), adj.; Gr. (1) God-bearing; bearing witness to God. (2) A procession in which the Blessed Sacrament is carried in a monstrance, unveiled.

**Theotocus** (thē·ō·tŏk′ŭs), n.; Gr. Literally the word means God-bearing and is used in regard to the Blessed Virgin who bore not only the man Jesus but the Son of God, the second Person of the Blessed Trinity.

**Third Order** (thûrd), num. adj. & n.; A.S. A religious rule and way of life interpreted for and made applicable to members of the laity and the secular clergy so that they may enjoy the fruits of a religious life; a religious rule or order taking its membership from the laity; tertiary.

**Thomism** (tō′mĭz’m), n. The system and interpretation of scholastic philosophy and theology which follows the teaching of St. Thomas Aquinas; the Thomistic system of scholastic philosophy and theology.

**Thomist** (tō′mĭst), n. & adj. One who follows the system of scholastic philosophy and theology of St. Thomas Aquinas; frequently applied to a neo-scholastic philosopher.

**Throne** (thrōn), n.; Gr., L., O.Fr. (1) The seat of a bishop, generally in the sanctuary of his cathedral. (2) An elevated platform for the exposition of the Blessed Sacrament; a thaborstand which may be permanent.

**Thrones** (thrōnz), n. pl.; Gr., L., O.Fr. One of the nine choirs of angels. (Cf. Angel.)

**Thurible** (thū′rĭ·b′l), n.; Gr., L. A censer; a vessel shaped like a bowl and usually supported on chains, in which incense is burned.

**Thurifer** (thū′rĭ·fẽr), n.; Gr., L. The acolyte or minister who tends the thurible in religious ceremonies.

A thurible

**Tiara** (tĭ·ār′á), n.; Gr., L. A round three-crowned headpiece about 15 inches high, worn by the Pope and signifying his sovereignty as the head of the Church.

**Tierce** (tērs), n.; L., O.Fr. Terce. One of the canonical hours of the Divine Office.

**Tithes** (tīthz), n. pl.; A.S. At present, that part of one's income or substance given to the support of the Church; formerly, a tenth part of the fruits or profits to be given to the Church.

Tiara

**Titular Bishop** (tĭt′ū·lẽr), adj. & n.; L. One who has been made a bishop, having the title of an ancient but now extinct diocese where once the faith flourished but where now there are few or no Catholics. (Cf. *In partibus infidelium* in the section on foreign phrases in the appendix.)

**Titulus** (tĭt'ū·lŭs), n.; L. (1) One of the quasi-parochial churches of Rome established in the fourth century. (2) The titular church of a cardinal. (3) A title or superscription.

**Tobias** (tō·bī'ăs), n.; Heb.; Bib. A book of the Old Testament; the name of the father and son whose story is related in this book.

**Toleration** (tŏl'ēr·ā'shŭn), n.; L. In canonical language, neither the approval nor disapproval of an act; permitting one to follow a planned course of action, usually given in Latin as, *Tolerari potest*, "It can be tolerated."

**Toleratus** (tŏl'ēr·à·tŭs), n.; L. Name given to an excommunicated person whose penalty permits the faithful to associate with him. (Cf. Excommunication, Vitandus.)

**Tonale** (tō·nä'lā), n.; It. The compilation of the right tone and ending for the singing of the psalms of the Divine Office; there are eight such modes.

**Tonsure** (tŏn'shēr), n.; Gr., L. A sacramental by which a man is raised from the lay to the clerical state. The shaving of the crown of the head, usually in the form of a circle, given as a mark of the rank of cleric in the Church; the clipping of the hair to symbolize that one has been raised to the clerical state. (Cf. Corona.)

**Torah** (tō'rä), n.; Heb.; Bib. Literally: instruction.

The revelation of God to the Israelites, particularly that contained in the Pentateuch, the first five books of the Old Testament.

**Touriѐre** (tōōr′ĭ-ĕr), n.; Fr. The sister who tends the portal or revolving door through which gifts or alms are given to a convent.

**Toussaint** (tōō-săn′), n.; Fr. The French for All Saints' Day, Nov. 1.

**T.P.**, abbre. The first letters of the Latin words *Tempore Paschale* meaning, literally, "in the paschal season" or the time of Eastertide.

**T.Q.**, abbre. The first letters of the Latin words *Toties quoties*, which mean "as often as"; used in regard to indulgences which can be gained as often as the conditions are fulfilled.

**Tract** (trăkt), n.; L. Passages of Sacred Scripture read after the Gradual, or sung by the choir, in all Masses from Septuagesima to Holy Saturday, on ember days, some vigils, and in requiem Masses.

**Tractarianism** (trăk·târ′ĭ·ăn·ĭz'm), n.; L. The principles and practices of the Oxford Movement of England begun in 1833.

**Tradition** (tră·dĭsh′ŭn), n.; L., O.Fr. The handing down by word of mouth from generation to generation doctrine or truths of the faith which were not written; the testimony of early nonscriptural writings and customs by which are known the various practices, the truths of faith, the moral teaching of Christianity, and facts of the life and times of Christ; teaching of the Church transmitted orally which has been proclaimed to be correct and free from error in being handed down; a source of revelation or of faith.

**Traditionalism** (tră·dĭsh′ŭn·ăl·ĭz′m), n.; L., O.Fr. The philosophical system which reduces all belief in the truths of religion to the direct revelation of God, received through tradition by means of language; a system of thought opposed to the rationalistic approach which holds that one acquires knowledge and instruction revealed to the first parents and handed down by them to all men.

**Traditores** (trăd′ĭ·tŏr′ĕs), n. pl.; L. Those Christians who during the Diocletian persecution became traitors by surrendering sacred books and vessels or by revealing the names of other Christians.

**Transept** (trăn′sĕpt), n.; L. The cross arms of a cruciform church. It is located between and to the sides of the choir and nave. Also called the confessional.

**Transfiguration** (trăns·fĭg′ū·rā′shŭn), n.; L., O.Fr. (1) The appearance of Christ in the glory of His divinity on Mount Tabor. (2) The feast commemorating this event on August 6.

**Transitus** (trăn′sĭ·tŭs), n.; L. A death; a service commemorating a death, especially of a saint.

**Translation** (trăns·lā′shŭn), n.; L. (1) Removal of a saint's relics from one place to another; on the anniversary of such transference the saint's feast is sometimes observed. (2) Postponement to another day of a feast which falls on the same day as another feast which is of higher rank. (3) The official transfer of a bishop from one diocese to another.

**Transubstantiation** (trăn′sŭb·stăn·shĭ·ā′shŭn), n.; L.

The changing of bread and wine into the Body and Blood of our Lord; the changing of one substance into another substance while retaining the accidents of the former thing.

**Trappists** (trăp′ĭsts), n. pl.; Fr. Cistercian monks who follow the reformed constitutions of La Trappe, a monastery in France. The reform was ordered by the abbot, Jean de Rancé, in 1664, and imposed strict silence, abstinence from meat the year around, and other mortifications.

**Trent** (trĕnt), n.; Fr. A council of the Church which derives its name from Trent, a city in Italy, where it was held. The sessions of this council began in 1545 and ended in 1563. It is known as the great Council of the Reformation. (Cf. Appendix: Ecumenical Councils.)

**Trental** (trĕn′tăl), n.; Fr. A series of thirty Masses said on consecutive days for the repose of the soul of a deceased person; more familiarily known as the Gregorian Masses.

**Tre Ore** (trāy ôr′ē), n.; L., Fr. Literally, three hours. A devotion, not prescribed, commemorating the three hours' agony of Christ on the cross, held from twelve noon to three o'clock on Good Friday.

**Triangle** (trī′ăng′g'l), n.; L., O.Fr. Name applied to the tenebrae hearse; the triangular candle rack used during tenebrae. (Cf. Hearse, 2.)

**Tricerion** (trī-sē′rĭ-ŏn), n.; Gr. Candlesticks having three lights which signify the Trinity. Also, trikerion.

**Tridentine** (trī-dĕn′tĭn), adj.; L. Of or pertaining to

the city, Trent, of Italy, or the ecumenical council of Trent.

**Triduum** (trĭd'ū·ŭm), n.; L. The preparation for a great feast day made for three days during which special prayers or devotions are offered. (Cf. *Triduum Sacrum* in Appendix I.)

**Trination** (trī·nā'shŭn), n.; L. Celebration of three Masses by a priest on the days permitted, the feast of All Souls and Christmas, or on holydays of obligation by special privilege in case of necessity.

**Trinitarians** (trĭn·ĭ·târ'ĭ·ănz), n. pl.; L. A religious order of brothers and priests founded in Rome in the twelfth century by St. John of Matha, under the title, The Order of the Holy Trinity. The members now engage in teaching and nursing.

**Trinity** (trĭn'ĭ·tĭ), n.; L. The three Persons in one God. The mystery whereby God, while being numerically one, exists in three divine Persons; the existence of the divine essence in three Persons, which Persons are distinct from each other and yet identical with the divine essence.

**Triple Candlestick** (trĭp''l), adj. n.; L., Fr. A candlestick so formed that three separate candles arise from one base. It is used in the liturgy of Holy Saturday and from it the Paschal candle is lighted; a single candle bearing three lights.

**Triptych** (trĭp'tĭk), n.; Gr. A three-leaved tablet with hinged leaves on which names of those offering

A triptych

intentions were inscribed. Sometimes these were highly ornamented and used as decorative panels on altars or church walls. (Cf. Diptychs.)

**Trisagion** (trĭs·ăg'ĭ·ŏn), n.; Gr. The brief hymn of three references or statements declaring the holiness of God. It is sung in both Latin and Greek in the Latin rite at the adoration of the Cross on Good Friday, and in English is: O holy God; O holy strong One; O holy immortal One, have mercy upon us.

**Triune** (trī'ūn), adj.; L. Literally, three in one. Said of God, there being the three Persons of the Blessed Trinity in the one God. (Cf. Trinity.)

**Trope** (trōp), n.; Gr., L., Fr. Literally, a turn of speech. The addition of clauses or long passages of notations in the singing of the Kyrie or Introit at High Mass.

**Tropology** (trŏ·pŏl'ŏ·jĭ), n.; Gr., L. The interpretation of the figurative language of sacred writings.

**Truce (of God)** (troos), n.; A.S. A law and custom in the Middle Ages which forbade all war and individual fighting between the times of Thursday evening to Sunday evening and during the seasons of Advent and Lent and all festival days.

**Tunic** (tū'nĭk), n.; L., Fr. The vestment worn by the subdeacon and proper to him, corresponding to the dalmatic and usually of the same color as the vestment worn by the celebrant; also called tunicle.

**Tutiorism** (tū'shĭ·ŏr·ĭz'm), n.; L. The system of moral theology which teaches that acts must be done according to the law unless the opinion in favor of the contrary is certain or at least most probable; a rigoristic doctrine, which in its extreme form has been condemned by the Church.

**Type** (tīp), n.; Gr., L. Person, thing, action, or event of the Old Testament which foreshadowed or pointed to the future or to an occurrence which was to be recorded in the New Testament.

# ☦ U ☦

**Unction** (ŭngk′shŭn), n.; L. The act of anointing. An oil for anointing; a name usually applied to the Oil of the Sick, *oleum infirmorum*, used in the sacrament of Extreme Unction.

**Uniat** (ū′nĭ·ăt), n.; L. Erroneously used as name for a Catholic belonging to one of the Eastern rites. The term is in disrepute and should not be used.

**Unigenitus** (ū′nĭ·jĕn′ĭ·tŭs), n.; L. Literally, one begotten or singly born. The Latin word applied to Jesus who was the only-begotten Son of God the Father.

**Unity** (ū′nĭ·tĭ), n.; L., O.Fr. (1) Oneness; indivision. (2) Said of God because only *one* can possess in utter simplicity the fullness of all goodness and all perfection, one Being without limitation. (3) One of the marks of the Church, because all its members, according to the will of Christ, profess the same faith, practice the same form of worship, and are joined under the Holy Father, the Pope, as the Vicar of Christ on earth and the head of the Church.

**Unleavened** (ŭn·lĕv′ĕnd), adj.; L., O.Fr. Without yeast. Used with reference to the bread from which the hosts to be consecrated during the Mass are made.

**Unliturgical** (ŭn′lĭ·tûr′jĭ·kăl), adj.; Gr., L. Some phase or aspect of public worship which in some way is contrary to the liturgical prescriptions of the Church.

**Ursulines** (ûr′sū·lĭnz), n. pl.; L., Fr. An order of nuns founded at Brescia, Italy, in 1537 by St. Angela Merici. The nuns devote themselves to the education of girls.

**Usury** (ū′zhoo·rĭ), n.; L., O.Fr. The gain or profit made from the lending of money; the lending of capital at interest, particularly an excessive interest. Today, in its more common use, the word has come to mean the unjust gain made by a loan of money.

**Utraquism** (ū′trȧ·kwĭz′m), n.; L. Communion under both species of bread and wine.

# ✠ V ✠

**Vagi** (vā′gī), n. pl.; L. Vagrants, wanderers, those with no domicile or quasi-domicile. They are bound to observe both the general and particular laws in force in the place where they find themselves.

**Valid** (văl′ĭd), adj.; L., Fr. Founded on truth or fact; in Church law, that which conforms to conditions essential to the efficacy of a sacrament; that is, the proper rite in administration, the intention and jurisdiction of the minister, and the moral fitness and intention of the recipient.

**Validation** (văl′ĭ·dā′shŭn), n.; L., Fr. The legal process or ecclesiastical action which rectifies an irregular marriage which is null because of defect of consent or one or another canonical impediment.

**Validity** (vå·lĭd′ĭ·tĭ), n.; L., Fr. The quality of being valid; that which fulfills all essential conditions.

**Vatican** (văt′ĭ·kăn), n.; L. The independent city and state within the city of Rome which is the seat of the Church, where the Pope resides and where the household of the Vatican lives; the entire group of buildings surrounding the residence of the Pope. The name by which the Council of the Vatican held in December of 1869 is known.

**Veil** (vāl), n.; L., Fr. (1) The long vestment worn by the celebrant at Benediction of the Blessed Sacrament, which is placed upon his shoulders and the ends of which he uses to hold the monstrance in his hands; the humeral veil; also called by its Latin name, *velum*. (2) A covering of the head and shoulders used by members of religious orders of women.

**Velatio** (vĕ·lá′sĭ·ô), n.; L. An ancient rite performed at the consecration of virgins to a life of religion. It would correspond today to the religious profession of nuns. (Obs.)

**Velleity** (vĕ·lē′ĭ·tĭ), n.; L. A desire of the mind which is not fully willed; a weak desire or one with incomplete volition.

**Velum** (vēl′ŭm), n.; L. The humeral veil; the scarf-like vestment worn over the shoulders of the celebrant at Benediction of the Blessed Sacrament.

**Venerable** (vĕn′ēr·à·b'l), adj. & n.; L. A title given to one whose cause for canonization is being advanced; a title of sanctity; a title of address applied to nuns and lay brothers.

**Veneration** (vĕn′ēr·ā′shŭn), n.; L. The admiration of, the imitation of, and prayer to the saints which is given to them by men because of their great sanctity, their supernatural excellence as the friends and familiars of God. (Cf. Dulia.)

**Venia** (vĕn′ĭ·å), n.; L. The act of satisfaction performed by a religious after the commission of a venial fault.

**Venial Sin** (vē′nĭ·ăl), adj.; L., O.Fr. An offense against God in a light matter or without full consent of the will which does not destroy grace or friendship with God or the right to eternal happiness, but is a partial or small aversion from God; venial sin may be so slight that it is called a venial fault rather than a sin. (Cf. Sin.)

**Vernicle** (vûr′nĭ·k′l), n.; L. Name sometimes given to the veil of Veronica or a representation of it.

**Verse** (vûrs), n.; L., A.S. (1) A subdivision of a chapter of the Bible or of a psalm or canticle. (2) During Mass, a sentence said by the priest to which a response is given. It may be sung with the choir giving the response. A versicle. (3) The solo portion of the Gradual of the Mass when it is sung.

**Versicle** (vûr′sĭ·k′l), n.; L. A prayer, usually brief, which is followed by a response. It is indicated by the symbol ℣.

**Vesperal** (vĕs′pĕr·ăl), n.; L. Latin: *Vesperale*. A book containing the office and music for Vespers throughout the year.

**Vesperal (cloth),** n.; L. The cloth used to cover the mensa when it is not in use so as to prevent soiling of the altar linens. Also called *stragulum*.

**Vespers** (vĕs′pĕrz), n. pl.; L. (1) The sixth canonical hour of the Breviary. (2) The devotion consisting of the public recitation of the Vesper hour of the

Breviary by the choir and the ministers of the service, during which incensing of the altar is performed.

**Vessels** (vĕs″lz), n. pl.; L., O.Fr. The various receptacles used in the ceremonies of divine service in the Church; usually they are made of gold or are gold-plated and are either consecrated or blessed. (Cf. Chalice; ciborium.)

**Vestibule** (vĕs′tĭ·būl), n.; L., Fr. An enclosed entrance. The back part of a church, usually just within the door and immediately before the door entering the main part of the church or the nave.

**Vestiges** (vĕs′tĭj·ĕz), n. pl.; L. Beings not having reason and so not made to the image and likeness of God; yet they reflect God because of His act of creating them.

**Vestments** (vĕst′mĕnts), n. pl.; L., O.Fr. The garments worn by the priest in celebrating the Mass or other acts of divine worship; the official garb or liturgical dress of priests and bishops in offering the divine sacrifice.

**Veto** (vē′tō), n.; L. An authoritative prohibition. The right formerly claimed by rulers or governments to prevent a particular cardinal or other candidate from receiving papal election because he was considered not acceptable. This has been canceled and is no longer permitted.

**Viaticum** (vĭ·ăt′ĭ·kŭm), n.; L. Holy Communion or the Eucharist, given to persons in danger of death. Originally the word was applied to food taken on a journey. The Viaticum may be received without fasting, and may be repeated during the time of the same illness.

**Vicar Apostolic** (vĭk′ēr), adj. & n.; L., O.Fr. A cleric, usually a titular bishop, who governs a territory not yet established as a diocese. (Cf. Vicariate Apostolic.)

**Vicar Capitular,** n.; L. The canon chosen by the chapter to administer a diocese during the period of vacancy caused by the death of the bishop.

**Vicar Forane,** n.; L. A rural dean; a senior priest entrusted with vigilance over Church discipline in the several parishes which constitute the deanery; he has the power of summoning and presiding at meetings of the clergy of this district.

**Vicar General,** n.; L. An official of a diocese appointed by the bishop and holding ordinary jurisdiction with the bishop; an assistant to the bishop, his jurisdiction is coterminous with the reign of the bishop. (Cf. Bishop.)

**Vicariate Apostolic** (vī·kâr′ĭ·āt), n.; L. An ecclesiastical district in a missionary country presided over by a vicar apostolic who is appointed by the Pope.

**Vigil** (vĭj′ĭl), n.; L., O.Fr. Originally this meant a watch in prayer and fasting kept on the night before a feast; later it included the day before the feast; a time of preparation for a feast; the day immediately preceding a feast day. It is also applied to the custom of watching over the bodies of the dead before burial; a wake.

**Vimpa** (vĭm′pà), n.; L. A veil of silk worn over the shoulders and down the arms of the acolytes who carry the mitre and the pastoral staff at a Pontifical Mass.

**Vincentians** (vĭn·sĕn′shănz), n. pl.; Fr. Members of the society of St. Vincent de Paul, a charitable organization founded by Frederic Ozanam in 1833 to care for the poor and administer to the sick. Also a name applied to the members of the Congregation of the Mission, or Lazarist Fathers.

**Violation** (vī′ō·lā′shŭn), n.; L., O.Fr. The act whereby a church, oratory, or cemetery is deprived of its consecration through the commission of one of the public crimes stated in Church law, such as murder.

**Virgin Birth** vûr′jĭn bûrth), n.; L., O.Fr. The miraculous bearing of Christ, the Son of God, by Mary while she, by divine intervention, remained a virgin.

**Virginity** (vĕr·jĭn′ĭ·tĭ) n.; L. The highest state of chastity; the state in which one avoids all indulgence in sexual acts; the state of being physically a virgin.

**Virtue** (vûr′tū), n.; L., O.Fr. (1) An essentially good habit giving one the power and the inclination to do good acts; briefly, a habit of right conduct. There are three classes of virtues: intellectual, moral, and theological. (Cf. Cardinal Virtues and Theological Virtues.) (2) In the plural, one of the choirs of angels. (Cf. Angel.)

**Vision** (vĭzh′ŭn), n.; L., O.Fr. The actual appearance of God or angels or saints, or also the devil, to living persons.

**Visit** (vĭz'ĭt), n.; L., O.Fr. (1) The practice or devotion of spending some time each day in prayer before the Blessed Sacrament; also the practice of going into a church whenever one chances to be near a church to pray before the Blessed Sacrament. (2) The periodic visit of a bishop to the Pope in the Vatican. (Cf. Visitation; *Ad limina*.)

**Visitation** (vĭz'ĭ·tā'shŭn), n.; L. (1) The journey of the Blessed Virgin to Elizabeth, the mother of John the Baptist, and her prolonged stay with Elizabeth. (2) Episcopal visitation: the obligation the bishop has to visit all parishes in his diocese every five years. (3) Visitation *ad limina:* the obligation which rests upon all bishops ruling a diocese to visit at prescribed periods of time, usually five or ten years, the tombs of the Apostles Peter and Paul in Rome and the Supreme Pontiff. This is also known simply as the *ad limina* visit.

**Visitatrix** (vĭz'ĭ·tā'trĭks), n.; L. The designated title of the sister or nun to whom is entrusted the duty of periodically visiting the several houses belonging to a religious community.

**Vitandus** (vĭ·tăn'dŭs), n.; L. An excommunicated person whose penalty demands that he be shunned or avoided by the faithful.

**Vitta** (vĭt'*à*), n.; pl. vittae.; L. Literally: a ribbon. One of the two pendants hanging from the back of a mitre. (Cf. Infula.)

**Vocation** (vō·kā'shŭn), n.; L. The calling or the disposition by which a person is inclined to serve God in a special state such as the priesthood or as a member of a religious order; the strong inclination or desire to serve God in a special manner. The elements of a vocation are: (*a*) the right intention to avoid all sins and to secure one's salvation; (*b*) freedom from impediments; (*c*) admission or call, by the superior of the order or the bishop. Also used in general to denote any calling in life, e.g., the vocation of marriage.

**Votive Mass** (vō′tĭv), adj.; L. A Mass which does not correspond to the office of a particular day but is said at the choice of the priest; the reading of a Mass not assigned to a particular day. (Cf. Mass.)

**Votive Offerings,** adj. & n. pl.; L. Objects dedicated to God or His saints; contributions dedicated to a particular devotion.

**Votive Office,** adj.; L. The reading of an office by the priest which was not prescribed for a particular day. Since 1911 such votive offices have been abolished.

**Vow** (vou), n.; L., O.Fr. A deliberate, free promise made to God by which one obligates himself under pain of sin by the virtue of religion to the performance of some act more pleasing to God than its opposite. Public vows are either solemn or simple. Solemn vows invalidate any act against the vows; simple vows merely forbid or render unlawful any act against the vows.

**Vulgate** (vŭl′gāt), n.; L. A Latin version of the Bible made up of a translation by St. Jerome in the fourth century of the protocanonical books of the Old

Testament and of a few of the deuterocanonical books, and a revision of all the other books of the Old and New Testaments, and recognized by the Church as an authentic and authorized version.

# ☩ W ☩

**Wake** (wāk), n.; Scand. The vigil or watch kept before the burial of a person.

**Whitefriars** (hwīt′frī′ērz), n. pl. (and sing.); A.S., O.Fr. (1) Name formerly applied to the Carmelites. (2) A Carmelite monastery in Fleet Street, London, till 1538 from which the vicinity derived its name.

**Whitsunday** (hwĭt′sŭn′dĭ), n.; A.S. Literally, White Sunday, a name applied to Pentecost or the feast of Pentecost.

**Wimple** (wĭm′p'l), n.; A.S. The linen or silk covering placed in folds about the neck, chin, and sides of the face, and worn by sisters or nuns of certain religious communities.

**Wisdom** (wĭz′dŭm), n.; A.S. (1) A book of the Old Testament written in the first century before Christ by an unknown author. (Cf. Books of Wisdom.) (2) One of the seven gifts of the Holy Ghost.

**Witchcraft** (wĭch′kráft), n.; A.S. The art of doing

things or performing certain feats which have the appearance of being supernatural but which are done without the aid of God; the power of doing unnatural things by aid of the evil spirit; trafficking with the devil or evil spirits; the casting of spells, curses, incantations to the devil, etc.

**Works (of Mercy)** (wûrkz), n. pl.; A.S. Meritorious deeds of Christian charity performed in the service of one's neighbor to relieve his needs of body or of soul. (*a*) Corporal works of mercy: to feed the hungry, to give drink to the thirsty, to clothe the naked, to shelter the homeless, to visit the sick, to visit the imprisoned, and to bury the dead. (*b*) Spiritual works of mercy: to counsel the doubtful, to instruct the ignorant, to admonish the sinner, to comfort the sorrowful, to forgive injuries, to bear wrongs patiently, and to pray for the living and the dead.

**Worship** (wûr′shĭp), n.; A.S. Honor shown to anyone because of superior excellence. Divine worship is the adoration of and prayer to God whereby we honor Him because of His infinite excellence. Veneration is the honor given to saints because of their great excellence. (Cf. Latria, Dulia, and Hyperdulia.)

✢ X ✢

---

**Xaverian Brothers** (ză·vēr′ĭ·ăn), n.; Fr. A religious order of teachers founded in 1839 at Bruges, Belgium, by Theodore James Ryken. Their chief work is teaching.

**Xerophagy** (zē·rŏf′à·jĭ), n.; Gr. Literally: dry food. A strict fast which permits only bread, salt, certain fruits and vegetables, and water.

✢ Y ✢

---

**Yule** (yo͞ol), n.; A.S. A name referring to Christmas, used among the early peoples of England.

**Yuletide** (yo͞ol′tīd), n.; A.S. The Christmas season or Christmastide.

# ✠ Z ✠

**Zacharias** (zăk′*a*·rī′*a*s), n.; Heb., Gr. The Greek form of the Hebrew name Zechariah, and the title of a prophetical book of the Old Testament.

**Zeal** (zēl), n.; L., O.Fr. The active and ardent pursuit of an objective; perseverance in doing good for the promotion of God's glory.

**Zelator** (zĕl′*a*·tēr), n.; L., Fr. One who works for the furthering of a cause; sometimes referred to a particular nun or sister.

**Zephaniah** (zĕf′*a*·nī′*a*), n.; Heb., Bib. The Hebrew form for the name of the prophet Sophonias.

**Zimarra** (zĭ·mär′*a*), n.; It. Simar (sĭ·mär′). The black cassock with a purple cape, sash, buttons, and piping worn in the house by a bishop.

**Zucchetto** (tsook·kĕt′tō), n.; It. A skullcap worn by bishops and other prelates. Also, Berrettino; pileolus.

# APPENDIX

I Words and Phrases from Foreign Languages

II The Ecumenical Councils and Their Chief Doctrines

III Abbreviations Used in General and Among Scholars

IV List of the Popes and Dates of Their Reigns

V Titles and Terms of Address Given to Ecclesiastical Persons

# 1

# WORDS AND PHRASES FROM FOREIGN LANGUAGES*

**Ab homine** (L.), *By man*—an ecclesiastical censure imposed by a judge which can be removed only by the one who imposed it or by his superior or successor.

**Acta Apostolicae Sedis** (L.), *The Acts of the Apostolic See*—the official publication of the Holy See.

**Acta Martyrum** (L.), *The Acts of the Martyrs*—the official record of the trials and deaths of the martyrs.

**Acta Sanctae Sedis** (L.), *The Acts of the Holy See*—a Roman publication discontinued in 1909.

**Acta Sanctorum** (L.), *The Acts of the Saints*—the lives of the saints originally published in the seventeenth century.

**Actus charitatis** (L.), *Act of charity.*

**Actus contritionis** (L.), *Act of contrition.*

---

* The literal translation appears in italics after each word or phrase.

**Actus fidei** (L.), *Act of faith.*

**Actus hominis** (L.), *Act of man*—used specifically in scholastic philosophy to denote an act of a man not under direction of reason and will, as opposed to a "human act" which is under direction of reason and will.

**Actus primus** (L.), *First act*—in Thomistic writing it is that primary perfection whereby a thing is constituted in its essence or nature.

**Actus secundus** (L.), *Second act*—in Thomistic writing that perfection added to something finite for attaining its ultimate end.

**Actus spei** (L.), *Act of hope.*

**Ad hominem, argumentum** (L.), *Argument to man*—an appeal to the individual; an argument based not on the facts at issue but on the character of the one who doubts or denies them.

**Adiutorium nostrum in nomine Domini** (L.), *Our help is in the name of the Lord.*

**A divinis** (L.), *From divine functions*—a penalty which may be imposed upon clerics, depriving them of right to say Mass, etc.

**Ad libitum** (L.), *To please* or *as to please*—the expression of : (1) a choice offered on the ferial days of Lent up to Palm Sunday, the ember days (exclusive of those days within the octave of Pentecost), the Monday of the Rogation Days, etc., of saying either the Mass of the feria with a commemoration of the feast or *vice versa.* (2) A choice offered in the *Ordo* of selecting one of several orations. (3) Any free choice.

**Ad limina Apostolorum** (L.), *To the threshold of the Apostles*—the required periodic visit of bishops to the Vatican. (Cf. Visitation.)

**Ad maiorem Dei gloriam** (L.), *To the greater glory of God*—often abbreviated A.M.D.G.

**Ad nutum sanctae sedis** (L.), *At the will of the Holy See*.

**Adonai** (Heb.), *My Lord*—term used by the Jews for the word God.

**Adoro Te devote, latens Deitas** (L.), *Hidden God, devoutly I adore You*—a hymn written by St. Thomas Aquinas.

**Advocatus diaboli** (L.), *The devil's advocate*—the title, arising from a slang name, given to the Promoter of the Faith in the process of beatification or canonization.

**Aeterni Patris** (L.), *Of the eternal Father*—(1) The apostolic letter of Pius IX in 1868 calling the Vatican Council. (2) An encyclical of Leo XIII issued in 1879.

**Agios O Theos, Agios Ischyros, Agios Athanatos** (Gr.), *Oh Holy God, Holy Strong One, Holy Immortal One*—words of the trisagion recited on Good Friday.

**Agnus Dei** (L.), *Lamb of God*.

**A iure** (L.), *By law*—an ecclesiastical censure, imposed by the law itself, or opposed to a censure imposed by a superior court.

**Aleph, Beth** (Heb.), The letters *A* and *B* of the Hebrew alphabet.

**Alma redemptoris mater** (L.), *Beloved Mother of the Redeemer*—the first antiphon of the Blessed Virgin.

**Alpha, Omega** (Gr.), The first and last letters of the Greek alphabet: A. Ω. *The beginning and the end.*

**Altum dominium** (L.), *The supreme dominion.*

**Anima Christi** (L.), *Soul of Christ*—beginning of a prayer written by St. Ignatius.

**Anniversarium Eucharistiae** (L.), *Anniversary of the Eucharist*—a name sometimes applied to Maundy Thursday.

**Anno Domini** (L.), *In the year of the Lord*—abbreviated A.D.

**Aperitio aurium** (L.), *The opening of the ears*—the Latin name for that part of the Baptismal service known as the Ephpheta.

**A posteriori** (L.), *From the following*—argumentation from effects to cause, from particulars to general, reason based on induction.

**Apostolicae Curae** (L.), *Of apostolic care*—a bull of Leo XIII issued in 1896 declaring Anglican Orders invalid.

**A priori** (L.), *From the foregoing*—argumentation from general principles to particulars, the deductive system.

**Ave Maria** (L.), *Hail Mary*—first words of the prayer named the Angelical Salutation.

**Ave Regina Coelorum** (L.), *Hail, Queen of the Heavens.*

**Benedicamus Domino** (L.), *Let us bless the Lord.*

**Berrettino** (It.), *The zucchetto*.
**Bona mors** (L.), *Good death*.
**Breviarium Romanum** (L.), *The Roman Breviary*.

**Caeremoniale Episcoporum** (L.), *The ceremonial of bishops*—a liturgical book. (Cf. Ceremonial.)
**Caeremoniale Romanum** (L.), *The Roman ceremonial*.
**Calotte** (It.), *A zucchetto*.
**Cameriere Segreto** (It.) *Private servant*—title of chamberlains of the private apartments of the Pope.
**Canon sanctorum** (L.), *List of the saints*.
**Capella ardente** (It.), *The glowing chapel*—the chapel wherein the body of the deceased lies in state.
**Casus conscientiae** (L.), *A case of conscience*.
**Casus perplexus** (L.), *A perplexing case* or *a doubtful case*.
**Causae maiores** (L.), *The greater causes*.
**Censor librorum** (L.), *The censor of books*.
**Censura ab homine** (L.), *Censure by man*—an ecclesiastical censure imposed by precept, sentence, or an ecclesiastical court.
**Censura a iure** (L.), *Censure by law*—an ecclesiastical censure determined by law.
**Cessatio a divinis** (L.), *Suspension of divine services*—the stopping or forbidding of the holding of divine services in a church.
**Christe eleison** (Gr.), *Christ, have mercy*.
**Ciborium magnum** (L.), *The great ciborium*—the canopy over an altar. (Cf. Canopy.)

**Codex Iuris Canonici** (L.), *The Code of Canon Law.*

**Coena Domini** (L.), *Supper of the Lord*—Holy Thursday.

**Commune Sanctorum** (L.), *Common of the Saints*—services for feast days of saints grouped under the classes of feasts.

**Communicatio idiomatum** (L.), *The communication of attributes*—affirming the same properties of the Word and Christ the Man.

**Communicatio in sacris** (L.), *Taking part in sacred acts*—e.g., a Catholic joining in the acts of worship in a Protestant church (forbidden).

**Communio Sanctorum** (L.), *The Communion of Saints.*

**Confiteor** (L.), *I confess.*

**Congregatio Caeremoniarum** (L.), *Congregation of Ceremonies.*

**Congregatio Concilii** (L.), *Congregation of the Council.*

**Congregatio Consistorialis** (L.), *Consistorial Congregation.*

**Congregatio de Disciplina Sacramentorum** (L.), *Congregation of the Sacraments.*

**Congregatio de Negotiis Ecclesiasticis Extraordinariis** (L.), *Congregation for Extraordinary Ecclesiastical Affairs.*

**Congregatio de Propaganda Fide** (L.), *Congregation for Propagation of the Faith.*

**Congregatio de Seminariis et Universitatibus Studiorum** (L.), *Congregation of Studies for Seminaries and Universities.*

**Congregatio Negotiis Religiosorum** (L.), *Congregation of the Affairs of Religious.*

**Congregatio pro Ecclesia Orientali** (L.), *Congregation for the Oriental Church.*

**Congregatio Reverendae Fabricae S. Petri** (L.), *Congregation of the Basilica of St. Peter.*

**Congregatio Sacrorum Rituum** (L.), *Congregation of Holy Rites.*

**Congregatio Sancti Officii** (L.), *Congregation of the Holy Office.*

**Coram Cardinale, Episcopo** (L.), *In the presence of a cardinal or bishop.*

**Coram ministello** (L.), *In the presence of a minister.*

**Cor Jesu** (L.), *Heart of Jesus.*

**Corpus Christi** (L.), *Body of Christ.*

**Corpus mysticum** (L.), *The mystical body.*

**Corriere Vaticano** (It.), *Vatican Courier*—a newspaper of the Vatican State.

**Credo** (L.), *I believe*—first word of both the Apostles' and Nicene creeds.

**Credo in Deum** (L.), *I believe in God*—the opening words of the Apostles' creed.

**Credo in unum Deum** (L.), *I believe in one God*—the opening words of the Nicene creed; this creed is sung during Mass.

**Cuius regio, eius religio** (L.), *Whoever rules, his is the religion*—the principle used in northern Europe which intended that the people ruled would embrace the religion professed by the ruler.

**Cultores Sanctae Sindonis** (L.), *Protectors of the Holy Shroud*—an Italian organization for promoting the scientific and spiritual cause of the Holy Shroud of Turin.

**Cultus disparitas** (L.), *Difference of worship*—a diriment impediment to marriage.

**Curia Romana** (L.), *The Roman Court*—usually all the tribunals of the Church.

**De condigno** (L.), *Out of worthiness*.

**De congruo** (L.), *Out of suitableness*.

**Decreta Authentica Congregationis Sacrorum Rituum** (L.), *The Authentic Decrees of the Congregation of Holy Rites*.

**Decretum laudis** (L.), *Decree of praise*—the temporary decree of approval issued by the Holy See to a diocesan congregation.

**Defensor fidei** (L.), *Defender of the faith*.

**Defensor vinculi** (L.), *Defender of the bond* (of matrimony).

**De fide** (L.), *Of faith*—said ot a dogma of the Church which is revealed and must be believed.

**De haeretico comburendo** (L.), *Concerning the burning of a heretic*.

**Deo gratias** (L.), *Thanks be to God*.

**Depositum fidei** (L.), *Deposit of the faith*.

**De profundis** (L.), *Out of the depths*—opening words of Psalm 129.

**Der liturgische Choral** (Ger.), *The liturgical chant*.

**De tempore** (L.), *Of the time* or *of the season*—term

used in regard to liturgical seasons of the Church calendar.

**Deus in adiutorium meum intende** (L.), *O God, come to my assistance*—the first words of Psalm 59.

**Dies irae** (L.), *Day of wrath*—the first words of the sequence of the requiem Mass.

**Dies natalis** (L.), *Day of birth*—referred to the day of martyrdom, the day the Christian's soul went to heaven.

**Disparitas cultus** (L.), *Disparity of cult* or *worship*.

**Doctor Angelicus** (L.), *Angelic Doctor*—title of St. Thomas Aquinas.

**Domine, non sum dignus** (L.), *Lord, I am not worthy*—prayer before the Communion of the Mass.

**Dominica** (L.), *Sunday*.

**Dominica de Passione** (L.), *The Sunday of the Passion* or *Passion Sunday*—the name applied to the fifth Sunday of Lent.

**Dominica de Rosa** (L.), *The Sunday of the Rose*—the name by which Laetare Sunday, the fourth Sunday of Lent, is sometimes known.

**Dominica Hosanna** (L.), *Hosanna Sunday*—a name sometimes applied to Palm Sunday.

**Dominica in Albis** (L.), *White Sunday*—the Sunday following Easter. Also called Low Sunday. Historically, the Sunday when the newly baptized catechumens put on white garments.

**Dominica in Ramis** (L.), *Palm Sunday*—the Sunday preceding Easter.

**Dominica Resurrectionis** (L.), *Sunday of the Resurrection*—the Latin name for Easter Sunday.

**Dominus vobiscum** (L.), *The Lord be with you*—early form of salutation found in the Mass.

**Ecce Agnus Dei** (L.), *Behold the Lamb of God.*

**Ecce Agnus Dei; ecce qui tollit peccata mundi** (L.), *Behold the Lamb of God; behold Him who taketh away the sins of the world.*

**Ecce homo** (L.), *Behold the man.*

**Ecce lignum crucis** (L.), *Behold the wood of the cross*—first words of the chant sung by the priest at the unveiling of the crucifix on Good Friday.

**Ecce Panis Angelorum** (L.), *Behold the Bread of Angels.*

**Ecclesia discens** (L.), *The learning Church.*

**Ecclesia docens** (L.), *The teaching Church.*

**Ecclesia orans** (L.), *The praying Church.*

**Ephphetha** (Aramaic), *Be thou opened* (Mark 7:34).

ἐπίκλησις (Gr.), *Invocation*—used in reference to a prayer to the Holy Ghost, formerly a part of the Mass.

**Epistolarium** (L.), *An epistolary.*

**Evangelium** (L.), *The Gospel.*

**Ex cathedra** (L.), *From the throne* or *chair* (meaning the chair of St. Peter)—infallible pronouncement by the Pope.

**Ex informata conscientia** (L.), *From an informed conscience.*

**Ex opere operantis** (L.), *In virtue of the one performing* *the action*—the effect of sacramentals depending upon the minister's sanctity or the disposition of the one receiving it, or the effect of grace produced through the sacramentals.

**Ex opere operato** (L.), *In virtue of the action performed*—effect of grace of the sacrament taking place regardless of the disposition of the minister or recipient.

**Ex toto genere suo** (L.), *From its entire nature*—said of a sin which is mortal and can never be considered otherwise.

**Ex voto** (L.), *Out of a promise* or *according to one's wish*.

**Ferendae sententiae** (L.), *Sentence to be imposed*—used in reference to certain crimes that may be punished by certain censures, but only by the actual passing of sentences by a court or superior.

**Fête-Dieu** (Fr.), *Festival of God*—the feast of Corpus Christi.

**Fidei defensor** (L.), *Defender of the faith*.

**Flectamus genua** (L.), *Let us kneel down* or *bend the knee*.

**Forum competens** (L.), *The proper* or *competent court*.

**Forum ecclesiasticum** (L.), *The ecclesiastical forum* or *court*.

**Fractio panis** (L.), *The breaking of bread*.

**Frère** (Fr.), *Brother*.

**Frères des Ecoles Chrétiennes** (Fr.), *Brothers of the Christian Schools*.

**Gloria in excelsis Deo** (L.), *Glory to God in the highest*—the opening Latin words of the prayer of praise in the Mass.

**Gloria laus** (L.), *Glory and praise*—the title of a hymn composed by Theodolphy about 810 A.D. and sung during the procession on Palm Sunday.

**Gloria Patri** (L.), *Glory be to the Father*.

**Graduale Romanum** (L.), *The Roman Gradual*—book containing the chants for the Proper and Ordinary of the Mass for the year.

**Gratiae gratis datae** (L.), *Graces of extraordinary character*, literally, *graces gratuitously given*—St. Augustine's name for those graces given not for the recipient but for the salvation of others.

**Gratiae gratum facientes** (L.), *Graces making one pleasing*—(i.e., holy in the sight of God)—name given by theologians to designate the grace which is known as sanctifying grace and actual grace.

**Habemus pontificem** (L.), *We have a pope*—the formal announcement after the election of a pope.

**Hebdomada** (L.), *The week*—sometimes a single day of the week.

**Hic est enim calix Sanguinis Mei . . .** (L.), *For this is the chalice of My Blood . . .*—the first words of the consecration of the wine said in the Mass.

**Himmel, Der** (Ger.), *The heaven*—name applied to the Baldachin in German.

**Hoc est enim Corpus Meum** (L.), *For this is My Body*

—the words said at the consecration of the host in the Mass.

**Honorarium** (L.), *Gift*—a term sometimes applied to a stipend.

**Horae diurnae** (L.), *Day hours of the Breviary.*

**Hostia** (L.), *Host* or *sacrificial gift.*

**Humanum genus** (L.), *The human race*—an encyclical of Leo XIII written in 1884 condemning Freemasonry.

**Identitas mysterii** (L.), *Identity of mystery.*

**Imprimi potest** (L.), *It may be printed*—the approval to print granted by the head of a religious order to one of his members who wishes to have something he has written published.

**In articulo mortis** (L.), *At the moment of death.*

**Index Librorum Prohibitorum** (L.), *Index of Prohibited Books*—the Roman Index.

**Ineffabilis Deus** (L.), *Ineffable God*—the papal bull declaring the Immaculate Conception of the Blessed Virgin to be of faith. It was issued December 8, 1854.

**In foro externo** (L.), *In the external forum.*

**In foro interno** (L.), *In the internal forum*—the confessional, or under the seal of confession.

**In globo** (L.), *In a lump*—i.e., all together.

**In media parte altaris** (L.), *In the middle part of the altar.*

**In nomine Patris** (L.), *In the name of the Father.*

**In partibus infidelium** (L.), *In places (regions) of unbelievers.* (Cf. Titular bishop.)

**In perpetuum** (L.), *Forever.*

**In plano** (L.), *On the level.*

**In principio** (L.), *In the beginning.*

**In radice** (L.), *In the root.* (Cf. Sanatio in radice.)

**In saecula saeculorum** (L.), *For ages of ages* or *forever and ever.*

**In se** (L.), *In itself.*

**Instaurare omnia in Christo** (L.), *To restore all things in Christ.*

**Instructio Clementina** (L.), *Clementine Instruction*—the regulations of Forty Hours' Devotion of Pope Clement VIII issued in 1592.

**Instrumentum Pacis** (L.), *Instrument of Peace*—the pax-brede.

**Inter vivos** (L.), *Among the living.*

**Ipso facto** (L.), *By that very fact.*

**Ite, missa est** (L.), *Go, it is the dismissal*—the words said during the Mass by the priest to the congregation following the postcommunion.

**Iuris Canonici** (L.), *Of Canon Law.*

**Jejunia** (L.), *A fast.*

**Jeunes Ouvrière Chrétienne** (Fr.), *Young Christian Workers*—title of the organization of those belonging to the Jocist or J.O.C. movement for **Catholic Action**.

**Jeunesse Agricole Chrétienne** (Fr.), *Young Christian Rural Workers*—the title of the group of **French**

Catholic Actioners who are known as members of the Jocist movement.

**Jeunesse Ouvrière Chrétienne** (Fr.), *The Young Catholic Worker*—the name of the Jocist Movement in Canada. It is called Young Christian Workers in the United States.

**Judicium Dei** (L.), *The judgment of God*—ordeal by trial or suffering in proof of one's innocence.

**Kyrie eleison** (Gr.), *Lord, have mercy!*

**Latae sententiae** (L.), *Sentence imposed*—censure immediately incurred by the commission of a crime.

**Laudate Dominum** (L.), *Praise the Lord.*

**Laus perennis** (L.), *Endless praise.*

**Laus tibi Christe** (L.), *Praise be to Thee, O Christ.*

**Lavabo** (L.), *I will wash*—first word in the Latin version of Psalm 25.

**La vie liturgique** (Fr.), *The liturgical life.*

**Lectio brevis** (L.), *Short lesson.*

**Legatus a latere** (L.), *Legate from the side*—a confidential envoy of the Pope.

**Legatus natus** (L.), *Born legate*—an envoy of the Holy See by virtue of the office he holds.

**Le Salut** (Fr.), *Benediction of the Most Blessed Sacrament.*

**Levate** (L.), *Rise up!*

**Lex dubia non obligat** (L.), *A law that is doubtful does not oblige*—a principle of moral.

**Liber Pontificalis** (L.), *Pontifical book* or *book of the* *popes*—it contains accounts of the lives of the popes from St. Peter to Stephen VI who died in A.D. 891; there are three exceptions but otherwise it is complete.

**Liber Usualis** (L.), *A book of practice*—a compendium of chants to be sung on Sundays and on greater feasts. It is compiled principally from the *Graduale Romanum*, *Antiphonale Romanum*, and the Missal.

**Ligue Ouvrière Chrétienne** (Fr.), *The Christian Worker League*—a league begun in 1937 for Christian working-class people who carry on a well organized, practical program of Catholic Action and have a truly apostolic spirit. It is an adult group continuing the work of the Jocist groups of France.

**Los von Rom** (Ger.), *Away from Rome*.

**Lumen Christi** (L.), *The light of Christ*.

**Maestro di camera** (It.), *Master of the room*—the chief chamberlain of the Pope.

μάρτυρ (Gr.), *A witness*—the Greek word from which the term martyr is derived.

**Matrimonium ratum non consummatum** (L.), *Marriage ratified but not consummated*.

**Memoriale Rituum** (L.), *Collection of Rites*—a liturgical book compiled by Benedict XIII in 1725 for the carrying out in simpler form the ceremonies of Candlemas, Ash Wednesday, Palm Sunday, and the last three days of Holy Week in smaller parochial churches.

**Mi-carême** (Fr.), *Mid-lent*—name of Laetare Sunday.

**Miserere** (L.), *Have mercy*—the first word of the Latin version of Psalm 50.

**Missa cantata** (L.), *Sung Mass*.

**Missa de Angelis** (L.), *Mass of the Angels*.

**Missa dialogata** (L.), *A dialogue Mass*—one in which the members of the faithful answer as a group and aloud the responses of the server.

**Missale Romanum** (L.), *The Roman Missal*.

**Missa Pontificalis** (L.), *Pontifical Mass*.

**Missa pro defunctis** (L.), *Mass for the dead*—a requiem Mass.

**Missa pro pace** (L.), *Mass for peace*.

**Missa pro populo** (L.), *Mass for the people*.

**Missa pro sponsis** (L.), *Mass for the spouses*—the simple votive Mass read for marriages, the nuptial Mass.

**Missa quotidiana defunctorum** (L.), *The "daily Mass" of the dead*.

**Missa recitata** (L.), *Recited Mass*—a dialogue Mass.

**Missa sicca** (L.), *A dry Mass*—name given to the ceremonies preceding the Mass proper on Palm Sunday.

**Missa solemnis** (L.), *High Mass*—with deacon and subdeacon.

**Mons pietatis** (L.), *A mount of piety*—a fund for pious purposes (Cf. Entry in main dictionary.)

**Motu proprio** (L.), *Of his own accord*—a written document of the Pope done on his own initiative and signed by him.

**Munda cor meum** (L.), *Cleanse my heart*.

**Mysterium Fidei** (L.), *Mystery of Faith*.

**Nihil obstat** (L.), *Nothing stands in the way*—the certification given by a diocesan censor to a book before publication.

**Nobis quoque peccatoribus** (L.), *And to us sinners*.

**Non consummatum** (L.), *Not consummated, not completed*.

**Non expedit** (L.), *It is not expedient*.

**Notre Dame** (Fr.), *Our Lady*.

**Nunc dimittis** (L.), *Now do you dismiss*—the first two words in the Latin version of the canticle of Simeon recorded in Luke 2:29–30 which have come to be the name of this canticle.

**Oleum charismata** (L.), *Chrism*.

**Oleum infirmorum** (L.), *Oil of the sick*.

**Oleum sanctorum** (L.), *Oil of Saints*, or *Oil of catéchumens*.

ὁμοούσιος (Gr.), *Of the same substance*. (Cf. Homoousion.)

**Opus Dei** (L.), *Work of God*.

**Opus redemptoris** (L.), *Work of redemption*.

**Orans** (L.), *Praying*.

**Orate, fratres** (L.), *Pray, brethren*—the first two words by which the priest bids the people to pray immediately after the Lavabo of the Mass.

**Oratio imperata** (L.), *Commanded prayer*—usually an

extra Collect to be added in the Mass by order of the Pope, Ordinary, or religious superior with the permission of the Ordinary. It is added to the other Collects of the Mass.

**Orationes diversae** (L.), *Various prayers.*

**Oratio super oblata** (L.), *Prayer over the oblation*—the Secret of the Mass.

**Oratio super populum** (L.), *Prayer over the people*—a prayer added after the Postcommunion in the weekday Masses of Lent.

**Ordinarium Missae** (L.), *Ordinary of the Mass.*

**Ordo Missae** (L.), *Order of the Mass*—that portion of the Missal made up of the Ordinary and Canon of the Mass.

**Oremus** (L.), *Let us pray.*

**O Salutaris Hostia** (L.), *O Saving Host*—the opening words of a common hymn sung at Benediction of the Blessed Sacrament.

**Osservatore Romano** (It.), *The Roman Observer*—a daily evening newspaper published in Vatican City and a semiofficial paper of the Holy See.

**Pain Bénit** (Fr.), *Blessed bread.*

**Pallium altaris** (L.), *Cover of the altar*—the antependium.

**Parvitas materiae** (L.), *Smallness of matter*—in moral theology, that lack of gravity of the material of a human act which makes that act a venial sin.

**Pascha annotina** (L.), *Easter of last year.*

**Pastor Aeternus** (L.), *Eternal Shepherd*—the constitution of the Vatican Council treating of the primacy and infallibility of the Pope.

**Pater noster** (L.), *Our Father*—the first two words of the Lord's Prayer in Latin.

**Pax Dei** (L.), *The peace of God*.

**Pax Romana** (L.), *Roman peace*.

**Pax vobis** (L.), *Peace be to you*.

**Per accidens** (L.), *Through an accident*—not of the nature of a thing but from an accident or outside of the thing itself.

**Per Dominum nostrum Jesum Christum** (L.), *Through our Lord, Jesus Christ*.

**Per modum suffragii** (L.), *Through suffrage*.

**Per se** (L.), *Through itself*—from the nature of a thing.

**Pontifex maximus** (L.), *The supreme Pontiff*—the Pope.

**Pontificalia exercere** (L.), *To perform pontifical functions*, that is: (1) Those which according to the requirements of liturgy demand pontifical insignia, namely, mitre and crosier; (2) celebration of the Divine Office according to the rite proper to prelates.

**Preces** (L.), *Prayers*.

**Preces et Pia Opera** (L.), *Prayers and Acts of Devotion*—the official book containing prayers and devotions indulgenced by the Church, published by the Vatican Press in 1938.

**Preces feriales** (L.), *Ferial prayers*.

**Primus** (L.), *First*.

**Pro aliquibus locis** (L.), *For some places.*

**Pro Armenis** (L.), *For the Armenians*—name given to a decree contained in the bull *Exultate Deo* addressed to the Armenians in 1439 giving instruction on the seven sacraments.

**Pro Ecclesia et Pontifice** (L.), *For the Church and the Pope.*

**Promotor fidei** (L.), *The promoter of the faith*—also called *Advocatus diaboli* or devil's advocate.

**Proprium de tempore** (L.), *The Proper of the season or time*—the Proper of the Mass for Sundays and certain great feasts of the Church.

**Proprium sanctorum** (L.), *The Proper of the saints*—the Proper of the Mass of Saints' feast days and other holydays which do not find place in the *Proprium de tempore.*

**Pro re gravi** (L.), *For a serious matter.*

**Pro Sponsis** (L.), *For the Spouses*—the title of the special Mass read for a marriage.

**Providentissimus Deus** (L.), *The Most Provident God*—an encyclical of Leo XIII in 1893 on the study of the Bible.

**Quicumque vult salvus esse** (L.), *Whoever wishes to be saved*—the opening words of the Athanasian Creed.

**Ratio Studiorum** (L.), *Method of Studies*—abbreviated title of the "Method" of education of the Society of Jesus first published in 1599, entitled: "*Ratio atque Institutio Studiorum Societatis Jesu.*"

**Ratum non consummatum** (L.), *Ratified but not consummated.*

**Recto tono** (L.), *The right tone* or *the same pitch*—singing on the same note without modulation or melodic inflection.

**Regina Caeli** (L.), *Queen of Heaven*—a prayer substituted for the Angelus prayer during Eastertide.

**Requiem aeternam dona eis, Domine, et lux perpetua luceat eis** (L.), *Eternal rest grant unto them, O Lord, and let perpetual light shine upon them.*

**Requiescant in pace** (L.), *May they rest in peace.*

**Rerum novarum** (L.), *Of the new things*—an encyclical of Pope Leo XIII published in 1891 on the question of labor.

**Rituale Romanum** (L.), *The Roman Ritual*—the liturgical manual giving the rubrics for the administration of the sacraments, churching, exorcising, processions, the burial rite, and a wide range of blessings for many and various objects.

**Ritus servandus** (L.), *The custom observed*—**Ritus servandus in celebratione Missae**—*the custom observed in the celebration of Mass*—the section in the front of the Missal containing the rubrics for the celebration of Mass.

**Rubricae Missalis Romani** (L.), *Rubrics of the Roman Missal.*

**Sabbatum in Albis** (L.), *White Saturday*—the Saturday following Easter.

**Sacra Congregatio** (L.), (See under Congregatio.)

**Sacra Penitentiaria** (L.), *The sacred Penitentiary.*

**Sacra Romana Rota** (L.), *Sacred Roman Rota.*

**Sacra supellex** (L.), *Holy vestment*—in the code of canon law this term includes all liturgical vestments.

**Salve Regina** (L.), *Hail, holy Queen*—first words of a widely used prayer and antiphon of the Blessed Virgin.

**Sanatio in radice** (L.), *Healing in the root*—term applied to revalidation of a marriage from its beginning or the dispensing of an impediment from the time the marriage was contracted.

**Sanctum Chrisma** (L.), *Holy chrism.*

**Sanctus Deus** (L.), *O holy God*—the first invocation of the trisagion recited on Good Friday, the other two being: *Sanctus Fortis, Sanctus Immortalis* (O holy brave One, O holy immortal One).

**Scala sancta** (L.), *The holy stairs*—the 28 marble steps leading to the palace of Pilate upon which Christ walked.

**Schola Cantorum** (L.), *School of singers*—(1) A special group of male singers who sing the more complex chants. When they have become proficient in Gregorian Chant, they may, according to Pius X, undertake the rendition of classical polyphony. (2) In a wide sense, any group of singers at a liturgical service.

**Scrutatores** (L.), *The watchers*—the three cardinals appointed to preside over the voting at the election of a new pope.

**Secundum quid** (L.), *In some way*.

**Sedia Gestatoria** (It.), *Portable chair*—a chair on a platform upon which the Pope is carried when making solemn entry into St. Peter's or elsewhere.

**Semaines Liturgiques** (Fr.), *Liturgical weeks*—weeks devoted to the study of the Liturgy held at Louvain, France, under the auspices of the famous Abbey of Mont Cesar.

**Servus servorum Dei** (L.), *The servant of the servants of God.*

**Signatura Apostolica** (L.), *Apostolic signature.*

**Sine qua non** (L.), *Without which not*—said of a condition which must be fulfilled in performing some act.

**Speciali modo** (L.), *In a special manner.*

**Specialissimo modo** (L.), *In a most special manner.*

**Stabat Mater** (L.), *The mother stood*—the first two words of a hymn commemorating the sorrow of the Blessed Virgin which was written by Giacopone da Todi.

**Statio** (L.), *Station*—a place of assembly.

**Sub gravi** (L.), *Under grave (penalty).*

**Sub levi** (L.), *Under light (penalty).*

**Sub voce** (L.), Literally, *quietly* or *in a low voice.*

**Summa theologica** (L.), *Theological summary*—the principal but unfinished theological writing of St. Thomas Aquinas.

**Tabella secretarum** (L.), *Altar cards.*

**Talitha, cumi** (Aramaic), *Maiden, I say to thee, arise*

(Mark 5:42)—words said by Jesus when He brought back to life the daughter of Jairus.

**Tantum ergo** (L.), *All therefore*—the first words of the second last stanza of the hymn *Pange, Lingua* which is the benediction hymn of the Church and which has come to be called by these words.

**Te Deum laudamus** (L.), *We praise You, O God*—the first Latin words of the hymn of praise.

**Te igitur** (L.), *You therefore*—first words of the first prayer of the Canon of the Mass.

**Terminus ad quem** (L.), *The end to which*.

**Terminus a quo** (L.), *The end from which*.

**Theologice certum** (L.), *Theologically certain*—said of a teaching of the Church which is to be believed but which has not been directly revealed.

θεοτόκος (Gr.), *God-bearing*.

**Tolerari potest** (L.), *It can be tolerated*—a canonical term stating that a thing is not forbidden but only permitted.

**Tolerati** (L.), *Tolerated*—term applied to those excommunicated by whose penalty it is permitted for the faithful to associate with them.

**Tonus peregrinus** (L.), *Wandering tone*—a tone for singing the psalms having two dominant notes for the verse recitation.

**Toties quoties** (L.), *As often as*—indulgence gained *as often as* the prescribed prayers and the attached conditions are fulfilled.

**Tre ore** (L.), *Three hours*—the devotion commemorating the three hours agony of our Lord on the cross.

**Triduum Sacrum** (L.), *The holy triduum*—namely, Maundy Thursday, Good Friday, and Holy Saturday.

**Tunica taloris** (L.), *Garment reaching to the ankles*—the alb.

**Typographia polyglotta Vaticana** (L.), *The Vatican polyglot press.*

**Unam sanctam** (L.), *The one holy* (Church).

**Urbi et orbi** (L.), *To the city and to the world.*

**Vade mecum** (L.), *Go with me*—sometimes used as a title for a book of meditations or any brief manual frequently used by priests.

**Veni Creator Spiritus** (L.), *Come, Creating Spirit*—opening words of the hymn of the Holy Ghost.

**Veni Sancte Spiritus** (L.), *Come, Holy Spirit.*

**Venite adoremus** (L.), *Come, let us adore.*

**Vexilla Regis** (L.), *The Banner of the King*—the title of the vesper hymn.

**Via Crucis** (L.), *Way of the Cross*—Latin name for the Stations of the Cross.

**Via dolorosa** (L.), *Sorrowful way*—the name applied sometimes to the Stations of the Cross.

**Via media** (L.), *The middle way.*

**Vidi aquam** (L.), *I beheld the water*—antiphon said in place of the Asperges during Eastertide.

**Vis et metus** (L.), *Force and fear.*

**Visitatio ad limina Apostolorum** (L.), Visit to the threshold of the Apostles. (Cf. Visit.)

**Vitandi** (L.), *To be shunned*—term applied to those excommunicated whose penalty demands that they be avoided by the faithful.

**Volto santo** (It.), *The holy face.*

**Votum** (L.), *A wish.*

## II

## THE ECUMENICAL COUNCILS AND THEIR CHIEF DOCTRINES

THE TWENTY General Councils are presented here in their chronological order. Several General Councils were held in the same places at different times and so are named first, second, etc., after the particular place where they were held. Of necessity only a very general statement can here be made of the various actions of the Councils and we limit this to the more important doctrinal questions.

1. *The First Council of Nice* (A.D. 325)

This Council, the first Ecumenical Council of the Catholic Church, was held in order to bring out the true teaching of the Church as opposed by the heresy of Arius. It formally presented the teaching of the Church declaring the divinity of God the Son to be of one substance and one nature with that of God the Father. There were twenty canons drawn up, in which the time of celebrating Easter was clarified and a denunciation of the Meletian heresy made, also various matters of discipline or law were dealt with and several decisions advanced. From this Council we have the Nicene Creed.

## 2. *The First Council of Constantinople* (A.D. 381)

Again the true faith was maintained against the Arians. Answer was also given against the Apollinarian and Macedonian heresies. In answering the latter which denied the Godhead of the Holy Ghost, the dogma of the Church was again stated and the words inserted into the Nicene Creed declaring the truth that the Holy Ghost proceeded from both the Father and the Son.

## 3. *The Council of Ephesus* (A.D. 431)

The third General Council of the Church defined the Catholic dogma that the Blessed Virgin is the Mother of God and presented the teaching of the truth of one divine person in Christ. The Council was convened against the heresy of Nestorius.

## 4. *The Council of Chalcedon* (A.D. 451)

Held twenty years after the third General Council, this was to answer the Eutychian or Monophysite heresy and affirm the doctrine of two natures in Christ. This followed as a result of the growing controversy among the early theologians who were being led into error by a confused idea of the one divine person being both God and Man. It affirmed the truth that Christ is both God and Man or that there are two natures, human and divine, in the one person of the Word.

## 5. *The Second Council of Constantinople* (A.D. 553)

This Council is sometimes referred to as the Council of the Three Chapters because its chief work was to condemn the writings and teachings of Theodore of Mopsuestia, the erroneous portions in the writings of Theodoret, and the letters of Ibas. It reaffirmed the dogmas stated by the third and fourth General Councils.

## 6. *The Third Council of Constantinople* (A.D. 680)

This Council gave the definition of two wills in Christ as the true teaching against the Monothelite heresy which claimed only one will.

## 7. *The Second Council of Nice* (A.D. 787)

Here was defined the veneration due to holy images, that we give honor only to those they represent and not to the image itself as such; it presented the answer to the image breakers or iconoclasts. It also gave twenty-two canons regarding the clergy.

## 8. *The Fourth Council of Constantinople* (A.D. 869)

This was a disciplinary Council to heal the threat of Schism which was separating the East and Rome. This was done by deposing the usurper, Photius, and restoring the patriarch, Ignatius. The Greeks finally refused acknowledgment of the Council.

## 9. *The First Council of the Lateran* (A.D. 1123)

The Lateran is the Cathedral Basilica of Rome. This was the first General Council held in the West. It was convened to confirm the peace between the Church and State and to give final settlement to the problem of Investiture between Emperor Henry V and the Holy See. It was agreed that the Church has all rights to choose and consecrate prelates and invest them, and Church goods were restored to the Church.

## 10. *The Second Council of the Lateran* (A.D. 1139)

This Council took disciplinary action and excommunicated Roger of Sicily who championed the antipope, Anacletus II, and imposed silence on Arnold of Brescia. Canons against simony, incontinence, breaking the "Truce of God," dueling or group feuding were advanced, and regulations concerning clerical dress were given.

## 11. *The Third Council of the Lateran* (A.D. 1179)

After forty years again a General Council took action against simony and abuses of the clergy. Also defense of the true teaching was made in answer to the Albigenses and Waldenses.

## 12. *The Fourth Council of the Lateran* (A.D. 1215)

Besides disciplinary action the seventy decrees of this Council answered prevailing heresies, gave pronouncements in favor of the Crusades, prescribed the duty of annual confession and Easter Communion, offered additional definitions on the absolute unity of God, and presented definition of the doctrine of the Church regarding sacraments, and in particular that the bread and wine, by transubstantiation, become the Body and Blood of Christ.

### 13. *The First Council of Lyons* (A.D. 1245)

This Council was called to bring disciplinary action against Emperor Frederick II and at the same time sentence of the solemn renewal of excommunication was passed on the emperor.

### 14. *The Second Council of Lyons* (A.D. 1274)

Effort was made at this Council under Pope Gregory X to bring about union between the East and West. It also defined that the Holy Ghost proceeds eternally from the Father and the Son. The discipline governing the election of the Pope was formulated.

### 15. *The Council of Vienne* (A.D. 1311 and 1312)

The purpose of this Council was to settle the affair of the Templars, to advance the rescue of the Holy Land, and to reform abuses in the Church. The doctrinal decrees of the Council were: condemnation that the soul is not "in itself and essentially the form of the human body"; that sanctifying grace is infused into the soul at Baptism; and denial that a perfect man is not subject to ecclesiastical and civil law.

### 16. *The Council of Constance* (A.D. 1414–1418)

This Council can be regarded as ecumenical only in so far as it was in union with the Pope. The heretical teachings of John Huss and Wyclif were answered. It was here that communion to the laity under one species was prescribed.

17. *The Council of Ferrara-Florence* (A.D. 1438-1439)

This was convened to unite the Greeks and other oriental sects with the Latin Rite. It was defined that "the Holy Apostolic See and Roman Pontiff hold the primacy over all the world; that the Roman Pontiff is the successor of Peter, prince of the Apostles; that he is the true vicar of Christ, the head of the whole Church, the Father and teacher of all Christians."

18. *The Fifth Council of the Lateran* (A.D. 1512-1517)

It defined the Pope's authority over all Councils and condemned errors regarding the human soul, namely, that the soul with its intellectual power is mortal.

19. *The Council of Trent* (Opened under Pope Paul III in 1545, continued under Pope Julius III, and concluded under Pope Pius IV in A.D. 1563)

The doctrine of original sin was defined; the decree on Justification was declared against the Lutheran errors that faith alone justifies and that man's justice merely consists in imputing to man the merits of Christ; the doctrine of the sacraments of Penance and Extreme Unction was defined; decrees relating to the censorship of books were adopted; the doctrine of Christian marriage was defined and decrees on Purgatory and indulgences adopted. Besides many refutations against the so-called reformers were given and measures of true reform advanced.

20. *The Vatican Council* (Opened under Pope Pius IX in 1869 and adjourned on October 20, A.D. 1870)

This last General Council has never been closed and could be reopened. At this Council the primacy and infallibility of the Pope were defined.


21. *The Vatican Council II* (Opened under Pope John XXIII October 11, A.D. 1962 closed during the papacy of Paul VI on December 8, A.D. 1965.

This council was convened to present the Faith in terms pastorally acceptable to the modern world.

## III

## ABBREVIATIONS USED IN GENERAL AND AMONG SCHOLARS

**A.A.S.**—*Acta Apostolicae Sedis*
**ADDIT.**—*Additiones et Variationes* in *Rubricis Missalis*. (To be found at the beginning of the Missal, after *Rubricae Generales*, since the reform of the Missal by Pius X in the bull *Divino Afflatu* of 1911.)
**A.B.**—Bachelor of Arts.
**Abp.**—Archbishop.
**A.D.**—*Anno Domini* (Year of our Lord).
**A.M.**—Master of Arts.
**A.M.D.G.**—*Ad maiorem Dei Gloriam* (For the greater glory of God).

**B.A.**—Bachelor of Arts.
**B.C.**—Before Christ.
**B.C.L.**—Bachelor of Canon Law or Bachelor of Civil Law.
**Bp.**—Bishop.

# Appendix III

**Bro.**—Brother. (pl. Bros.)
**B.V.M.**—Blessed Virgin Mary.


**Card.**—Cardinal.
**C.**—Canon.
**C.E.**—*Caeremoniale Episcoporum.*
**C.J.C.**—*Codex Juris Canonici* (Code of Canon Law).
**Conf.**—Confessor.
**C.Y.O.**—Catholic Youth Organization.


**D.**—*Decretum* (decree)—chiefly one of the Congregation of Sacred Rites.
**D.C.L.**—Doctor of Canon Law, or Doctor of Civil Law.
**D.D.**—Doctor of Divinity.
**Doct.**—Doctor.
**D.O.M.**—*Deo Optimo Maximo* (To God, the best and greatest).
**D.V.**—*Deo volente* (God willing).


**Fr.**—Father.


**I.C.**—*Instructio Clementina* (The Clementine Instruction).
**I.H.S.**—First three letters of the name of Jesus in Greek. (Cf. dictionary proper.)
**I.N.R.I.**—*Iesus Nazarenus Rex Iudaeorum* (Jesus of Nazareth, King of the Jews). (Cf. dictionary proper.)


**J.A.C.**—*Jeunesse Agricole Chrétienne* (The Young Christian Farmer). (Cf. dictionary proper.)

**J.C.D.**—Doctor of Canon Law, or Doctor of Civil Law.
**J.M.J.**—Jesus, Mary, Joseph.
**J.O.C.**—*Jeunesse Ouvrière Chrétienne* (The Young Christian Workers). (Cf. dictionary proper.)
**J.U.D.**—Doctor of Both Laws (canon and civil).

**K.S.G.**—Knight of St. Gregory.
**K.H.S.**—Knight of the Holy Sepulchre.

**Lect. Glis. Phil.**—Lector General of Philosophy (Franciscan degree, conferred Ph.D.).
**Lect. Glis. S.S.**—Lector General of Sacred Scripture (Franciscan degree, conferred S.T.D.).
**Lect. Glis. Sac. Theo.**—Lector General of Sacred Theology (Franciscan degree, conferred S.T.D.).
**L.O.C.**—*Ligue Ouvrière Chrétienne* (The Christian Workers' League). (Cf. dictionary proper.)

**M.A.**—Master of Arts.
**MM.**—Martyrs.
**Msgr.**—Monsignor.
**M.P.**—*Motu Proprio* (of Pius X regarding the Reform of Church Music).
**M.R.** or **Mem. Rit.**—*Memoriale Rituum*.

**N.C.C.M.**—National Council of Catholic Men.
**N.C.C.W.**—National Council of Catholic Women.
**N.C.R.L.C.**—National Catholic Rural Life Conference.
**N.C.W.C.**—National Catholic Welfare Conference.

# Appendix III

**N.D.**—Our Lady.
**N.T.**—New Testament.

**O.M.**—*Ordo Missae* (found, normally, in the center of the Missal after "Holy Saturday").
**O.S.**—Old Style.
**O.T.**—Old Testament.

**P.A.**—Protonotary Apostolic.
**P.C.**—*Pax Christi* (Peace of Christ).
**Ph.D.**—Doctor of Philosophy.
**Phil.**—Philosophy.
**Pont. Max.**—*Pontifex Maximus* (Supreme Pontiff).
**P.T.**—*Paschale Tempore* (The Easter time). (Cf. dictionary proper.)

**Rev.**—Reverend.
**R.G.**—*Rubricae Generales Missales* (General rubrics of the Missal).
**R.I.P.**—*Requiescat in Pace* (May he, or she, rest in peace).
**R.P.**—*Reverendus Pater* (Reverend Father).
**R.R.**—*Rituale Romanum* (Roman Ritual).
**R.S.**—*De Ritibus Servandis in cantu Missae* (from the Gradual).
**Rt. Rev.**—Right Reverend.

**Sr.**—Sister.
**S.R.C.**—Decrees of the Congregation of Sacred Rites.
**SS.N.D.**—Our Most Holy Lord (also a title of the Holy Father).
**S.**—Saint.

**St.**—Saint (pl. Sts.).
**SS.**—Saints.
**S.S.**—Sacred Scripture.
**S.T.B.**—Bachelor of Sacred Theology.
**S.T.D.**—Doctor of Sacred Theology.
**S.T.M.**—Master of Sacred Theology.

**Theo.**—Theology.
**T.P.**—*Tempore Paschale* (also P.T.) (The Easter time.)
**T.Q.**—*Toties Quoties.*

**Ven.**—Venerable.
**V.F.**—Vicar Forane.
**V.G.**—Vicar General.
**Vig.**—Vigil.
**Virg.**—Virgin.
**V. Rev.**—Very Reverend.
**V.T.**—Old Testament.

# IV

# LIST OF THE POPES

1. St. Peter, d. 67
2. St. Linus, 67–79
3. St. Anacletus I, 79–90
4. St. Clement I, 90–99
5. St. Evaristus, 99–107
6. St. Alexander I, 107–116
7. St. Sixtus I, 116–25
8. St. Telesphorus, 125–36
9. St. Hyginus, 136–40
10. St. Pius, 140–54
11. St. Anicetus, 154–65
12. St. Soter, 165–74
13. St. Eleuterius, 174–89
14. St. Victor, 189–98
15. St. Zephyrinus, 198–217
16. St. Callistus I, 217–22
17. St. Urban I, 222–30
18. St. Pontian, 230–35

19. St. Anterus, 235–36
20. St. Fabian, 236–50
21. St. Cornelius, 251–53
22. St. Lucius I, 253–54
23. St. Stephen I, 254–57
24. St. Sixtus II, 257–58
25. St. Dionysius, 259–68
26. St. Felix I, 269–74
27. St. Eutychian, 275–83
28. St. Caius, 283–96
29. St. Marcellinus, 296–304
30. St. Marcellus I, 304–09
31. St. Eusebius, 309–11
32. St. Melchiades, 311–13
33. St. Sylvester I, 314–35
34. St. Marcus, 336
35. St. Julius I, 337–52
36. St. Liberius, 352–66
37. St. Damasus I, 366–84
38. St. Siricius, 384–98
39. St. Anastasius I, 398–401
40. St. Innocent I, 402–17
41. St. Zosimus, 417–18
42. St. Boniface I, 418–22
43. St. Celestine I, 422–32
44. St. Sixtus III, 432–40
45. St. Leo I, 440–61
46. St. Hilarius, 461–68
47. St. Simplicius, 468–83
48. St. Felix II, 483–92
49. St. Gelasius I, 492–96
50. St. Anastasius II, 496–98

51. Symmachus, 498–514
52. St. Hormisdas, 514–23
53. St. John I, 523–26
54. St. Felix III, 526–30
55. Boniface II, 530–32
56. John II, 533–35
57. St. Agapetus I, 535–36
58. St. Silverius, 536–38
59. Vigilius, 538–555
60. Pelagius I, 556–61
61. John III, 561–74
62. Benedict I, 575–79
63. Pelagius II, 579–90
64. St. Gregory I, 590–604
65. Sabinianus, 604–06
66. Boniface III, 607
67. St. Boniface IV, 608–15
68. St. Deusdedit, 615–18
69. Boniface V, 619–25
70. Honorius I, 625–38
71. Severinus, 638–40
72. John IV, 640–42
73. Theodore I, 642–49
74. St. Martin I, 649–55
75. St. Eugene I, 655–57
76. St. Vitalian, 657–72
77. Adeodatus, 672–76
78. Donus, 676–78
79. St. Agatho, 678–81
80. St. Leo II, 682–83
81. St. Benedict II, 684–85
82. John V, 685–86

## Appendix IV

83. Conon, 686–87
84. St. Sergius I, 687–701
85. John VI, 701–05
86. John VII, 705–07
87. Sisinnius, 708
88. Constantine, 708–15
89. St. Gregory II, 715–31
90. St. Gregory III, 731–41
91. St. Zacharias, 741–52
92. St. Stephen II, 752–57
93. St. Paul I, 757–67
94. Stephen III, 768–72
95. Adrian I, 772–95
96. St. Leo III, 795–816
97. St. Stephen IV, 816–17
98. St. Paschal I, 817–24
99. Eugene II, 824–27
100. Valentine, 827
101. Gregory IV, 827–44
102. Sergius II, 844–47
103. St. Leo IV, 847–55
104. Benedict III, 855–58
105. St. Nicholas I, 858–67
106. Adrian II, 867–72
107. John VIII, 872–82
108. Marinus I, 882–84
109. Adrian III, 884–85
110. Stephen V, 885–91
111. Formosus, 891–96
112. Boniface VI, 896
113. Stephen VI, 896–97
114. Romanus, 897

115. Theodore II, 897
116. John IX, 898–900
117. Benedict IV, 900–03
118. Leo V, 903
119. Christopher, 903–04
120. Sergius III, 904–11
121. Anastasius III, 911–13
122. Lando, 913–14
123. John X, 914–28
124. Leo VI, 928
125. Stephen VII, 928–31
126. John XI, 931–36
127. Leo VII, 936–39
128. Stephen VIII, 939–42
129. Marinus II, 942–46
130. Agapetus II, 946–55
131. John XII, 955–64
132. Leo VIII, 964–65
133. Benedict V, 965
134. John XIII, 965–72
135. Benedict VI, 973–74
136. Benedict VII, 974–83
137. John XIV, 983–84
138. Boniface VII, 984–85
139. John XV, 985–96
140. Gregory V, 996–99
141. Sylvester II, 999–1003
142. John XVII, 1003
143. John XVIII, 1003–09
144. Sergius IV, 1009–12
145. Benedict VIII, 1012–24
146. John XIX, 1024–32

## Appendix IV

147. Benedict IX, 1032–45
148. Gregory VI, 1045–46
149. Clement II, 1046–47
150. Damasus II, 1048
151. St. Leo IX, 1049–54
152. Victor II, 1055–57
153. Stephen IX, 1057–58
154. Benedict X, 1058–59
155. Nicholas II, 1059–61
156. Alexander II, 1061–73
157. St. Gregory VII, 1073–85
158. Victor III, 1087
159. Urban II, 1088–99
160. Paschal II, 1099–1118
161. Gelasius II, 1118–19
162. Callistus II, 1119–24
163. Honorius II, 1124–30
164. Innocent II, 1130–43
165. Celestine II, 1143–44
166. Lucius, 1144–45
167. Eugene III, 1145–1153
168. Anastasius IV, 1153–54
169. Adrian IV, 1154–59
170. Alexander III, 1159–81
171. Lucius III, 1181–85
172. Urban III, 1185–87
173. Gregory VIII, 1187
174. Clement III, 1187–91
175. Celestine III, 1191–98
176. Innocent III, 1198–1216
177. Honorius II, 1216–27
178. Gregory IX, 1227–41

179. Celestine IV, 1241
180. Innocent IV, 1243–54
181. Alexander IV, 1254–61
182. Urban IV, 1261–64
183. Clement IV, 1265–68
184. St. Gregory X, 1271–76
185. Innocent V, 1276
186. Adrian V, 1276
187. John XXI, 1276–77
188. Nicholas III, 1277–80
189. Martin IV, 1281–85
190. Honorius IV, 1285–87
191. Nicholas IV, 1288–92
192. St. Celestine V, 1294
193. Boniface VIII, 1294–1303
194. Benedict XI, 1303–04
195. Clement V, 1305–14
196. John XXII, 1316–34
197. Benedict XII, 1334–42
198. Clement VI, 1342–52
199. Innocent VI, 1352–62
200. Urban V, 1362–70
201. Gregory XI, 1370–78
202. Urban VI, 1378–89
203. Boniface IX, 1389–1404
204. Innocent VII, 1404–06
205. Gregory XII, 1406–09
206. Alexander V, 1409–10
207. John XXIII, 1410–15
208. Martin V, 1417–31
209. Eugene IV, 1431–47
210. Nicholas V, 1447–55

# Appendix IV

211. Callistus III, 1455–58
212. Pius II, 1458–64
213. Paul II, 1464–71
214. Sixtus IV, 1471–84
215. Innocent VIII, 1484–92
216. Alexander VI, 1492–1503
217. Pius III, 1503
218. Julius II, 1503–13
219. Leo X, 1513–21
220. Adrian VI, 1522–23
221. Clement VII, 1523–34
222. Paul III, 1534–49
223. Julius III, 1550–55
224. Marcellus II, 1555
225. Paul IV, 1555–59
226. Pius IV, 1559–65
227. St. Pius V, 1566–72
228. Gregory XIII, 1572–85
229. Sixtus V, 1585–90
230. Urban VII, 1590
231. Gregory XIV, 1590–91
232. Innocent IX, 1591
233. Clement VIII, 1592–1605
234. Leo XI, 1605
235. Paul V, 1605–21
236. Gregory XV, 1621–23
237. Urban VIII, 1623–44
238. Innocent X, 1644–55
239. Alexander VII, 1655–67
240. Clement IX, 1667–69
241. Clement X, 1670–76
242. Innocent XI, 1676–89

243. Alexander VIII, 1689–91
244. Innocent XII, 1691–1700
245. Clement XI, 1700–21
246. Innocent XIII, 1721–24
247. Benedict XIII, 1724–30
248. Clement XII, 1730–40
249. Benedict XIV, 1740–58
250. Clement XIII, 1758–69
251. Clement XIV, 1769–74
252. Pius VI, 1775–99
253. Pius VII, 1800–23
254. Leo XII, 1823–29
255. Pius VIII, 1829–30
256. Gregory XVI, 1831–46
257. Pius IX, 1846–78
258. Leo XIII, 1878–1903
259. Pius X, 1903–14
260. Benedict XV, 1914–22
261. Pius XI, 1922–1939
262. Pius XII, 1939-1959
263. John XXIII, 1959-1963
264. Paul VI, 1963-1978
265. John Paul I, 1978-1978
266. John Paul II, 1978-(now reigning)

## V

## TERMS OF ADDRESS FOR ECCLESIASTICAL PERSONS

BECAUSE of the dignity and honor of their calling ecclesiastical persons are entitled to proper and special titles and terms of address. The following offers, progressively according to rank, the strictly formal manner of addressing these persons in (*a*) direct speech or conversation; (*b*) correspondence. The abbreviation *add.* = the address upon the envelope (addressing letters to priests, brothers or sisters of religious orders or communities, the initials of their order or community should be given after their names); *sal.* = the salutation of a letter. The close of a letter may be given in any accepted and dignified manner.

**The Pope,** (*a*) Your Holiness. (*b*) *Add.:* To His Holiness, Pope....... *Sal.:* Most Holy Father.

**Cardinal,** (*a*) Your Eminence. (*b*) *Add.:* His Eminence (Christian name) Cardinal (surname). *Sal.:* My Lord Cardinal.

**Latin Patriarch,** (*a*) Your Excellency. (*b*) *Add.:* His Excellency the Patriarch of....... *Sal.:* Your Excellency *or* Most Reverend Excellency.

**Eastern Patriarch,** (*a*) Your Beatitude. (*b*) *Add.:* His Beatitude the Patriarch of....... *Sal.:* Most Reverend Lord.

**Apostolic Delegates and Nuncios,** (*a*) Your Excellency. (*b*) *Add.:* His Excellency Archbishop (or Monsignor)....... *Sal.:* Your Excellency.

**Archbishop,** (*a*) Your Excellency. (*b*) *Add.:* The Most Rev.........., D.D., Archbishop of....... *Sal.:* Your Excellency.

**Bishop,** (*a*) Your Excellency. (*b*) *Add.:* The Most Rev..........., D.D., Bishop of....... *Sal.:* Most Reverend.

**Abbot,** (*a*) Father Abbot *or* My Lord Abbot. (*b*) *Add.:* The Rt. Rev..........., Abbot of....... *Sal.:* Right Reverend Abbot.

**Abbess,** (*a*) Lady Abbess *or* Mother Abbess. (*b*) *Add.:* Lady Abbess.........., Abbess of....... *Sal.:* Dear Mother Abbess.

**Protonotaries Apostolic, Domestic Prelates and Vicars General,** (*a*) Monsignor. (*b*) *Add.:* The Rt. Rev. Monsignor.........., P.A. *or* V.G. *Sal.:* Right Reverend and Dear Monsignor.

**Provosts and Canons,** (*a*) Provost *or* Canon. (*b*) *Add.:* The Very Rev. Provost (or Canon). *Sal.:* Very Reverend Provost *or* Dear Canon.

**Papal Chamberlain,** (*a*) Monsignor. (*b*) *Add.:* The Very Rev. Monsignor........... *Sal.:* Very Reverend Monsignor.

**Rectors of Seminaries,** (*a*) Father (or title). (*b*) *Add.:* The Very Rev............ *Sal.:* Very Reverend and Dear Father (or title).

**Provincials of Religious Orders,** (*a*) Father Provincial. (*b*) *Add.:* The Very Rev. Father Provincial........ *Sal.:* Very Reverend and Dear Father Provincial.

**Priors,** (*a*) Father Prior. (*b*) *Add.:* The Very Rev. Father Prior........... *Sal.:* Very Reverend and Dear Father Prior.

**Prioresses,** (*a*) Mother Prioress. (*b*) *Add.:* The Very Rev. Mother Prioress........... *Sal.:* Very Reverend and Dear Mother Prioress.

**Rural Dean,** (*a*) Father. (*b*) *Add.:* The Very Rev. ..........V.F. *Sal.:* Very Reverend and Dear Dean.

**Priests, diocesan,** (*a*) Father. (*b*) *Add.:* The Rev. ........... *Sal.:* Reverend and Dear Father.

**Priests, religious,** (*a*) Father. (*b*) *Add.:* The Rev. Father............... *Sal.:* Reverend and Dear Father.

**Clerics** (below order of priesthood), (*a*) no title. (*b*) *Add.:* The Rev. Mr.............*Sal.:* Reverend Sir.

**Brothers,** (*a*) Brother. (*b*) *Add.:* Venerable Brother ............ *Sal.:* Venerable and Dear Brother.

**Sisters.** (*a*) Sister. (*b*) *Add.:* Venerable Sister........ ....... *Sal.:* Venerable and Dear Sister.

**Papal Knights,** (*a*) Sir. (*b*) *Add.:* The Honorable .........., K.S.G. (or K.H.S.). *Sal.:* Honored and Dear Sir.